The Acceptable Year of the Lord

Karen A. Hamilton

The Acceptable Year of the Lord

Preaching the Old Testament with Faith, Finesse and Fervour

NOVALIS

© 2008 Novalis, Saint Paul University, Ottawa, Canada

Cover design: Julie-Anne Lemire
Cover image: iStockphoto
Layout: Audrey Wells

Business Offices:
Novalis Publishing Inc.
10 Lower Spadina Avenue, Suite 400
Toronto, Ontario, Canada
M5V 2Z2

Novalis Publishing Inc.
4475 Frontenac Street
Montréal, Québec, Canada
H2H 2S2

Phone: 1-800-387-7164
Fax: 1-800-204-4140
E-mail: books@novalis.ca
www.novalis.ca

Library and Archives Canada Cataloguing in Publication

Hamilton, Karen A.
    The acceptable year of the Lord : preaching the Old
Testament with faith, finesse and fervour / Karen A. Hamilton.

Includes bibliographical references.
ISBN 978-2-89646-032-8

    1. Bible. O.T.—Homiletical use. 2. Bible. O.T.—Sermons.
3. Preaching. 4. Church year sermons. I. Title.

BS1191.5.H34 2008   251'.6   C2008-905790-2

Printed in Canada.

We acknowledge the financial support of the Government of Canada through the Book Publishing Industry Development Program (BPIDP) for our publishing activities.

5   4   3   2   1   12   11   10   09   08

Dedication

This book is dedicated to the widows, the orphans and the sojourners – to all the world's vulnerable ones for whom our calling is to care.

They are inscribed on the palms of God's hands. (Isaiah 49:16b)

Proceeds realized from the sale of this book will go towards HIV/AIDS relief in Africa.

Contents

Preface

This book is for Christian preachers. It arises out of the conviction that the Old Testament is essential to the life of the church, to Christian faith and witness.[1] This has been the general consensus throughout the history of the Christian church, though it has not always been unanimous. For early Christian preachers, the Old Testament was foundational to the proclamation of the Gospel. The same was true, of course, for the apostle Paul, the gospel writers and all those who shared their deep faith in Christ through the New Testament texts. The genealogies in Matthew and Luke, for example, are key to our faith in Jesus as Messiah, and are much more comprehensible with some knowledge of Old Testament faith and messianic prophecies. Jesus himself made frequent references to Old Testament figures and

---

1   How to refer to the scriptures is a thorny issue. "The Hebrew Scriptures" is inaccurate, since the text was written in both Hebrew and Aramaic. (Following this logic, the New Testament would have to be called the Greek Scriptures.) Using the term "the Hebrew Scriptures" does not honour and respect our Hebrew roots or our Jewish sisters and brothers, for they call their scriptures "the TaNaKh," an acronym for Torah, Nevi'im (prophets) and Kethubim (writings). (Sometimes the whole thing is referred to as "the Torah.")

   More important, what we refer to as the Old Testament is not the TaNaKh. The ordering of the biblical books for Jews and Christians is the same until we get to the end of 2 Kings; then a significant reordering has been done for Christians for theological reasons. The TaNaKh ends with 1 and 2 Chronicles, while the Old Testament ends with the Book of the prophet Malachi, whose name means "my messenger." This leads Christians into a direct proclamation of the Messiah in the New Testament.

   In this book I use "Old Testament" and "New Testament" to describe the parts of the Christian Bible.

stories. In the church's view, these scriptures provide vital truths about God, the nature of Messiahship, the Spirit, the world and the church itself. To limit the scriptures to the New Testament would be to miss much of God's revelation.[2]

This book is for *busy* Christian preachers. Many sermons, mine included, are thought out while a preacher waits to see a parishioner in hospital, or are written on a Saturday evening on the train back from a meeting. Many preachers these days do not – and we might as well admit it – know very much about the Old Testament. Some of us come to seminary and theological college with little biblical knowledge to start with. Theological college and seminary are packed full of other essential courses, leaving little time and space in the schedule for many Old Testament ones. Once we are launched into ministry it is hard to find time to pick up those wonderful Old Testament commentaries in religious bookstores, in theological college libraries or even on our own bookshelves.

I spent ten years as a kind of itinerant guest preacher and Bible study leader. Whenever and wherever I spoke or preached, I would root my reflections in the Old Testament texts because they speak deeply to my faith, heart and experience. The reaction was startling. Time after time, older participants would tell me how good it was to hear those Old Testament texts that they had not heard since they were children. Time after time, younger participants would tell me how good it was to hear those Old Testament passages and stories that they had never heard before.

It has become clear that Christians need to take a good look at how we articulate Christian theology. How does this theology reflect the teachings of the Old Testament? Does this theology honour our relationship with our Jewish sisters and brothers? We sometimes seem to forget that our Old Testament contains the complete and revelatory

_____
2   Using "Yahweh" to refer to God is offensive to Jewish people: in the Jewish tradition, God's name is too holy to be pronounced or written in full. (This term takes the consonants of God's name [YHWH] in the biblical text, which originally was not "pointed" with vowels, and guesses which vowels would be most likely.) Use the noun "God," as I do in this book. You may, if you are reading contemporary Jewish materials, see "G_d" as the way of referring to the Holy One. That is one way of expressing the inexpressible and a reminder of God's holiness. Orally, you may hear "adonai," which means "lord."

scriptures of living Judaism, both of Jesus' time and now. We may even have thought of ourselves as somehow replacing the people of Israel in the providence of God, even though the Old Testament clearly states that God has a covenant with the people of Israel, and that God never breaks covenant.

Since the Shoah,[3] however, some Christians who had forgotten have become aware again that the Old Testament scriptures are the ones that Jesus knew in his earthly life, and that the church has always officially recognized them for the wondrous, myriad ways they reveal God to us. The early church, searching its Jewish scriptures (which have a very close, though not identical, relationship to what Christians call the Old Testament today – see footnote 1), found them to witness to Jesus Christ in ways that spoke to their experience of his resurrection and enabled them to proclaim that experience. The church's faith in the one God was first spoken of in the Old Testament; we continue to see the face and hear the voice of God in those texts. Now we must share that knowledge in our preaching. This book will help you do that.

---

3   Because they did not offer themselves to the Nazis, Jewish people prefer the term "Shoah" to the term "Holocaust." (A shoah, from the Hebrew, is a ruin; a holocaust, from the Greek, is a burnt offering.)

Introduction: Setting Things in Context

Nearly every week, the lectionary brings us texts from the Old Testament: almost 150 texts in the three-year cycle. Many excellent Old Testament resources are available, but they tend to be long and detailed. Lectionary preaching resources often emphasize the gospels, with the Old Testament text as a kind of sidebar.

In this book, I offer an accessible resource for preachers, encouraging you to preach from those Old Testament texts with faith, finesse and fervour. It reflects, in a way that is directly applicable to preaching, on the richness, diversity, complexity, context, and deep, broad, up-close and personal revelation of God in the Old Testament. Because this book can easily and quickly be used on a weekly basis, it dances through many topics, themes and details. To be faithful to the Old Testament, however, we must explore two topics in some depth before we begin to look at the weekly readings: the Book of the prophet Isaiah (because a third of the lectionary texts are taken from it) and the theology of two covenants (because past misunderstandings of this theology have led to unfaithful interpretations and even unfaithful behaviour that is anti-Judaic or even anti-Semitic).[4]

I have referred to a number of commentators in the writing of this book – not relying on them heavily, but taking a bit of a dance through their thoughts. (If I had relied on them heavily there would

---

4   It is important to distinguish between these two terms. "Anti-Judaic" refers to being against something that is particularly a part of the Jewish tradition. "Anti-Semitic" – "semitic" was originally used in ethnology and linguistics to refer to a family of Middle Eastern languages, including Arabic, Aramaic and Hebrew, and the cultures and ethnic groups associated with them – means to be against those of Jewish origin or lineage, whether or not they practise any elements of Judaism.

have been no point in writing this book: you could have read those commentators yourself.) Sometimes I do this to provide background, sometimes as a frame for what I want to say about these lectionary passages. I have deliberately used Jewish commentators for the first five books of the Old Testament, because a lot of great work has been done by Jewish scholars, and many Christian preachers do not have the opportunity to see it. I have used Walter Brueggemann for the Isaiah passages because I am familiar with his work, because we have a similar methodological approach and because he is just plain good.

The Book of the Prophet Isaiah

> The Spirit of the Lord is upon me, because he has anointed me to bring good news to the poor. He has sent me to proclaim release to the captives and recovery of sight to the blind, to let the oppressed go free, to proclaim the acceptable year of the Lord's favour. (Luke 4:18-19)

The fact that approximately one-third of the Old Testament lectionary readings are taken from Isaiah has both positive and negative aspects. Positive aspects include Isaiah's wonderful poetry and universalism, and especially its ability to speak to Christians profoundly and in detail about their faith in Jesus Christ. Focusing on the writings of one prophet can be overwhelming for preachers, however. To prepare, try reading the passage from Isaiah over and over again, starting early in the week you will preach on it. Two minutes a day will suffice. And reading a chapter and a half of Isaiah most days will easily get you through the whole book in a year, which would also be helpful. Let the Spirit of God in the Word and the words wash over and through you.

Many biblical commentaries contain fascinating, in-depth discussions of the historical-critical, form critical, text critical, redaction critical, rhetorical critical, and other issues, including which parts of the book may be identified as First, Second or Third Isaiah.[5] (Walter Brueggemann's two-volume Isaiah commentary, *Isaiah 1–39*, *Isaiah*

---

5   Based on such things as historical references and literary style, many biblical scholars see the Book of Isaiah as being in three parts, perhaps written or edited by three individuals or groups. First Isaiah is thus chapters 1–39, Second Isaiah is chapters 40–54, and Third Isaiah is chapters 55–66.

14

40–66, is an excellent one for preachers as well as biblical scholars.) This section on Isaiah, however, does not deal with those issues in any depth; rather, it portrays some of the ways that the book is witness to the revelation of God. The entire book of Isaiah is a vital scripture for Jewish faith, past and present. The early church, in striving to understand the meaning of the Risen Christ for its life, began to seek meaning for its faith in texts from Isaiah. The church today also proclaims its faith in word and action, informed, nurtured, challenged and comforted by Isaiah's writings.

The church's use of the Book of Isaiah

I intentionally began this section on Isaiah with a quotation from Luke's gospel. The quotation comes from that part of the gospel in which Jesus is portrayed as setting out the nature and content of his ministry, of his messiahship. Whether Jesus chose to read Isaiah 61:1-2a himself, or, as is more likely, whether he was given the Jewish lectionary prophetic text (technically the "haftorah" text for the day) to read, the gospel writer believed that this passage from Isaiah well portrayed the reality of Jesus' ministry and its inauguration.

The New Testament contains up to 250 quotations of and allusions to Isaiah: more than from any other scriptural book, with the possible exception of the Psalms.[6] Isaiah has also been used throughout Christian church history in art and music, as well as a proof for theology and doctrine. For these reasons, Isaiah's prominence in the lectionary is no surprise. Through the ages, the church has used Old Testament texts to teach and inspire in a variety of contexts. As Walter Brueggeman says frequently in his *Theology of the Old Testament*, the Old Testament is both elusive and able to speak to the church's memory and its continuing sense of the transforming presence of Jesus Christ.

---

6   It is sometimes difficult to tell whether something is a quotation or is a phrase common to the faith context. This is further complicated by the fact that the Greek translation of the Old Testament, used by many of the New Testament writers, often differs from the Hebrew translation.

The historical context of Isaiah

The book of Isaiah is named after the prophet whose words and actions it relates, at least in part. The lectionary texts from Isaiah are all taken from the poetic parts of the book. Though prophetic poetry (both "prophecy" and "poetry" are defined below) makes up the majority of the book, some important narrative sections left out of the lectionary deal with the prophet's historical context and prophetic actions.

This historical prophet lived until at least 681 BCE, during the time when the nation of Israel, after Solomon, was divided into two kingdoms: Judah in the south, and Israel in the north.[7] It was a difficult and turbulent time. The empire of Assyria was expanding and the two kingdoms of Israel were declining. Complex political alliances and uncertainties were rife. Isaiah speaks of a coming captivity for the people, seeing it as a result of their sin: their reliance on political alliances, their lack of justice towards the poor and vulnerable, and their unfaithfulness to God. However, the book also moves forward, towards the future of God's kingdom on earth, with its righteous ruler and righteous subjects. As the introduction to Isaiah in the NRSV Bible states, "The restored earth and the restored people will then conform to the divine ideal, and all will result in the praise and glory and fulfillment of the justice and peace of the Holy One of Israel."

In 701 BCE, Sennacherib, the ruler of Assyria, invaded the land and was poised at the gates of Jerusalem to conquer the city. Something (perhaps plague among his soldiers, or a miracle, or both) caused Sennacherib to abandon the siege and head home. Seen by the people – writers, theologians and prophets of Israel – as a sign of God's great power and grace, this event was a major influence not only on the book of Isaiah, but on the whole Old Testament canon. (Read the story in Isaiah chapters 36–39, which do not make it into the lectionary.)

---

7   The abbreviations BCE and CE are used in this book. These stand for "Before the Common Era" and "Common Era," and cover the same period as BC ("Before Christ") and AD ("Anno Domini" = "The Year of the Lord"). BCE and CE are more commonly used by biblical scholars than are BC and AD.

Eventually the nation falls to the Empire of Babylon. Many texts in this prophetic book reflect that Exile and the return from exile, in all their complexity and in time periods later than that of the historical prophet.

It is popular to speak of biblical prophets as always railing against the institutions of Israel – disparaging the sacrificial system while calling Israel back to actions of justice, which is seen as superior to or disconnected from the sacrificial system. This is an incorrect way of viewing the prophets in general and Isaiah in particular, and leads to anti-Judaism and anti-Semitism. To talk about "replacing" the sacrificial system with justice misses the integral connection between the two in the biblical text, and particularly in the person of Isaiah. Isaiah understood that acknowledging the Lordship of the Creator through sacrifice is bound up with the Creator God's imperative for justice. Isaiah called for justice and care for the needy – the widow, the orphan and the sojourner – which is the biblical phrase referring to the most vulnerable ones in society. Isaiah also had the ear of the king and the king's institutional structure, and could and did try to influence politics. Isaiah, who may have been a priest in the Temple (note the context of his call, as described in chapter 6: only a priest would probably be that familiar with such details around the inner sanctuary of the Temple), would have understood that human beings, called as we are to live in community, need structures and institutions. We need ritual to express our relationship to the divine. All these are part of our complex relationship with God.

After the fall of the Temple in 70 CE, the purpose of the sacrificial system was transformed into the home ritual of Judaism. This home ritual, which is still practised today, understands deeply God's call to words and deeds of justice.

Particular parts of the book of Isaiah deserve comment: they have been chosen for major liturgical seasons of the Christian year, and they have been used (and sometimes misused) by Christian interpreters for much of Christian history.

Isaiah 42:1-4 (5-9), Isaiah 49:1-6, Isaiah 50:4-9 and Isaiah 52:13–53:12 are four poems concerning the role and work of the servant. For Jews past and present, these texts are interpreted to speak about either the role of an individual, possibly the coming Messiah, or the nation as a whole. Very early on, Christians understood these poems to be about Jesus. The poems speak of "vicarious suffering" – the belief that the suffering of one can atone for the guilt of others. (It is not required, but it can have that effect.) Isaiah 52:13–53:12 was crucial to the early church's understanding Jesus' life, and especially his death and resurrection, as events that healed the world. New Testament interpretation and theology affirm that Jesus has re-enacted the vocation of Israel in suffering for the sake of others. The suffering servant texts in Isaiah therefore permit Jewish and Christian interpretations to stand side by side: the key is the belief that one may – not must, but may – suffer for the sake of others.

Biblical prophecy

The Old Testament contains fifteen books of prophets out of a total of 39 books, which equals about one-fifth of the entire Bible. As a whole, these prophetic books speak of such themes as economic disparity; injustice; war; unrelieved suffering; unfaithfulness to God; repentance; restoration; the constant, faithful love of God; and the acceptable year or kingdom of God. Briefly, these are themes of judgment and salvation, with the continual possibility of repentance and choice on the part of the people.

It is important to define "repentance" and to keep that definition in mind throughout this book. Repentance does not mean just giving up bad behaviour. It means turning 180 degrees, in a whole new direction, and it is always done in reference to God. It means acknowledging that whatever the behaviour was, because of God's intimate relationship with all people, it was primarily bad behaviour towards God.

The prophets proclaim the majestic power of God and God's intimate, personal involvement with people. The books of the prophets are to a great extent collections of speeches. These speeches are rarely in chronological order, as chronology is not relevant to their message. Sections of narrative may be interspersed with poetry. The prophets sometimes say and do strange, eccentric things. As a result, their lives can be signs and symbols of their message that God loves all and that God's love requires justice and right behaviour. Prophets are not fortune-tellers busily looking into the future and predicting dire consequences for those who are not in right relationship with God.

Prophets are always centred in the now. They name what they see. They remind the people that repentance – turning in a new direction – is always possible with God.

Biblical poetry

Many of the Old Testament lectionary texts are poetic in form, though a much higher percentage of these are poetry than is the Old Testament as a whole. Like poetry in any language, biblical poetry uses symbol, a particular vocabulary and what might be called short forms in grammatical structure. It can seem harder to understand poetry than narrative texts. Biblical courses often spend much time on the parallelism structure of Hebrew poetry. Poetic phrases frequently appear in pairs that seem repetitive but are deliberately structured to reinforce their point. Hear poetry as poetry, read poetry as poetry, preach on biblical poetry as biblical poetry.

The Two Covenants

God is faithful

The Old Testament describes the covenant God established with the people of Israel. God has acted in the lives of a particular people, calling them into relationship and faithfulness to God's way as a way of life. The people of Israel continually fell short of God's will for life and justice, as we do today. God's love, which is passionate and deep, always calls people back into relationship. The Old Testament frequently repeats the refrain that is found in Psalm 103:8: "The Lord is merciful and gracious, slow to anger and abounding in steadfast love."

There are repercussions for behaviour that is not in line with God's will for justice. Yet the love that calls people back into right relationship is very real. The people of Israel and all their descendants, including Jews today, have believed this.

It is a false dichotomy to speak of the Old Testament as "Law" (as is often pejoratively done) and the New Testament as "Grace." Each testament contains both features of relationship with God. Furthermore, the people of Israel and their descendants, including our

19

contemporary Jewish sisters and brothers, consider the parts of the Old Testament commonly referred to as laws – such as the ten commandments and the other mitzvoth – as good news. As an act of grace, God freed the people from slavery in Egypt. Then God gave the people the ten commandments – laws that reveal that God cares deeply about the people and how they live in relationship both to God and to each other.

God never breaks covenant. Even the most dire judgments on human sin in the Old Testament allow for repentance. In Romans 9–11, Paul reminds us that the Jews remain in covenant with the God who makes covenant forever.

We know from scripture that Jesus was a Jew, the disciples were Jews and the first followers of Jesus were Jews. Jewish law, Jewish traditions and Jewish Temple worship were foundational and integral to the life of the early church. (Go to a Christian Orthodox church today with a Jewish colleague and you will be told how much Christian ritual worship resembles Jewish worship.) Many details of Jesus' ministry portray him as being in line with his Jewish traditions and faith. We may miss such subtle remarks: the possible reference to the fringes of his prayer shawl in Luke 8:44, for example. Luke's gospel (as mentioned earlier) records the story of Jesus in the synagogue in Nazareth, reading Isaiah 61 from the scroll handed to him. The gospels also record criticisms – sometimes sharp criticisms – that Jesus makes about his tradition, but he is making them from the inside. As someone who is immersed in the tradition, he can see where it has strayed from what it is called to be.

Living side by side

"Supersessionism," a pejorative term meaning that the church has replaced the people of Israel and in fact is the new Israel, is not a position to which faithful Christians can subscribe. Judaism has not been replaced. Rather, in Jesus Christ's life, ministry, death and resurrection, God opened the door to those previously outside the covenant. Judaism and Christianity both took much of the shape that is recognizable today after the Romans destroyed the Temple in 70 CE. They are two sibling religions living sometimes in great understanding and sometimes in great tension. The two faiths have lived side by side amid both these realities for nearly two thousand years. Because

Christianity became aligned with the state early on in its history (with Constantine's Edict of Toleration in 313 CE), Judaism has borne the worst of the tension in the relationship.

Judaism is a living, sustaining faith. Jewish teachers and scholars have constantly read and interpreted the scriptures, both in worship and in study, through lived experience. Unfortunately, Christians have long overlooked Jewish scholarship and the central importance of scripture in Jewish worship. Christian use of and interpretation of the Old Testament has at times led to anti-Judaism and anti-Semitism. For example, for long periods of time Christians have paid little attention to Leviticus, the central book of the Torah, which reveals that God is in the details, and that God cares very much about the ways people live in relationship to God and to each other. Christians have also misread or rejected the meaning and importance of the sacrificial worship of the Temple, as portrayed in Leviticus and other biblical texts. As a result, Christians have misrepresented even current-day Judaism as ritualistic and legalistic.

The lectionary has allowed for this kind of disparaging of Judaism past and present by leaving out many of the Old Testament texts and almost all of the narrative prophetic texts. It includes mostly prophetic texts that can be interpreted as referring to a coming messiah and the justice that such a messiah requires. This can give readers and hearers the impression that all the prophets do is predict Jesus, when in fact many Old Testament books, especially Leviticus and Deuteronomy, along with the prophetic books, describe justice in the life of the people of Israel. Making matters worse is the fact that for people living in the northern hemisphere, a number of the lengthy Old Testament stories fall during the summer months of lectionary readings, when a lot of people are away. Also, the lectionary always tries to line up Old Testament texts thematically with the Gospels. While the latter are read in order, the former are frequently out of sequence.[8]

God is faithful. The biblical witness to which we must be faithful is to two covenants living, standing and worshipping side by side.

The Old Testament is a wondrous collection and variety of texts all revealing the presence and intimacy of God in life. Narrative, po-

---

8   Even when the Old Testament passages are read more continuously, many of these texts occur during the summer months in North America, when church attendance

etry, prophecy, wisdom literature and proverbs overlap and intertwine. A high percentage of Old Testament scripture is narrative; stories of the joys and challenges of the people of God and all the ways in which God is calling them into gracious and just relationship. The texts, the variety of books that make up the Old Testament, reflect centuries of life for the people, centuries of working out their relationship with God.

The Old Testament begins with the theological statement that God is the Creator and has created into relationship. God's creation of free will as the way for authentic relationship between humanity and divinity is revealed, as is God's sovereignty over and care for all peoples. The texts, the stories, then narrow to focus on a particular people with particular joys and challenges – lots of challenges – as they try to understand their relationship with God. It is a relationship that involves every aspect of the life of the people – how they govern themselves, their relationship with other peoples, what they eat and wear, and especially how they will strive to reflect the will of God for Shalom – peace, justice, health, wholeness, prosperity for all people – even though at times they will fail.

Narrative, poetry, song, psalm, prophecy, proverb, wisdom, instruction – the Old Testament texts are wondrously diverse, often very challenging to us in our context, sometimes very challenging in their relationship to each other, not always letting us be comfortable.[9]

But they are always, always about human life grounded in the passionate reality of God.

Old Testament genealogies

It is rare for a preacher to preach on the genealogies of the Old Testament, or those of the New Testament, for that matter. Yet for

---

may be lower. As a result, many people may rarely or never hear these texts. There is no easy solution to that problem, but focusing a bible study on these texts during non-summer months every five years or so would be helpful. It could be presented as a "summer in the winter" kind of faith experience.

9   It is the nature of Scripture, despite its own claims to be fully comprehensible, to remain obscure enough to elicit a deep striving on behalf of its audience to understand. It is unrealistic to expect Scripture to be truly understood if it is the sublime will of God conveyed in the limiting language of humanity. Scripture thus demands

centuries, people of faith considered genealogies to be very important to the expression of their belief in the living God. Genealogies, which are used at significant places in the biblical text, reinforce the understanding of the God of history in particular lives and places. Some people think that oral traditions, like a game of broken telephone, are not reliable. Scholars show, however, that, in time before accessible written texts, oral tradition indeed transmitted detail over generations.

The beginning of the New Testament, the first seventeen verses of the Gospel according to Matthew, is a genealogy. This marks the transition from the Old to the New Testament, and sets up one story of the Incarnation. The New Testament writers deliberately began the book that way because they believed that was how the reality of God becoming flesh needed to be told. (And yet those key New Testament verses are rarely preached in Advent.)

Reading the Old Testament

That is not to say that Christians should read the Old Testament the same way as our Jewish sisters and brothers. We read Old Testament passages, always, in the light of the life, ministry, death and resurrection of Jesus Christ. But in the preaching context, it is always worth noting the huge gaps in what is chosen from the Old Testament for the purposes of the lectionary. It is always worth pushing forward the question of what gets little emphasis and why. John Sawyer's book *The Fifth Gospel* makes very clear specifically with reference to Isaiah that Christian commentators have always chosen to emphasize particular biblical passages which they saw as being relevant to their context. Different passages have been emphasized in different times and places and the lectionary choices are not immune to that reality.

---

humility according to both Judaism and Islam – humility, diligence, striving, and patience, all for greater understanding and improved deeds. (Rabbi Reuven Firestone, in *Noah's Other Son*, Brian Arthur Brown, Continuum, New York, London, 2007, page 238.)

How to Use This Book

This book is set up to be preacher-friendly. Each Old Testament lectionary passage for the three-year cycle of the Revised Common Lectionary and the Roman Catholic lectionary has an entry. You can read just that one page or so for the preparation of your weekly sermon. The lectionary entries deliberately focus almost entirely on the Old Testament, to sharpen your prayerful reflection as you prepare for your sermon on the Old Testament in and of itself, rather than as a prelude to the gospels.

This book is not a thorough, in-depth commentary of all the historical-critical, form-critical or other methodologies that could be discussed with any particular Old Testament text. Plenty of books discuss those and other interpretive issues. Since I am trained as an Old Testament scholar, you may notice such issues occasionally lurking in the background of the entries, but the purpose of every entry is to explore, prompt, challenge and encourage you, the preacher, to proclaim to and with your congregation how God is speaking, how the Word is revealed, how God is present in these texts. My hope is that you will do so in a way that lives in love, respect and understanding of covenant with our Jewish sisters and brothers.

Each entry covers some, but not all, of the key issues that arise from the text. These issues are always theological, but may also be historical, homiletical, rhetorical, contextual, narrative, poetic or contemporary. My aim is to let the nature of the text itself determine what I say about it. I use the terms "text," "lectionary passage," "reading," and so on synonymously to keep us all awake.

Those who, for some reason, read the entire book in one sitting will find that there is a certain amount of repetition. The repetition is unavoidable; entries are accessible when preachers preach the Old Testament every week or only occasionally.

A word about preaching from narratives. There are not a lot of Old Testament narrative texts in the lectionary, considering the large amount of narrative in the Old Testament overall. The lectionary contains a much higher percentage of poetry than is found in the Old Testament. When the narrative texts do surface, treat them as the wondrous stories they are – complex, sometimes a bit incomprehensible from our perspective, but wondrous. Often just telling the story is the most effective way to preach narratives. Resist the temptation to add a moral.

Should one have favourite biblical passages? We all do. Some passages resonate for us throughout most of our lives; others speak to particular times and seasons of our lives. But do we tend to hear only what we want to hear in favourite passages? The lectionary tries to alleviate that very human tendency by calling us to read beyond what we might choose.

Sometimes the lectionary omits verses that it considers difficult. The realities of busy pastoral life mean that many preachers do not perceive that they have the time to wrestle with passages they think are very difficult. Some preachers lack biblical scholarship. But we must wrestle with all scriptural texts – the difficult ones as well as the ones we perceive to be easy.

When it comes to pronunciation of unfamiliar biblical names, pronounce them exactly the way that they look and you will usually be correct. The words are transliterated from the Hebrew or the Greek meaning that the sound of them in Hebrew or Greek is put into the English letters to elicit the same sound in English.

The same and yet different

Roman Catholics and Protestants who use the lectionary for weekly preaching and liturgy – and some Protestant denominations do not – will find that although many of the Old Testament texts are the same for both traditions, many are different. This book includes both sets of Old Testament lectionary texts. Readings particular to the Roman Catholic lectionary are found in the Appendix: Roman Catholic Readings, following the readings for Year C of the Revised Common Lectionary.

Year A

In the beginning

Across the street from the United Nations building in New York is a small park. Inscribed on a stone wall in that park are these very words from the Book of the Prophet Isaiah that were chosen to begin the Lectionary for Advent 1, Year A. It is a deep privilege to stand in that park and to let those words from Isaiah burrow into the core of one's being, and to hope, pray and work that they will burrow into the core being of the world's nations. It is a deep privilege, but in spite of – or perhaps because of – this passage, it is a challenging moment for many of us who preach at this time of year.

Advent is a time of high expectations. While Christians are waiting in hope for the Messiah, most are also dealing with the stresses of the pre-Christmas season. For some, this means shopping, entertaining, and having too much to do. For others, this season is a difficult one, where poverty, loss or loneliness becomes more obvious in light of the festive mood of others. For preachers, this may be a challenging time since, for the next twelve weeks, the lectionary's Old Testament passages are all from the prophet Isaiah. That is a lot of Isaiah!

A number of the Year A lectionary readings from Isaiah are judgment passages from the first twelve chapters. The people and the ruler have fallen short of all that God intends them to be, fallen short of faithful response to God. Disregard for God's will in public life leads to trouble in public life. These are often hard passages to explore, especially in the pre-Christmas frenzy; no one really wants to hear them. But these passages are always being "punctuated and reshaped" by passages of hope revealing that, ultimately, the promise of God's presence will prevail.[10] The judgment is real; so is the powerful promise of hope. Isaiah 2:1-5, this passage chosen for this first Sunday of Advent in Year A, is one of those powerful promises of hope. It follows the long

---

10   Walter Brueggemann, *Isaiah 1–39* (Louisville, KY: Westminster John Knox Press, 1998), 10.

judgment passage of chapter one as a pointed reminder that, while the judgment is real, from God's point of view, promise and hope are the ultimate outcome for all peoples of the earth.

Note the use of the term "instruction" (depending on your translation) in verse 3. This is the same word as "Torah." However it is translated, it is always a positive term in the Old Testament. Torah, the instruction, is a wondrous gift of God, showing the people how to live in relationship to holiness. Verse 4 is, of course, well known in the Christian tradition – a proclamation of God's vision for the world. It also occurs in Micah 4:3. Perhaps it was a familiar saying or passage in the time of the prophets. For an extra-challenging sermon some year, note that the Isaiah/Micah passage also occurs in Joel 3:10, but in Joel the ploughshares are beaten into swords. Delve deeply into why. And by the way, pray for the United Nations!

Who, what, where, why and how?

The first twelve chapters of Isaiah are primarily ones of judgment, but always include reminder passages about the power of hope. Today's reading is one of those reminder passages. Take a quick look at the end of chapter 10. It is a graphic and difficult judgment passage, axes and all. Then comes this passage with its promise that we can start over; God is making something new. We have appropriated this text to serve the proclamation of our faith. Isaiah 11:1-10 is, in the Christian canon, a messianic passage, a text that proclaims for us the coming of Jesus Christ. My good colleague Rabbi Tannenbaum says, "You Christians appropriate the texts. That is what you do and that is fine as long as you do not denigrate us, the Jews, in doing so."

In this passage we hear of the coming of a new, unidentified figure, upon whom the Spirit of the Lord rests. In this text, the shoot coming out from the stump of Jesse tells us that this restorative person is in David's royal line. This messiah will judge with righteousness and with favour for the poor and oppressed so that there is security and well-being for all. The reign of righteousness and faithfulness will also bring order and peace to the relationships of the natural world. (We will discuss this concept later in this book; for now, keep in mind that the biblical text always states clearly that the presence or absence of peace, justice and good order in humanity is integrally connected with what happens in the natural order.)

Although Christians can appropriate this text as speaking about the coming of Jesus Christ, we must remember that it has another context and meaning for our Jewish sisters and brothers: we remain faithful to the original meaning when we incorporate it into our understanding of the passage: the coming of the new Davidic ruler, the coming of Jesus Christ as Messiah, brings about real, concrete changes in the world. He decides with equity for the meek of the earth. In wisdom, understanding, counsel and might, and in "the fear of the Lord" – responding to God's holiness and power – things will change on earth. Christians are to be bearers of that change.

Here is your God

Chapter 35 is a lovely, lyric part of Isaiah's poetry. The poetic closing of a part of the book, this chapter is immediately followed by three narrative chapters. These lead directly into what is often designated as Isaiah's chapter 40 and beyond; they are not in the lectionary. Chapter 35 must be read in the context of chapter 34, because the two together paint a picture of the completeness of God's vindication and recompense. God will not leave the world in bondage, drought and oppression. That God is present, real, restorative and redemptive is set in contrast to the graphic painting of God's intolerance for the forces that work against peace, justice, security and blossoming for all.

The lectionary includes all of chapter 35. Verse 4 proclaims the refrain that we hear so often throughout both the Old and the New Testaments. "Be strong, do not fear! Here is your God." For Christians, "Fear not, for behold, I bring you good tidings of great joy." It is easy to see why the lectionary compilers thought Isaiah 35 a good passage to read in the third week of Advent. Note in verse 5 that this is not an abstract coming. Things will change for those who are vulnerable and hurting.

This might be a good time for a preacher to wrestle with the connections between restoration and redemption for people, and restoration and redemption for Creation and the natural world. The passage starts out by saying that "The wilderness and the dry land shall be glad, the desert shall rejoice and blossom; like the crocus it shall blossom abundantly, and rejoice with joy and singing." Years ago, I was the teaching assistant for homiletics professor Paul Wilson of Emmanuel College in Toronto. He used to say that in sermons we were not just to talk about some abstract phrase like "the kingdom of God." Instead, we were to show what that looked like. So what does it look like for the wilderness and the dry land to be glad? What does the rejoicing and blossoming desert look like? What does a "singing" desert look like?

To test or not to test

This familiar and well-loved passage from Isaiah is proclaimed on the Sunday before Christmas, a time when our congregations expect to hear a sermon about great hope. This text has given much comfort and has been a channel for the presence of God for many Christians for millennia. Yet reading it out of context has devastating effects on faithful interpretation.

Chapter 7 of Isaiah is a tough chapter. This passage falls right in the middle of it. Ahaz, the king of Judah, the southern kingdom, and Isaiah are in the midst of major conflict. Judah is being seriously threatened by Israel, its northern neighbour. Ahaz hopes to escape the threat by making an alliance with the superpower of the day, Assyria. Isaiah wants him to have faith in God instead. In the second verse of this passage, God challenges Ahaz to ask for a sign that faith in God will be enough, that God is truly faithful. Ahaz refuses to ask for such a sign but gets it anyway: the sign of the child. God's claim to faithfulness is going to be made concrete and inescapable. There is even a timeline provided: by the time the child knows the difference between good and evil, the threat from the northern neighbour will be over. Assyria will remain a threat, and the repercussions of the Assyrian invasion will be dire. Nonetheless, the call is to remain faithful to the Lord. The child's very name is positive and reassuring: "God is with us." The child is to be a visible, physical, concrete reassertion of the core conviction of royal Israel that God is present in and with and for Israel as defender, guardian and protector so that Israel need not be afraid. Indeed, Ahaz in this conflict need not be afraid and therefore need not turn to the savage resource of Assyria.

The point of the text is the conflict between King Ahaz and Isaiah over the issue of faith versus secular alliances. The sign of the child overcomes their conflict and is a visible summons to faith.[11] To use

---

11   Brueggemann, *Isaiah 1–39*, 70.

this text as a proof or a battleground over the doctrine of the Virgin Birth is to miss the point.

One way to preach this text faithfully is to point out that the sign Ahaz gets is one that he did not want or ask for. As we approach this time of the manger, the star, the shepherds and the angels, are we sure we can face the truth that they proclaim? As we wrap the last of the presents and finish the last of the baking, are we ready for a messiah who turns the world and all our expectations upside down? Born into poverty, cold and darkness, this messiah comes into the world knowing how to choose the good (God's will for justice, peace and economic security for all) and refuse evil (materialism, self-reliance, self-centredness). Are we able to do the same?

"The times they are a-changing"

It is Christmas Eve. There are probably more people in church tonight than at any other time in the church year. And they have come to hear … What have they come to hear? Someone once came up to me after I preached a Christmas Eve service and said, "I just come to church once a year, just on Christmas Eve, and I expect you to give me every-thing I need in that one service to get me through the whole year. You didn't do that." An extreme example? I am not so sure. Expectations are high on Christmas Eve. People want to hear both the familiar and sustaining as well as a slightly different take on the familiar. Many of those present will not be back for a while.

This text from Isaiah is one of those reminders of hope that are sprinkled throughout the first twelve judgment chapters.[12]

In its original context, this text proclaims, using rich imagery and liturgical poetry, that the times are changing. Things have not been good for the people of Israel under King Ahaz. Walter Breuggemann refers to Ahaz in this part of Isaiah as the embodiment of failed leader-ship.[13] A new Davidic king is coming and things are going to be differ-ent, better, glorious from then on. No matter how grim things might have become, God can always call new possibilities into being.

Do not skip over verse 4 and the day of Midian. It is important. It refers to a story that Isaiah's original hearers would have known well, as would Jesus, who had a solid education in the scriptures. Judges 6:2-6 tells of the great victory that the judge Gideon won over the oppres-sive Midianites. Isaiah 9:4, then, is an important reminder that God acts in human lives and that oppression can be overcome. Be sure to

---

12 The five lectionary texts from Isaiah that we have dealt with so far do not appear in the lectionary in the canonical order.

13 Brueggemann, *Isaiah 1–39*, 82.

take a quick look at Matthew 4:13-17, where this passage speaks to the Christian understanding that Jesus is the one proclaimed in the text.

In preaching on this Eve of such high expectations, a preacher might choose to emphasize the terms "justice and righteousness" in verse 7. The words "justice and righteousness" come up often in the Bible. God is ushering in social and power arrangements that are fair to all: we are invited and, indeed, enthusiastically encouraged to participate.

Seeing a "great light" always means particular things in particular times and places. Making extravagant purchases for family and friends while the single mom down the street has no turkey for Christmas dinner is a manifestation of the deep darkness that this passage describes. Complaining about too many Christmas parties while there are people in Africa who have no paraffin to light against the twelve-hour darkness of the night is another. Presents and parties are not wrong – especially not at Christmas, when we celebrate the coming of Christ, who came to bring life and bring it in abundance. The key is to find a balance: to celebrate *and* to share our blessings so that we help to shine light in the darkness.

You better watch out!

For Christmas Day, the lectionary jumps from the early chapters of Isaiah, with their primary emphasis on judgment and their reminders of hope, to a late part of the book. (Some might call this Third Isaiah, and stress that it was written or edited in the time when the people of Israel had been released from exile in Babylon and were establishing themselves again in the land of Israel. This is entirely possible.)

The imagery of the passage is that of a city, the city of Jerusalem being rebuilt. It is worth reminding ourselves here that the image of city is an important one in the Bible. There is no escaping to a peaceful, romantic, bucolic countryside or wilderness for the culmination of salvation if one is trying to be faithful to the biblical text. We do need to spend time in the wilderness – the desert, in fact – from time to time. Our lives are intertwined with the natural world. But the Temple is in Jerusalem. Jesus set his face to Jerusalem. And there will be a new heaven and new earth, a holy city, a new Jerusalem.

The time of exile is over, the time for re-establishing community is now, and sentinels are being posted on the rebuilt city walls. But these sentinels are not there to watch for either enemies or trade caravans.[14] The sentinels serve as reminders to God that Jerusalem needs God, and that God has an obligation to the city. We may find it somewhat disturbing that God should need such a concrete reminder of relationship, but it is not a faithful reading if we smooth over the biblical images that we find uncomfortable. The prayers of the people of Israel are always an urgent reality, reminding God of what God has continually promised.

---

14 Jerusalem was built close to the trade routes. There is not a lot of natural water, which is highly unusual for an ancient city, but it is connected to the routes from Egypt to all parts east and accessible to the north/south trade route. This is one reason for conflict in this part of the world. The final battle taking place at Mount Meggido (Armageddon) that the biblical text speaks of is close to two major trade routes.

Verse 12 of this passage contains wonderful Christmas Day kinds of imagery: the coming of salvation, redemption, reward, being sought out (with reminders), not being forsaken. Verse 9 is also to be noted for its definition of what salvation, redemption, reward, and so on "look like." This is the opposite of the futility referred to in other places in the Bible, such as Ecclesiastes 2:18-23, Deuteronomy 28:30 and Amos 5:11. Now there is the promise of stability, justice and righteousness. People will enjoy the fruits of their labours. Enough to eat, enough to drink. Not excess, just enough.

One foot, two foot

This passage, from what some scholars call Deutero-Isaiah or Second Isaiah, probably had its origins in the exile of the people of Israel to Babylon – sometime after 586 BCE and before the return of the people from exile about 40 years later.[15] Again we find sentinels, but in this passage, their purpose is somewhat different than in Isaiah 62. These sentinels watch for and then sing out the coming of God, who returns to dwell in Jerusalem, between the wings of the cherubim on the ark of the covenant in the Holy of Holies of the Temple. God is truly present in the world that God created. The conflict between God and Babylon is resolved; God is the victor. The people are free and Jerusalem is again made the new centre of God-governed reality.[16]

"How beautiful upon the mountains are the feet of the messenger who announces peace." In his book *Wishful Thinking*, Frederick Buechner writes about feet. He refers to this very passage, reminding us that the messenger's feet bring him up to the mountain to proclaim the good news of the coming of God. In Matthew 28:9, when the disciples first encounter the Risen Christ, they take hold of his feet as they worship him. Buechner concludes by telling us to discover who we really are by paying attention to where our feet take us.[17]

If you want more for the sermon for this day, when those who truly, deeply need or want to be in church are here, note that the word in verse 7 that in many translations is given as "good news" is the same word for "gospel" in the New Testament. Isaiah 40:9 offers

---

15 Many biblical references to 40 years are seen as highly significant theologically rather than as historically accurate. In the case of the exile, however, "40 years," while also theologically significant and resonating with other references to "40 years," is probably historical.

16 Walter Brueggemann, *Isaiah 40–66* (Louisville, KY: Westminster John Knox Press, 1998), 139.

17 Frederick Buechner, *Wishful Thinking: A Seeker's ABC* (San Francisco: Harper Collins, 1993), 31.

the first use of the term. This is the second. The good news/gospel being proclaimed is that God, as ruling sovereign, has come to decisive power. God has overcome the powers of captivity and oppression; a new world has begun. And where will your feet take you?

Context is everything

This is a very difficult Sunday for preachers. Between the two high points of Christmas Eve and the Epiphany, the New Testament lectionary passage for today is the massacre of the innocents. This book usually, deliberately, refers only to the Old Testament passages, to emphasize them, to try and inspire preachers with possibilities for using them to proclaim the Gospel. However, for this Sunday I break the pattern. How can preachers shed light on the lectionary's combination of the massacre of the innocents with the Isaiah passage, which sounds like a kind of general doxology recounting God's gracious, loving and faithful mercies to the people? One answer is context.

As noted earlier, the first twelve chapters of Isaiah are primarily chapters of judgment upon the people, interspersed with reminders of hope. Chapters 40 to 66 are primarily chapters of hope, interspersed with reminders of judgment. Verses 7 to 9 of chapter 63 are a kind of doxology set into a section of judgment in chapters that primarily resonate with comfort. Reading on into verse 10 sets the context of difficulty between God and Israel. Everything that verses 7 to 9 say is true, as the biblical context and as the glory and power of the resurrection show. But we live in in-between times: between the inauguration of all God's gracious deeds and the absolute fulfillment of that reality. God is mercy and the abundance of steadfast love. But we live in a world in which there is corrupt power and in which children die.

Isaiah 63:7-9 is a "general doxological opening that lacks specificity," Brueggemann says.[18] That is what makes it so powerful and why it needs to be counterpoised to the story of the massacre of the innocents. People need to hear the story of the massacre of the innocents. They know that power can corrupt and that children die for reasons that are unjust. This passage is crucial because it is the truth that resonates around and through the tough stuff and proclaims God's ultimate purposes.

---

18   Brueggemann, *Isaiah 40–66*, 229.

Jeremiah was not a bullfrog

Isaiah, Jeremiah and Ezekiel are called major prophets in the biblical tradition. The rest are called the minor prophets, or the Book of the Twelve – Hosea, Joel, Amos, and on through Malachi.[19]

What we have here is a reading from the prophet Jeremiah in the midst of a lot of readings from Isaiah. The historical Jeremiah prophesied in the southern part of the kingdom of Israel, Judah, during the later years of its existence. He did so from the time of King Josiah onward, living to see the destruction of Jerusalem by the Babylonians in 586 BCE. (Numerous colourful stories told in the Bible about Jeremiah do not make it into the lectionary. One describes the time he spent in a cistern, where the king thought he would cause less trouble.) To the religious and political establishments of the day, prophets were mostly a pain, definitely not to be invited for dinner! Jeremiah was always prophesying judgment to come because of the people's bad behaviour. He was always calling for repentance and turning back to God, for he believed that by repenting, the people could avoid the destruction. He clearly expressed in his words and actions (prophets often perform symbolic actions to make their points – they are not just abstract poets) that God is the God of all power and all times and places.

Jeremiah also makes it clear that God is very concerned about and involved with individual people. Individuals are accountable to God. The Old Testament creates a balance between collective and individual rights, responsibilities and accountabilities. Both are present in the text and both are important. Avoid slipping into the frequently heard and biblically inaccurate view that the Old Testament is about collective responsibility, and that phrases about individual responsi-

---

19   The major prophets were not called "major" because they were more important than the minor prophets, but rather because of the length of the books. In the days of scrolls, the major prophets would need one scroll each, while all twelve minor prophets could be copied onto one scroll.

bility are few and far between, foretastes of the "better way" to come in the New Testament.

In passages such as this one, Jeremiah does prophesy disaster if the people refuse to repent. But he also describes the ultimate return home. In Isaiah 49:15, God is likened to a mother. Here, God has become a father to the people.

The people have been scattered, but now is the time for them to be gathered back, as a great company. Note in verse 8 that the blind and the lame, those with child and those in labour – that is, the vulnerable – are particularly mentioned. They are an integral part of the great company for Jeremiah – may that be so for us!

In the realm of the God of justice, there may be "scattering" – that is, repercussions for injustice, but God's ultimate will is always that of compassion and comfort.

Two out of three

It is Epiphany! We all want to delve into the visit of the Magi.[20] The adoration of the Christ child by the Magi is a wonderful story, which makes it harder to preach from the Isaiah text. But in the tradition of the lectionary and church, this passage from Isaiah is seen in the context of Matthew 2. As people who help to shed light on the biblical texts, preachers need to tackle this Old Testament text.

This chapter of Isaiah is a long one of sustained good news to the restored community of Jerusalem. It comes in that part of the book that some scholars refer to as Third Isaiah. The people of Israel had been threatened with the dire realities of the trauma of the exile. They were comforted while in exile with the promise of return and restoration. They ultimately did return home; chapters 56 to 59 describe some of the contentious issues involved in resettlement. Isaiah always holds these two experiences in balance: the challenges and the sustaining promise of God's love and hope. Then comes the ringing affirmation of good news in this chapter. It is God's resolve to work for the good of Jerusalem. (In the biblical text, where peace, justice, righteousness and healing are proclaimed as God's great goodwill, these are not abstract qualities but involve concrete security, prosperity and offspring – all the things Israel needed to be a continuing people and presence in the world. We may find it strange to see these as signs of God's favour or goodness, but a people cannot survive without them.)

God is the light of Jerusalem, of the people. God as light is restoring Jerusalem (the city is often used as a symbol for the people), and all nations and rulers will stream towards it. Phrases such as the "wealth of nations" may trouble us; the point is to indicate reversal. For so long, Israel and Jerusalem have been subject to or conquered by a superpower – Assyria, Babylon, Persia. Tribute has been paid in

---

20 Traditionally, we talk about three of them. This is likely a parallel to the three sons
of Noah, and the idea that three encompasses the three major regions and divisions
of the world as well as the fact that there are three gifts mentioned.

taxes, plunder, even lives. The vision now is for a restored Jerusalem, a great centre into which trade and wealth – such as camels and flocks, the wealth of the desert – will flow.

As Christians, we immediately notice the reference to "gold and frankincense" in verse 6: gold for the one who would be king, and frankincense for the one who is both the great high priest and the sacrifice. But where is the myrrh, the embalming spice for the one who was to die? It is not here in Isaiah because that is not the point of the passage. The sacrifice motif is found in the "suffering servant" passages. This glorious, hope-filled passage, interspersed as it is with Isaiah's other passages on hope, judgment and of the suffering servant, points to God's future. According to Isaiah, the community is to be restored as a highly visible witness to God. God's all-encompassing reign of peace, justice, stability and enough of what is good for life for all is a guide to perfect light.

The servant is as the servant does

This general section of Isaiah, called in the terms of historical criticism "Second Isaiah," celebrates God's powerful intervention on behalf of Israel.[21] God's work in the world is to be done through human agency. This is the first reference in the book to "the servant" – commonly known as "the suffering servant" – and is one of many such passages in the lectionary. (For more on the servant passages, see the Introduction to this book.)

Over the centuries, scholars have debated whether the servant is an individual or the collective people. Christians tend to interpret this figure in messianic terms: the servant is Jesus. Jewish interpretation sometimes sees the servant as an individual, but more often as the collective people of Israel. Both interpretations are valid and can stand side by side.

Preachers may wish to examine verse 7, asking how we as Christians can follow this mandate. The point is not to interpret it literally, but to frame current situations in these terms. In the ancient world, the poor were the ones who mainly ended up in prison. Who are today's "prisoners"? What is keeping them captive? How can we help to set them free?

Another helpful reflection would be on the definition of "servant." This term is used frequently in the Old Testament. In the New Testament, Jesus is frequently described as a servant whom we are to emulate. How do we understand this term today? What does it mean to be served? What does it mean to serve others? Be specific.

---

21   Brueggemann, *Isaiah 40–66*, 11.

"To the ends of the earth ..."

Biblical scholarship – reading the Bible, exploring what others have thought upon reading the Bible, and delving deep into the issues of time, place and intention in the writing of the texts – is a good thing. Along with preaching, biblical scholarship helps congregations connect with the text. In it they hear the voice of God speaking and calling to their lives. Yet this passage from Isaiah is one that has been pored over in ways that are sometimes not helpful for preaching. There has been much debate about the identity of the servant. Is it an individual – for Christians, perhaps a casting forward to Jesus – or the nation of Israel as a whole? Walter Brueggemann suggests that we forget about the quest for the servant's identity and hear what the text is saying: "It is enough to see that [God] has designated some human agent to be about the work of healing and emancipation in the world with particular reference to Israel."[22] In other words, if the poet does not seem to care about the identity of the servant, why would we?

The servant is clearly portrayed as having a large mandate. The servant has been called and commissioned by God, given skills and kept in God's care until it is time to come forth. The language of verse 1 sounds very much like the language of the call narratives of the prophets. The servant has been called and sent out by God so that God will be glorified. And yet verse 3 clearly details the servant's discouragement, weariness and despair. What was to be accomplished seems not to have been done. Things look bleak to the servant. But in the face of that bleakness lies the certainty that the call is right and the servant is still and continually held by God. Many parallels exist between verse 3 and verse 7. No matter how bleak it may look now for the work and call of the servant, one who is deeply despised by many, the work and call of God will be vindicated because God is faithful and makes intentional choices.

---

22   Brueggemann, *Isaiah 40–66*, 110.

For the purposes of preaching, verse 6 is an important and rich part of this passage. It marks a turning point in the faith of the people. It is not enough, God clearly proclaims in and through the servant, that he or she should only be about the restoration of the particular community. The message of light and salvation is for all nations, to the ends of the earth. This message is not about conversion! It is about a God who is wider and deeper and higher and broader than we can imagine. This God truly loves all people. God calls us to proclaim that love – a love that brings with it certain just standards, certain mani-festations of righteousness and fairness for all. How does and will your congregation do so?

Before and after

Here we go again! On Christmas Eve we read this same passage, or almost. As you mull over what to say, think about why this text appears for the second time in a few weeks when so much of the Old Testament is not included in the lectionary.

If you tire of that question, ask yourself what difference it makes to preaching that on Christmas Eve we read verses 2 to 7, while for this week it is verses 1 to 4. Verse 1 sets the context of a transition from former times to latter times. Given the historical context of chapters 6 to 8, the former times are those of the reign of King Ahaz. During this time, rulers relied on political alliances rather than God, despite Isaiah's constant urgings to do otherwise. The latter times will therefore be those where there is new leadership: political and royal. This may refer to the rule of King Ahaz's son, King Hezekiah, who is always portrayed – pointedly in later chapters of Isaiah (36–39) – as a ruler who was faithful to God. This is a time of peace and prosperity. (Zebulun, Naphtali and "the way of the sea" are all used to name the land and the people of Israel.)

Walter Brueggemann constantly reminds us that the Old Testament text is multi-layered. These former and latter times can also be read as the pre-exilic and exilic times of judgment, despair and hard times, and the post-exilic times of restoration, healing and wholeness. God, as always, can make a new thing. Unqualified and unconditional new possibilities abound.

As we have noted, this passage ends with verse 4 rather than verse 7. Verse 4 is a strong declaration that in the times to come, the transformation to be wrought is a historical one. The actual oppression by an actual oppressor is to end. This is not a spiritual transformation; rather, the people's physical realities will be transformed. The "day of Midian" refers to a story told in Judges 6:2-6, where the judge Gideon won an unexpected victory over the oppressive Midianites. God can and does use people to overcome oppression. And that includes us.

The saving acts of the Lord

This passage from Micah is one of the best known texts of the minor prophets. We all love verse 8, but there is much richness and challenge in the text as a whole. I encourage you to preach on the whole text, verses 1 through 8. Much less is known about the historical prophet Micah than is known about Isaiah and Jeremiah, but scholars date him sometime around 721 BCE. This would place him around the time of the Assyrian deportation of the northern part of Israel.

Micah was a prophet in the southern part of the country, Judah, but would have been aware of the devastation of the northern part of the country. Micah alternates between messages of doom and messages of hope. He speaks out on God's perspective against idolatry, injustice, rebellion and empty worship, as noted in the NRSV's introduction to Micah, but he also proclaims firmly God's delight in pardoning the penitent.

Verses 1 and 2 offer a wonderful opportunity to preach on the interconnection of humanity and Creation. God has a controversy with the people and the mountains and the foundations of the earth – the heights and depths of Creation are called to hear the case. What happens in the human realm affects what happens in the natural realm; the two are bound together. The witness of both the Old and New Testaments has always been so. As people of faith, we are to lead in that witness.

Verses 3 to 5 offer a mini-recital of God's actions on behalf of the people. It would make a great congregational Bible study to study Moses, Aaron and Miriam, and then to study King Balak of Moab and Balaam son of Beor, and what happened at Shittim and Gilgal, so that we too might know those saving acts of the Lord. The Old Testament records for us and gifts us with these stories for a reason. What are they saying to us in our time and place? Why are they placed in such close proximity to the beloved verse 8? What light do they shed on it?

Preaching this text also means remembering the biblical truth that worship, ritual and sacrifice are ways of connecting intimately and profoundly with God. Problems arise when worship – bowing and offering before God – is not directly connected with how we are in the world. Our worship must be created in its telling of the biblical stories, in its music, in its preaching, in its silences, to give us the strength and the creativity and the passion to do justice, and to love kindness and walk humbly with our God.

The acceptable day of the Lord

Things are not as they should be! Tension is touching the life of the community to whom this passage is first addressed. It is one of those tensions that is alive and well in our time and place: the way the community professes in worship that it is living its life, and how it actually lives its life. They are seeking God in worship "as if they were a nation that practised righteousness and did not forsake the ordinance of their God" (verse 2). Verse 7 lays out in very specific language what exactly is in accordance with the purposes of God: the just, concrete meeting of people's needs as if they were one's own kin.

Because the people have not been doing that, God has not been paying attention to their acts and professions of worship. They have been serving their own interests on their fast days while oppressing their workers. If they loose the bonds of injustice that the true worship of God requires, the people will break forth like the dawn and they will hear and experience the close presence of God. Does what we do on Sundays slide into "feel-good" worship that is disconnected from the biblical imperatives set out in verses 6 and 7 of Isaiah 58? How do we carry our beliefs from worship to our daily lives?

In the weeks surrounding and including this week, the lectionary uses a number of texts from various prophets. This tends to blur the prophets together and makes it seem and sound as if they all are saying similar things. But they are not all the same, nor do they always proclaim social justice and denigrate empty, meaningless, ritualistic worship. Although many do speak out loud and long for social justice and many of them do denigrate empty, meaningless, ritualistic worship, they never sever the connection between social justice and worship. Both are always integral to each other and to our relationship with God.

It is easy for preachers to slip into condemning Israel for performing empty sacrificial worship that God does not want and for forgetting the meaningful pursuit of social justice that God does want, but this can be dangerous. The Old Testament practice of sacrifice was meaningful; it represented a holy sharing between God and the people. Through sacrificing the fruit of the land, the people offered something from Creation in thanksgiving for the blessings they received.

Isaiah may have been a priest in the Temple in Jerusalem. He may have administered the sacrificial system at the same time as holding firm to the social justice with which, in the biblical imperatives, it is intimately connected. Isaiah and the other prophets clearly state that worship and social justice go together.

Epiphany 6 – *Deuteronomy 30:15-20*

The choice is yours

Deuteronomy is the last of the five books of the Torah – the Five Books of Moses. Deuteronomy comes up in the lectionary cycle only a few times, so make the most of preaching on it when it does surface! As one of the five books of the Torah it has central importance in the Jewish faith. That means Jesus, a faithfully educated Jew of his time and place, was familiar with it. This book was as well known as, and perhaps better known than, all the prophetic, poetic passages that the Christian lectionary emphasizes.

The word "Deuteronomy" means "second law," and as a book functions as a repetition, with updates of the law. The narrative is set in the time after the Exodus – the 40 years of wandering in the wilderness are over. The people are about to re-enter the land of Israel. In Deuteronomy, Moses reminds them of their history, of all that God has done for them. He reminds them of the laws that they are to keep as their way of being in faithful relationship to God. The entire book is about God's relationship of love with the people, and the people's relationship of love with their God.

Chapter 30:15-20 is about choosing life. God has gifted the people with everything they need for living a relationship of love with God and with each other. The commandments promote love, life, relationship and blessing. God implores the people not to choose the ways of death, not to choose the false gods of fertility and materialism. These gods have no relationship with God or with all those made in God's image.

This passage, with its promise of land to the ancestors Abraham, Isaac and Jacob and the "possessing" of the land that is mentioned in verse 16, is problematic for some. What this means in terms of conflict in the Middle East needs to be resolved on the international scene. Jews, Christians and Muslims can contribute wisdom on this question. The biblical text is clear that there is a promise to the people of Israel. What that promise looks like, regarding the calling of Israel to be a light to the nations, is the issue that confronts our time and place.

Epiphany 7 – *Leviticus 19:1-2, 9-18*

Holiness it is

Of all the books in the Bible, the Book of Leviticus is the one that Christian preachers preach on least. Why? One answer, of course, is that Leviticus appears only once, for Protestants, in the three-year cycle of the lectionary. Also, some theological college or seminary programs spend little time on it, so as preachers we find its detail strange and overwhelming. We may think that the church does not need the rules and regulations set out in this, the third book of the Old Testament, because we believe that Christianity has set us free from what we perceive to be the legalistic attitudes of Leviticus. This perception has often led the church into words and actions that have denigrated Judaism past and present.

When Christians do speak on Leviticus, they tend it to pick one of its wide range of subjects and ignore all the rest. But to the Jews – before, during and after the time of Jesus – the book of Leviticus is a tremendous gift of grace from a loving God: a loving God who created all Creation and who cares deeply about the minutiae of their lives. All the details of the book of Leviticus are focused on defining life as a gift, and on God as the creator of that gift.

Leviticus in general, like today's text, is about the holiness of God and the holiness of the people. This passage says that the people are to be holy as God is holy; it goes on to define in concrete terms what that holiness looks like. Holiness equals care for the poor (vv. 9-10) and right relationships (vv. 11-15), based on the reality of God as the Lord of the people. Holiness is not abstract; it is concrete, justice-oriented behaviour based on Divine Imperative. These concrete terms resonate with other passages of scripture that are more familiar – the "ten commandments" – though with some differences, particularly in favour of the care of the poor and vulnerable. (Versions of the ten commandments are found in Exodus 20, Exodus 34 and Deuteronomy 5.)[23]

---

23 Although I discuss the fact that the English term "the ten commandments" is not the best translation of the Hebrew, I use it because it is well known.

Some verses are omitted in today's reading. It is interesting to read these verses. Leaving aside the issue of length, why would they have been left out? Often, as is the case with this passage, the omitted verses have to do with sacrifice. References to sacrifice in the Old Testament refer to the time of the Temple, before it was destroyed by the Romans in 70 CE. At the time, sacrifice acknowledged the supremacy of God. Through making animal sacrifices, the people gave back to God from the great gifts they had been given. The practice of making monetary offerings in Christian churches has a similar guiding principle. Some of the sacrifices offered were consumed by the priests; sacrifices provided nourishment to these servants of the Temple. Much was eaten communally, by all the people – a celebration in a time and place where food, especially meat, was often scarce.

In Leviticus, all of the rules – including rules about sexual behaviour – are about promoting life so that the people of Israel will reproduce and survive. Most of the people were poor, and many were malnourished. As a result, fertility was elusive. The sexual rules provided guidance for that time and place to increase fertility and thus increase the population.

"See, I have inscribed you on the palms of my hands."

This passage is the continuation of the passage used for Epiphany 2. Presenting the Old Testament texts out of order makes it harder to understand what they are saying to us today. (Isaiah – and, indeed, all the poetic and prophetic books of the Old Testament – were intended to be heard and experienced in the order in which they appear in the canon of Scripture.)

Since this is indeed a continuation of Chapter 49 of Isaiah, see this book's entry for Year A, Epiphany 2, for a short discussion of the nature of the servant who is referred to here. (See also Christmas 2, Jeremiah 31:7-14, which has many echoes in this week's text.) This Isaiah passage, verses 8-16a, is in what some scholars refer to as Second Isaiah – the part of the book that primarily speaks words of comfort and promise to a people in exile from what they knew and had held dear for so long. The servant is some kind of covenant partner who will make a new reality for the people. There is even a kind of travellers' guide of verses describing the trip home from exile. (Although the passage refers to the Babylonian exile, it speaks to other times and places, too.)

"See, I have inscribed you on the palms of my hands." These words offer further reassurance to the people. Their lingering doubts are met with the proclamation that, unlikely as it is for a nursing mother to forget her child, it is even less likely for God to forget or forsake the people. Even in the depth of exile, God has not forgotten or abandoned them. Like the ten commandments are carved onto stone tablets, Israel's name, the name of the people, is engraved on the very palm of God's hand. This visible sign and symbol attests to the eternal, faithful, sustaining and intimate – oh so intimate – attentiveness of God.

Now you see it

As mentioned earlier, the lectionary's Old Testament and epistle texts are chosen to complement the gospel lections. Sometimes this relationship is very easy to see, but not always. (For some general background on the book of Deuteronomy, look at the entry for Year A, Epiphany 6.)

Verses 18 to 21 refer to the Jewish practice of wearing phylacteries, which is followed by Orthodox Jews today. This practice involves strapping on to the forehead and arm, in a prescribed and ritual way, special containers that hold biblical verses at times of prayer. The words of God are to live in both heart and soul, physically visible in the prayer life of the believer in the world. Jesus, a practising, faithful Jew, attended, read in and spoke in the synagogue. He made the Passover pilgrimage to the Temple in Jerusalem with his disciples. Would he have prayed with phylacteries? Most likely. The words of God are to be taught continually to the next generation. Verse 20 refers to the Jewish tradition of the biblical mezuzah, a parchment on which a biblical verse is written. The parchment is sealed in a special container and attached to the door frame. People touch it each time they pass through the door to remind them of the holiness of God. Phylacteries and mezuzahs are visible and tangible signs of the holy.

What are the visible and tangible signs of the holy today, the reminders of our Christian identity? How do we connect ourselves physically with our God? Verses 22 to 25, which have been omitted from this text, are challenging: the driving out of nations, the dispossessing of nations, getting and keeping all the territory. Look at the earlier comments on Deuteronomy 30 and reflect prayerfully on these verses. Find a way to refer to them, even if they are not part of the reading. They remind us that for God, the concrete realities of life are important. God is a God of time and space and place. How we live where we live matters. How are these verses challenged or contradicted by the claims that run all through the Old Testament: that God is the God of peace, justice and economic security for all peoples?

3-D glasses

It is mighty tempting, before the temptations of Lent even begin, to see this Old Testament passage merely as a prefiguring or set-up of the Transfiguration passage in Matthew. It is also tempting, and has become far too common, to think of this story as an illustration of getting things wrong, while the Matthew text is an illustration of getting things right. Instead of leaping to the Matthew text, sit a spell with this passage from Exodus. What might it have meant in its original context? Why does God choose to be revealed to us in this text? Read the whole of chapter 24 to set things in context.

The people of Israel are wandering in the wilderness. The Exodus from Egypt, that supreme act of grace, has happened. Some rumblings of discontent against Moses have been heard. The ten commandments have been given. For the people of Israel and for the Jewish people now, the ten commandments have never been a set of legalistic rules and regulations. Rather, they are a gift: a sign of the wonderful relationship into which God has called the people, and a helpful, hopeful way to live in right relationship with God. This is the context for Exodus 24.

The prophets of Israel rail against meaningless sacrifice, just as we should rail against putting money in the offering plate without making a commitment to giving our time or to right, just and compassionate living. In the earlier verses of chapter 24, a sacrifice to God, offering all that the people were and had, was combined with reading the book of the covenant, setting out the paradigm by which right relationship was gifted and to be lived. Sacrifice in that time and place was a way of both honouring and giving back to God what God had given.

We need to keep all this in mind when we read today's text. When Moses and the elders go up the mountain, they experience the presence of God in an intimate and vibrant way. (Earlier in chapter 24, Moses reads to the people from the book of the covenant. He does not seem to have received the tablets of stone with the law and commandment written on them. There is no need to try to reconcile these two points; multiple sources and ancient traditions may have been combined. The point is the real and experienced presence of God, who gives revealed and written ways of relationship.)

Moses has a particular, intimate time with God. It is part of the vibrant relationship between the two of them that encourages him constantly to converse with and even challenge God. For six days, reminiscent of the six days of Creation, a cloud – a sign, symbol and reality of God's intimate and vibrant connection with Creation – rests on the mountain. The glory of God is revealed as living, vibrant fire. Moses enters into close proximity to God. The text goes on to describe in seven chapters their conversation about what it looks like to physically, in sign and symbol, represent God on earth – seven chapters about how the physical reality of created things helps us engage with the One who is the Lord of all Creation.

For better or for worse?

It is often easier to preach from a text that is not well known than to preach from one that is familiar to people. After the Christmas and Easter passages, the early Genesis texts are probably the best known in the Bible. At least on the surface. People think they know what is in these texts, but if you ask, for example, what kind of "forbidden" fruit Adam and Eve ate in the Garden, most people will say "an apple." Yet the text does not identify the fruit. Given the probable Mesopotamian setting for this story, apples are unlikely, albeit not impossible. The point is that hearers bring a lot of presuppositions to these readings: some of them useful and some of them not so useful.

Note the omission of verses here. It is easy to focus on the temptation aspects of this text; indeed, that is why it appears on the first Sunday in Lent – a time when the church focuses on temptation and how to overcome it. The biblical writers/editors deliberately placed in the middle of this story a description of the creation of humanity. As "every animal of the field and every bird of the air" were created, God also created humankind.

The woman had not been created when God commanded the man not to eat of the tree of the knowledge of good and evil, under pain of death. The woman therefore did not hear that conversation. But because 3:3 shows that she knows of it, women were long cast by the church as the cause of all evil and temptation. Numerous Christian and Jewish scholars, such as Phyllis Trible, have written on this passage and its negative repercussions on women through the ages.

This passage is not about sex, even though the words "naked" and "ashamed" appear together. The original sin is human pride and disobedience. Being suddenly aware that they are naked is a sign that the man and woman have lost their innocence through sin. They are ashamed that they have disobeyed God. Human beings are not meant to know all there is to know – the knowledge of good and evil. Only

God can know all. (Isaiah 7:15 uses a similar phrase to express the crucial definition of knowledge.)

Why did God make the crafty serpent? Another way of translating that word "crafty" from the Hebrew is "subtle." The serpent tries saying something that is not true – that the man and the woman may not eat of any tree in the garden – but when the woman rebuts that statement, the serpent tries another tactic. It says that God was lying in order to protect God's turf. That argument worked: both the man and the woman ate the fruit. Their eyes were opened. They saw themselves as they truly were, and did not like what they saw. In that way, giving in to temptation truly brought about an end to innocence. Stay tuned for the repercussions!

"The gifts of the Jews"

One week and nine chapters of Genesis later, we encounter the lectionary text chosen for the second Sunday of Lent. Having skipped over the rest of the Genesis stories, including the story of the Flood, we now meet Abraham – or Abram, as he is called here in chapter 12.

Names are significant in the Bible: every name means something. "Abram" means "exalted father." God calls Abram from his home and family, instructing him to set out for a place that God knows but that Abram does not. The promise that accompanies this journey is that God will make of Abram a great nation and will bless him and make his name great. In his own being and person, Abram will be a blessing. God will bless those who bless Abram, and curse those who curse him. By Abram, all the families of the earth will be blessed. His name becomes "Abraham," which means "father of a great nation."

This story is about how God works with people individually. Up to now, the stories in Genesis have been more general. They have dealt with the origins of humanity, the realities of the human condition, and the relationship with God and God's Creation. Chapter 12 of Genesis begins the story of a specific family in a specific place.

God does not work merely through general, cyclical rhythms and patterns (though these exist in both nature and human life, and God certainly created them). Rather, God speaks, acts and lives in and through particular people in particular times and places: Abraham, Sarah and Hagar, King David, Isaiah, Jonah, Huldah and countless others. For Christians, God comes in the person of Jesus of Nazareth. That is how God worked then, and that is how God works now. Jean Vanier, Mother Teresa and Archbishop Desmond Tutu are vibrant examples of God working in people today.[24]

---

24 For some more reading on particularity, see Thomas Cahill's *The Gifts of the Jews* (New York: Doubleday, 1998).

See, hear and proclaim the words of verse 3. Through God's word and work in particular people, "all the families of the earth shall be blessed." Accepting the call to new adventures and challenging work in God's name does not bring privilege. It did not bring privilege then, and it does not bring privilege now. So Abram went, so we go.

The God of life

Here we have a snippet of the long, detailed, dramatic, "chills and spills" saga of the Exodus. It is unfortunate that so little of the Exodus narrative made it into the lectionary; this saga is a key text for our Jewish sisters and brothers as they reflect on and bear witness to their faith, and is therefore significant for Christians as well.

At this point in the text, the people have already left Egypt to return to Israel. The plagues, the institution of Passover, the crossing of the sea, the songs of Moses and Miriam, the provision of manna and quail to eat in the desert – these things have happened. The people are complaining about life in the desert. Slavery in Egypt was starting to look pretty good – at least they had enough to eat when they were slaves. It is easy to dismiss the people at this point, to say that they did not have enough faith. Moses points out that the people are testing God. But it was not an idle, frivolous testing. The desert was a frightening place. It was terribly hot during the day and terribly cold at night. With no food or water, one's life could be over in days, or even hours. It would have been very hard for the people to trust that God was truly taking care of them. By chapter 17, they had been travelling for a long time with no water. Their thirst was not like the thirst we have on a hot day where we have gone without water for a few hours. It was the thirst that many of our African sisters and brothers know all too well: days and days without water, to the point of being on the edge of death. Children were especially vulnerable, and if the children died, the people would have had no future.

Moses, who is in a constant, vigorous, challenging conversation with God, cries out to God and gets his answer. Staff plus rock will equal water, and the people and their children and their livestock will live to complain another day. The livestock are important here; nature and humanity are closely bound together in the biblical text.

Moses calls the place by the Hebrew names that mean "test" and "quarrel." This is testing to the edge of death. Moses carries the faith of the people, but knows when to intervene for their sake.

This passage also lends itself to a discussion of the nature of miracles. One can seek and find a scientific explanation for the water flowing from rock, just as some have sought rational explanations for the manna and the quail. God is, after all, the God of all Creation, and that includes science. But it is the point of the telling that we are after. God frees. God listens. Life as God's people is filled with challenges and doubts. But in the end, it is clear that God is the God of Life.

A tale of two kings

This is one of the Old Testament passages that gets repeated in the lectionary. It is especially important to preach from these Old Testament narrative texts because there are so few of them in the lectionary.

This text is about the choosing of David as king of Israel. David, the divine choice over all others, is anointed by the prophet Samuel. The process is not without some difficulties, though. In choosing David, Samuel is clearly setting aside Saul, the first king of Israel. There is tension between David and Saul, as other stories in 1 Samuel describe. The notion of kingship in Israel is also fraught with tension. The people, wanting to be like the peoples around them, ask God, through Samuel, for a king. They have priests, prophets and leaders, but they want to be like the surrounding culture. God points out that monarchy, as a kind of earthly leadership, can be problematic. God warns the people of the demands that a monarchy will place upon them, but concedes when they say they want it anyway. An opposite stream in the history of the faith of the people sees human kingship as divinely appointed, with the kings set in their place and maintained in their place by God. Many biblical texts carry traces of both streams. The Bible does not tend to obliterate differing understandings; rather, it often includes them and lets the tensions stand as a reality of life.

When God chooses David, he is still a young man. The text says, "The spirit of the Lord came mightily upon David from that day forward." This does not mean that David was perfect. There was the Bathsheba incident, after all. It means that even though David forgot on occasion, he knew most of the time that he must keep God at the centre of his life. This text is about God choosing according to a different set of criteria than the world uses.

Ezekiel is weird

There is just no getting around it: the prophet Ezekiel is weird. Prophets do tend to be on the odd side, but even compared to prophets who wander around naked for three years in order to prove a message from God (Isaiah 20), Ezekiel is strange. He has bizarre visions, he eats scrolls, he spends a period of time speechless, and he uses images that were probably close to incomprehensible in his time and place and that are pretty much over the edge now. But Ezekiel, whose name means "May God strengthen," speaks with passion and certainty in his calling to proclaim, in that typically prophetic idiom, the "Word of the Lord."

Ezekiel was one of the later prophets. He was among the more than 3,000 Jews who were exiled to Babylonia in 597 BCE. The exile was a devastating event for the people of Israel. Many Old Testament texts are deeply coloured by the threat and then the reality of exile. Although we in Western churches sometimes cannot see the relevance of the Old Testament for our time and place, Christians who live in places where there is great political oppression or famine or plague see these Old Testament texts as vitally relevant. How disturbing it is to think that our comfortable existence can make us shrug off revealed Scripture!

Ezekiel received his call to be a prophet while he was among the exiles in Babylon. He was a priest-prophet. The notion that there was always enmity between the visionary social justice prophets and the "establishment," empty-ritual priests is false. Many prophets were priests, too, and those two roles were compatible. God's initiative and control over Creation are expressed clearly and pervasively throughout Ezekiel. God is not limited to the Temple or even to the city of Jerusalem. The Holy One can respond to the people anywhere and anytime. And God is the God of all people.

So out of all this context comes this dramatic, visual and visceral passage of hope and regeneration. God can bring life out of what looks like hopeless death. God will breathe life into the people, and release them from exile. They will know through these gracious and awesome actions that the Holy One is indeed the Lord. What could be more impossible than a valley of dry bones – long-dead, dry bones – should be revived? If the impossible can happen with a valley of dry bones, so can it happen with God's people. God is the God of life!

A question to ask ourselves is this: what are the driest, deadest parts of our lives? What would God's gift of life look like in those places? Be specific!

It's heck to be unpopular

This is another of the "suffering servant" passages in the Book of Isaiah. Because it appears in chapter 50, its original context may well have been the Babylonian exile. The servant of God has been equipped by God with all that is necessary for carrying out the divine calling – but this does not mean that those to whom the servant is called have any desire to listen. The servant has the tongue of a teacher, and has learned both how to instruct and to listen according to the model of the day and to the calling of God. And the servant is really good at it, apparently acquiring "A" grades in preaching, teaching and pastoral counselling. But no matter how well prepared or divinely called the servant is, this does not guarantee that people will listen.

The servant is probably addressing either the Babylonian authorities (who do not want to know about the will of the God of Life and Justice) or the exiled people themselves. Although being exiled was a devastating experience, Babylon was a civilized nation, an empire. The people may have adapted to living there and may have found it comfortable enough. Perhaps they were not interested in a teacher who reminded them of their God and their calling. Perhaps they did not want to think about heading home out of exile to the massive venture of rebuilding homes, cities and a nation that is called to be a light to the world.

But the servant is resolved and sustained. The servant will not give in. Starting in verse 8, the judicial language begins. The teacher is confident that no matter what accusations the accusers, the opponents and those resisting the teaching may bring, God, who is in charge of the court, will vindicate. (In Romans 8:33-34, Paul picks up this kind of language and certainty of vindication of vocation in the face of accusation and opposition.) The Isaiah passage ends in certainty (read the whole of verse 9 – there seems to be no reason for this verse to stop in the middle, other than wanting to end on a triumphant note rather than one that deals with what will happen to the opponents).

It ends in the certainty that made it obvious for Christians to use this text to help them reflect on, think about, pray on and preach about the Risen Christ. For Christians, Jesus Christ makes manifest all that resonates through this text. The one who vindicates Jesus is near. And so we cry, "Hosanna!"

Maundy (Holy) Thursday – *Exodus 12:1-4, (5-10), 11-14*

Get ready, get set

This evening, Maundy[25] or Holy Thursday, Christians begin the most intense three days of commemorating, of living deeply the last days of Jesus: his suffering, his death and then his glorious resurrection. On this night, Christians commemorate the last supper of Jesus and his disciples, along with the institution of the Eucharist and the agony of Jesus' night of prayer in Gethsemane. Since the gospels record that the supper was a Passover meal, with the details and rituals that would accompany such a celebration, the Old Testament passage that institutes the Passover is the obvious choice for an Old Testament reading.

The English language is one of the few languages in which the terms are dissimilar. In most languages, the names for the Jewish Passover and the Christian Easter resemble each other very closely.[26] Using similar terms would help us see the links between the two events more clearly.

For our Jewish sisters and brothers, Passover is an extremely important event. It marks the deliverance of the Hebrew people from slavery in Egypt. In the biblical text, the last of the ten plagues, which are being used through Moses to convince Pharaoh to let the Israelites go back to Israel, is interrupted and the focus shifts to the people. They are told to prepare for their liberation. Unleavened bread and roasted meat can be made quickly, for people on the move. (The bread and wine of the Christian communion resemble the wine and matzoh [unleavened bread] of the Passover meal.) There is no "magic" to the daubing of the blood on the doorposts and the lintels of the houses. Blood was a readily available colouring substance at that time, and it

---

25 "Maundy" comes from the Latin for "commandment," because of John 13:34.
26 Rabbi Gunther Plaut, *The Torah: A Modern Commentary* (New York: Union of Hebrew Congregations, 1981), 465.

symbolized the life essence. The deliverance of the Israelites into a life of freedom is an act of God.[27]

Many congregations have taken up the practice, with the best intentions, of honouring the Jewish tradition of Jesus by holding a Seder Supper on or around Maundy Thursday. Some of these Seders have, unfortunately, ended up denigrating the tradition of Jesus. Much sensitivity is necessary when one takes on the traditions of another faith, especially traditions that are very much alive today. It is always best to build a relationship with and consult a rabbi if you are intending on holding such a Seder. Even if there is no synagogue down the street, use phone or e-mail to further the conversation. Technology can be useful.

---

27   *The Jewish Publication Society Torah Commentary: Exodus* (New York: The Jewish Publication Society, 1991), 55.

He was wounded for our transgressions

One Good Friday, as I was writing both my Good Friday sermon and my Easter Sunday sermon (clergy tend to be immersed in both the death and the resurrection of Jesus at the same time), I had a phone call from a Jewish colleague. She said, "I don't know what to say to you today. I know that this is a very dark day in your tradition. I know that 'Happy Easter' is completely wrong. But I want you to know that I am thinking of you on this dark day."

What a blessing her words were to me! Good Friday is indeed a dark day. On this day, many of our churches spend time listening deeply to some of the poignant music that has been written for Good Friday. Some churches are full on this day; others are empty. Some congregations worship together with ecumenical partners. For some, this is the only day that the Christ candle is not lit. It is important to dwell in the darkness on Good Friday, not rushing too fast towards the flowers and trumpets and resurrection proclamations of Easter.

While Isaiah has been used to proclaim the Incarnation, it is also used to proclaim the suffering and death of the Christian Messiah. The passage for this Good Friday is one of the suffering servant songs. In the exquisite and painful poetry and imagery of such passages, Christians see and proclaim the painful, brutal death of Jesus. But the suffering servant passages had a different meaning for the people of Israel before the time of Jesus, and have meaning for our Jewish sisters and brothers today. Whether the suffering servant is meant to be an individual or the people of Israel as a whole does not really matter. The point is that although God never insists on vicarious suffering for the sake of another, it does happen sometimes. Christians believe that Jesus lived and taught, preached and healed, suffered and died and rose again, and that somehow a new relationship between God and the world has thus been established.

In preaching from the suffering servant songs, avoid getting caught up in a prolonged explanation of whether the details of the Passion narratives were artificially made to resemble these songs. Trying to show that this proves Jesus was who he said he was and who the disciples, through the light and life of the Resurrection, came to believe he was is to miss the point. Jesus suffered. The suffering was real and terrible.

Jews and Christians alike believe that this kind of suffering, freely offered, can be redemptive. How that is so is in the mysterious hands of God. We live even this dark and dire Good Friday knowing that by his wounds we are healed.

An alternative prophet

Jeremiah is apparently an alternative prophet, or at least so it seems, according to the Revised Common Lectionary. Today, churches may read this Jeremiah text or Acts 10:34-43 for the first reading. And for the next seven weeks, until Pentecost, there is no Old Testament reading in the prescribed lectionary texts. (There are Psalms, of course, but those are intended to be used differently in the liturgy and so are not counted as an Old Testament reading.) Between Easter and Pentecost, passages from the Book of the Acts of the Apostles replace Old Testament passages.

The point of this change is undoubtedly to the show the wondrous effect of the Resurrection on the early church: the growth of the church through words and acts of great power and life. Fair enough. But the fact that there is no Old Testament reading severs the wondrous power and love of the Resurrection from the wondrous power and love that is witnessed to throughout the Old Testament. While I encourage the church to reflect prayerfully on and preach on the Acts of the Apostles, I find it unfortunate that in the Sunday liturgy, the post-Resurrection period is severed from its basis and foundation.

But I turn to the Jeremiah passage for today, Easter Sunday. Jeremiah, as noted earlier, was a prophet in the southern part of the land of Israel. His prophetic career probably began about 626 BCE and ended sometime after the fall and the destruction of Jerusalem and the deportation of the people into exile in 586 BCE. Like many biblical prophets, Jeremiah was not popular. His primary proclamation was one of judgment against those who were being unfaithful to God. He could see that disaster lurked on the horizon, but he believed that repentance was possible. He spoke of God as being both all powerful and all encompassing, but also as caring about individuals and their relationship to God.

The passage for this Easter Sunday is a sort of love poem. It is a prophecy of return from exile. God loves the people – all the people

– with an everlasting love. God has always been and will continue to be faithful to them. That love and that faithfulness will be manifest in signs of wholeness, healing and restoration: the physical rebuilding of their home, and the celebration and plenty for all. In festive celebration, the people will go to meet God on the holy mountain. They have survived and found grace in hard times. And that grace is graphically portrayed. Those who plant vineyards will enjoy the fruits of their labours. No "multinational corporation" will do the harvesting. And there will be musical instruments and dancing. What does our response to the grace of God look like and sound like?

Hallelujah, Hallelujah, Hallelujah! Praise the Lord!

Do the math

The wandering continues. The people of Israel have been set free from slavery in Egypt; they have received the great gift of the commandments and laws at Mount Sinai/Horeb. Those commandments and laws show God's great care for the people, and the depth and strength of their relationship both with the Holy One and with each other. Numbers is quoted in the New Testament in a number of different books. Although Moses is said to have written it, most likely Numbers, like the rest of the Torah/Pentateuch, appeared in its final form later – possibly during the exile. Exile was a good time for the people to take stock of their traditions, beliefs and stories and to bring them together in a way that helped preserve the faith when they were far away from the Temple and the city of Jerusalem. Rabbinic Judaism and the early Christians did something similar later when the Romans destroyed the Temple in 70 CE.[28]

Numbers as a whole tells the story of wandering in the wilderness. The people complain and complain, and so are told that only their children will see and enter into the homeland and live the fulfillment of the promise. But for all the complaining and its consequences, it remains clear that God constantly cares for the people, loving and constantly forgiving them and meeting their needs. What they need in chapter 11 is leaders. The complaining has become too much for Moses to bear. The people have become a burden. In keeping with his always engaging and vital relationship with God, Moses speaks his mind. In a somewhat melodramatic moment that no doubt indicates the depths of his despair, Moses says he would rather die than continue to put up with the people. God proposes a solution. Seventy elders are to be gathered in a holy and sacred ceremony. During the ceremony, the people will be able to eat of an overabundance of what

---

28 For much more on this topic, read Donald Akenson's *Surpassing Wonder* (Chicago: University of Chicago Press, 2001).

they have been hungering for: meat. The elders will receive some of the spirit of God, which has until now rested on Moses, so that they may help him bear the burden of the people's misery.

Then comes that interesting little side story which shows so clearly the humanity of the biblical events and why they can be so engaging for us. Two of the seventy elders had not been in the right place at the right time, and may not have correctly received the spirit, at least in the minds of some. They prophesied like the others, but unlike the others, keep prophesying for a long time. Although some people find this behaviour suspicious, Moses affirms their ability and wishes that more had it. With the leadership burden shared, Moses is able to carry on, and the vision for returning to Israel is kept alive.

And God said and God did

I once did a pulpit exchange with a local rabbi. We each used the texts for the day from each other's tradition. The Jewish tradition is to read through the entire Torah every year. (A special holy day marks the ending of one cycle and the beginning of the next.) A long passage is read each Sabbath, with some readings from the prophets attached to the Torah readings thematically or theologically, much the same way that we attach Old Testament readings to the gospel cycle. When the rabbi sent me the text pages from his TaNaKh, I watched in shock and awe as page after page rolled off the fax machine. How was I going to preach on such a long passage, more than a chapter from the Noah saga? The rabbi had the opposite reaction when I sent him the lectionary passages for the Sunday he was preaching. How could one say anything, he asked me, based on such short bits of Scripture?

For this Trinity Sunday, the lectionary gives us a long section of scripture: the Creation story, the opening of the Bible. This story, well known both in church and in secular society, is a story that has been used and misused for millennia. It has been a battleground for the conflict between science and religion. But does such a conflict exist? Once scripture commentary explains:

> The biblical Creation narrative is a document of faith. It is a quest for meaning and a statement of a religious position. It enunciates the fundamental postulates of the religion of Israel, the central ideas and concepts that animate the whole of biblical literature. Its quintessential teaching is that the universe is wholly the purposeful product of divine intelligence, that is, of the one self-sufficient, self-existing God, who is a transcendent Being outside of nature and who is sovereign over space and time.[29]

---

29   *The Jewish Publication Society Torah Commentary: Genesis* (New York: The Jewish Publication Society, 1989), 3-4. A plethora of material is available on the relationship between science and religion. See the works of Sir John Polkinghorne, Episcopal

Much can be said about today's text. Here I will touch on a few homiletic possibilities. First, there is little point in spending a lot of time trying to prove this story over some scientific explanation or vice versa, or in a long discussion of the complex relationship between this story and the one that begins further in Genesis. As Clark M. Williamson says,

> The task of preaching is to enable each generation to hear that the word of God is a living and pertinent word, to interpret the events and insights, problems and dilemmas, of that generation in the light of the tradition and to reinterpret prior Christian tradition in the light of the contemporary situation ... Insofar as preaching does its job, proclamation is itself a living word of God, necessary to the life of the Church.[30]

The JPS Genesis commentary puts it this way:

> Genesis exhibits no interest in the question of God's origins. His existence prior to the world is taken as axiomatic and does not even require assertion, let alone proof. There is no definition of God or any mystical speculation about His nature. God's nature finds expression not in philosophical abstractions but through His acts and through the demands He makes on human beings.[31]

This last sentence could be a good jumping-off point for a sermon dealing with the whole Creation narrative. Some other jumping-off points could include verse 1:27 and the assertion that male and female, exactly equal in creation, are both made in the image of God; 1:28 and the command to rule the earth and what that means when set beside God's words to fish and fowl to multiply and increase (v. 22); or the relationship of the seventh day, where God rested, with the institution of a Sabbath for both humanity and all creatures. There are weeks' worth of sermons in this text!

priest and quantum physicist. I read his short book entitled *Searching for Truth: Lenten Meditations on Science and Faith* (New York: Crossroad Publishing Company, 1996) every Lent.

30 Clark M. Williamson, *A Guest in the House of Israel: Post-Holocaust Church Theology* (Louisville, KY: Westminster John Knox Press, 1993), 256.

31 *The Jewish Publication Society Torah Commentary: Genesis*, 5.

Not a nice story

While our Jewish sisters and brothers would read through the Noah story on a Sabbath, Christians break up the story and leave out large chunks of it. It might be interesting to mention this in a sermon and ask the congregation to read the omitted parts of the story when they get home. It may seem odd to give homework at a Sunday liturgy, but I suspect some people will take you up on it and will want to talk about the texts later.

One Sunday while I was telling the story of Noah as a children's story during the worship service, my young son piped up, "This is not a nice story!" He was right. It is not a story that can be explained by means of nice ark toys and songs about animals coming in by "twosies, twosies." God endowed humankind, made in the divine image, male and female, with free will. Humankind did not use the gift well. Divine tolerance, in a God who is the God of justice, can only go so far. The Flood undoes God's acts of creation.

Things must have been bad in Noah's day; what does God think of the world today? Rampant poverty, unrelieved suffering from HIV/AIDS, and other injustices prevail. Surely God weeps. Surely our God of acts and deeds calls us, who are made in the divine image, to acts and deeds. Proclaim loudly that HIV/AIDS, genocide, poverty and other calamities are *not* acts of God, not a kind of modern flood to wipe out "wickedness." Some people say such things: this is bad theology and is seriously lacking in compassion.

The end of the story, while not given in this text, is just a few verses on. We know it well. The God who is always faithful to the divine promises says that God will never again wreak such destruction on the earth and on human beings. We can blow ourselves up or destroy the earth, but it will not be God's work. Humanity, in relationship with creatures and with nature, has the chance to start again and to live according to the divine plan. What if we were to do it?

Who, me?

After 75 years of life with family in the area of Haran, Abram receives a call from God to uproot his immediate family and strike out for parts unknown. We have read part of this text in Lent 2 of this year; the fact that the lectionary repeats it so soon when so much of the Old Testament is omitted tells us that this text is highly significant in the minds of those who put together the lectionary. (See the entry for Year A, Lent 2, for more background on this text.)

The text tells us who Abram took with him and where they went. It would have been a slow journey with all those people and possessions and flocks. These were not just wilderness ramblings. The major highways and byways were well established in Abram's time; he would likely have followed the trade routes, which led through and around all the places mentioned in the text. So, at a creaky 75 years of age, at great inconvenience and with a major time commitment, Abram follows the call. He trusts in God and God's faithfulness: since the text gives us no hint that Abram had ever heard from God before, this was all pretty risky. He hears from God again at Shechem, at the oak of Moreh, where he receives a promise of the gift of the land. Abram responds by building an altar – a visible, physical sign and symbol of remembrance of divine encounter in that place.

Given the current geopolitical situation in the Middle East, this promise of the land of Israel/Palestine to Abram and his descendants raises questions. The biblical text always states clearly that there were other peoples there before – peoples that had migrated from other parts of the Ancient Near East. The books of Joshua and Judges speak harshly about how those peoples were to be dealt with. The biblical text also clearly states that God chooses, as we hear in this passage, a particular people to be in a particular place as a light to the nations. Although human frailty and sinful free will can cause much to go awry, so that the light flickers and may even seem to go out temporarily, the overall witness of Scripture tells us of the promise that the light is called to continue to shine.

Proper 6 – *Genesis 18:11-15*

God laughed

Fortunately for us, God has a great sense of humour. And what a wonderful witness to us that many of our biblical texts make this clear. They also remind us that we are laughably flawed in our calling to true humanity. God does not give up on humanity, however, but keeps on using us as agents and messengers.

Today's reading is one of those wonderful texts that bring together both God as subject who laughs, and humanity as the cause of that laughter. It is a new Abraham and Sarah adventure. Their names have been changed. Abram, exalted father, has become Abraham, father of a great nation. Sarai has become Sarah.

Read the eight verses that precede this text, even though they are omitted in the lectionary. They set up what happens in this reading and provide details about life for a wealthy Israelite living in an inhospitable land. Hospitality was extremely important in that time and place. Food and water could be in short supply, especially when people travelled. Hospitality – the sharing of food, water, and other essentials – was not just nice, it was a way of life.[32]

Back to the laughter. Earlier, God had promised Sarah and Abraham that they would have a son. Abraham had laughed at the time because he was 100 years old and Sarah was 90 – far too old to be having babies! God persisted and declared that Ishmael, Abraham's son by Hagar, would be the father of twelve princes. Kings would descend from another son, by Sarah.

Today, it is Sarah who is laughing. The three men have reiterated God's promise about Abraham and Sarah becoming parents, and Sarah finds this funny. When they catch her laughing, she denies it, but we hear about it. God laughs with us when we cannot believe, but fulfills the promise anyway. And God gets the last laugh. Sarah's son is named Isaac, which means "laughter."

---

32   Christians have sometimes used this text to proclaim the Trinity. Three visitors appear to Abraham and Sarah. It is hard to discern their identity: are they human or divine? This is a matter of faith and belief.

God uses whom God chooses

In the global context in which I write this entry, in the local context in which I write this entry, this passage could not be more relevant. It concerns the descendants of Abraham's sons – Jews, Christians and Muslims – an important issue for all of us today.

This narrative relates further challenging dynamics between Sarah and Abraham as they intersect through Isaac, the child of laughter. Complicating matters is Sarah and Abraham's relationship with Hagar and Ishmael. God has plans for them all. Sarah is not at her best: she wants Hagar and Hagar's son, Ishmael, cast out of the family compound. Sarah does not want Ishmael to have any chance of inheriting along with Isaac. God intervenes in a somewhat puzzling way. God tells Abraham to get over his distress and send Hagar and Ishmael out into the wilderness, as Sarah wants, because Isaac is indeed Abraham's heir. God also says that things will work out well for Ishmael.

When the supplies are gone and death is imminent, Hagar raises her voice and weeps. God hears the boy Ishmael and speaks to Hagar through an angel, promising her that Ishmael will be the ancestor of a great nation. The God of action then opens Hagar's eyes, and she sees the essential water. God remains with Ishmael as he grows up. He is considered to be the ancestor of Islam, of our Muslim sisters and brothers. Judaism and Christianity are descended through Isaac and Islam through Ishmael, but all three with the same father: Abraham. Much of today's interfaith dialogue is centred in this important relationship.

This passage has other noteworthy features as well. As in last week's Old Testament reading, the line between God and God's instruments – three men, an angel – can be somewhat fluid. (Reread Genesis 16:13 to see this fluidity.) Sometimes God is directly present; at other times, God seems to speak through others. We cannot be sure. God is not ours to contain, as the Old Testament shows.

Also to notice in this passage is that it describes God having a direct encounter with a woman. This does not happen often in the Old Testament. Sarah and Eve have experienced God's voice and presence – in Sarah's case, mediated through the three men – but a direct encounter between God and a woman is rare. What is more, Hagar is an outsider. She is not of the family of Abraham; she is an Egyptian. Abraham's roots are in Haran and Ur of the Chaldees. And yet it is Hagar the Egyptian to whom God relates directly and to whom God makes a wondrous promise. As can be seen in the opening passage of the New Testament, the genealogy of the Gospel of Matthew, where four women are mentioned, God uses whom God chooses.

The Akedah

We call this story the Binding of Isaac; in Hebrew it is the Akedah. Go gently with this narrative. Reading it with clarity, passion, inflection and import can have more impact on listeners than a sermon. This is Abraham's last theophany or encounter with God. He has had many such engaging, vital, dramatic encounters, and they have called him forward into new places and new realities. In this final encounter with the Holy One, God asks him to sacrifice his son Isaac. Isaac, whose name means "laughter," is the child of the promise. God has promised over and over again that Abraham will be the father of a great nation, that Abraham will have as many descendants as the stars in the sky and the grains of sand on the shore. God has promised that all this will happen through Isaac. And now God is asking Abraham to sacrifice this child!

What is worse, as we read last Sunday, God has sent Ishmael, Abraham's other son, to the wilderness of Paran. Is Abraham to lose both sons? What is God thinking? It seems a cruel test. We may argue that Abraham is the model of faith for us all; he offers us an example of the depth of the faith we are to manifest in our lives. This argument rings a bit hollow. I believe we must ponder and pray in the power of this story, carrying it with us on our faith journey. It is a challenge: our God may ask things of us that we do not understand and that push us beyond what we think are our limits.

The reader knows from the start that this is a test, that Abraham will not have to follow through with the sacrifice, that God does not really desire human sacrifice, but Abraham does not know this. Both Abraham and the first hearers of this story knew that human sacrifice was practised in that time and place, even by the people of Israel (see 1 Kings 18:34). In the Hebrew of verse 2, the verb "take" has a suffix on it that could be translated as "please." The testing is not a command, but a hard entreaty to hear, to be sure.

Abraham's agreeing to this entreaty is therefore an act of free will. As in the story about Ishmael, an angel intervenes at the last minute, and something appears that was not seen before: a ram in a thicket. The NRSV ends this story with Abraham calling the place "The Lord will provide." The text adds that it is said to this day, "On the mount of the Lord it shall be provided." Yet an additional reading from the Hebrew has Abraham naming the site "He/it shall be seen" – in the present, "On the mount of the Lord there is vision" or "On the mount the Lord appears." In the Jewish tradition, it is on this mount, Mount Moriah, that the Temple was built.

Christians interpret this story in terms of God's decision to sacrifice his own son, Jesus. That free decision and Jesus' willingness to die make this act a redemptive one.

God is in the details

This story of the faith comes from Genesis, the first book of Scripture for both Christians and Jews. It tells the story of our ancestors in the faith, those people descended from Abraham, the people of Israel.[33] Jesus, who lived as a faithful Jew, would have known the book of Genesis and the stories of Isaac and Rebekah. Genesis, like the other books of the Torah, may have been assembled in the time of King David (around 1000 BCE). At that time, the people were becoming a nation with a distinct and articulated faith in the one God. Stories such as the one we hear today would have been an important part of the tradition for a long time before the text was formed. Such stories were passed down and cherished as oral tradition or in other, smaller written formats for hundreds of years.

For many centuries, the church believed it was important that Christians know these stories, including this one about Isaac and Rebekah. As preachers we do not always need to be ransacking our sacred texts for moral lessons that fit with our contemporary values. Sometimes, we just need to tell the story in the kind of vivid detail we encounter in this narrative and remind the people and ourselves that God cares about individuals, and God has been and is active in the particularity of human life. Most important, God uses human beings who live in families and communities, who have traditions and particular customs, and who have doubts, fears and other emotions, to be lights and witnesses in the world. The particularity and detail of this story of the people of God remind us of our calling, too, in the particularity and detail of our stories.

---

33 A number of verses are omitted from the lectionary passage. In this case, the reason seems to be one of length. While omitting these verses damages the beauty and flow of the narrative, it does not have any other major effect.

Sibling rivalry, or a "mess of pottage"

With this story, the biblical text moves into a series of narratives about Isaac. Isaac is often eclipsed in the Genesis narratives by either his father, Abraham, or his son Jacob, but he is much more than a transition between those two men. In Isaac's day, the social history of the people was determined by the conflicts between two ways of life: hunting and agriculture. Isaac is the only patriarch to engage in agriculture. He is also the only one never to leave the land of Israel. The emphasis in today's narrative is on the births of Isaac's twin sons, Esau and Jacob, and the tension and struggle between them. This narrative reflects an ancient belief that long-term, historical and very real bitter rivalry between the people of the land of Israel and the people of the land of Edom started even before birth!

The story begins with the statement that Rebekah, the wife of Isaac, was barren. Barren women abound in the Old Testament – Sarah, Rebekah, Rachel, Hannah, to name just a few. Due to poor nutrition and regular famines, many women must have been barren in those days. A live, healthy birth would have been a tremendous event indeed. Yet God is the God of Life, and God will do what God will do to fulfill divine purposes. We human beings are not in control; we are not gods. Rebekah eventually does become pregnant, though she has a difficult pregnancy (the only difficult pregnancy mentioned in the Bible).

Verse 23 tells us, in God's words, of the ancient tradition that the seeds of the enmity between the people of Israel and the people of neighbouring Edom were sown in the womb. Esau was born first, with hairy, red skin. Jacob, born second, gripped Esau's heel with his hand. Jacob's name is given as meaning "takes by the heel" or "surplants," giving us a hint of what is to come. What happens is this: Esau sells his birthright to Jacob. This is a significant act. The firstborn son, along with the first fruits of the field and the firstborns of the flocks and herds, were considered to have a particular sanctity – not in and of themselves, but because they were the first. This was a way of rec-ognizing God as the creator and the origin of all life. All such firstborn creatures or first fruits belonged to God. As a result, firstborns came to be seen as the primary guarantor of the future of the family. They had status as well as certain rights and responsibilities. This is what Esau sells away, seemingly without any second thoughts or regrets. He despises his birthright, even. Both Jacob, who trades for the birthright, and Esau appear to be shady characters.

The Old Testament does not whitewash our ancestors in the faith. For the most part, they come to us in all their strengths and weak-nesses. In both they serve the Lord. We can do no less.

Perchance to dream

Genesis now moves to focus on the stories of Jacob, and colourful stories they are. The conflict between Jacob and his older twin, Esau, has increased. Both continue to be scoundrels; Jacob is now on the run from Esau. Because it was too dangerous to travel by night, Jacob stopped on his way back to the family home of Haran. As he slept, he received a dream-revelation. God takes Jacob by surprise. Jacob did not stop in Bethel because he expected to encounter God there; it just happened to be as far as he got when the sun went down.

The Hebrew word for the ladder in the dream is used only once in the Old Testament, so it is hard to translate exactly. It could mean a mound or ramp or steps or a ladder, and may have some connection with Egyptian and Hittite religion, in which the souls of both mortals and the gods travel between heaven and earth by means of a ladder. Or it may have a connection with the Babylonian ziggurat temple design referred to in the Tower of Babel story. Whatever it is, the ladder does not function as a channel of communication between God and humanity. It is also not clear what those angels are doing there aside from going up and down and down and up. Are they a visible manifestation of their role, which is to be engaged with the earth and its people?

God appears and stands beside Jacob, clearly identified as the God of Abraham and Isaac. God is not to be confused for a moment with "El," the head of the Canaanite pantheon. God promises to Jacob and to his multitudinous offspring the land on which he is lying. Again, as we heard with Abraham, we hear that the people of the earth will be blessed, this time because of Jacob. How reassuring those next words must have been, too, to one who knew that all was not well with his family relationships. God would be with him, protect him wherever he went and bring him back home.

When Jacob woke up, he realized the import of what he had seen and heard. God was in that place, and Jacob had had no idea! It was an awesome place: the house of God and the gate of heaven. None of the other ancestors in the faith, including Hagar the Egyptian woman, were as astonished to encounter God as Jacob was. He of the dysfunctional family relationships, fleeing for his life, conscious perhaps of his bad behaviour and totally ignorant of the sacredness of the spot, lies down at night in mid-flight, guilty, anxious and exhausted, and is awestruck by the arrival of God.

Jacob commemorates this encounter with the living God by setting up a pillar and pouring oil over top of it. Pillars as idols or as containing a divinity or spirit, which some of the peoples of that time and place believed in, were forbidden to the people of Israel. Pillars as a witness, as a mark of a momentous occurrence happen in a number of biblical stories. The pillar of Bethel is a pillar of witness. (The pouring of oil over the pillar may have its roots in international treaty relationships or contracts.) Bethel becomes for the early Israelites an important, sacred spot for divine encounter. (Much later, it has difficult political dynamics, too, and is a part of the breakup of the kingdom of Israel under Solomon's son.)

God does not approve of scurrilous behaviour, but it is good news for us all that God can and does use scoundrels.

Scoundrels both! Or, love story

We are right in the middle of one of the few sustained uses of Old Testament narrative texts in the lectionary. These texts are given in canonical order, but with many sections omitted. Because some members will not have been there on the previous few Sundays, or may miss some of the following ones, try to offer enough repetition to set the context for those not familiar with the story, but not too much for the people who have just heard the stories.

This week, the scoundrel meets another scoundrel. Jacob, in his flight from his dysfunctional family relationships and his fear of his older twin brother, Esau, has fled to the place of his mother's brother, Laban. It seems to be a good idea to stay there for a while. And so the love story begins.

Laban has two daughters. Jacob loves the younger one, Rachel. The wedding feast and wedding night are held seven years later, as stated in the agreement between Laban and Jacob, under the cover of darkness or a veil. But Laban substitutes his older daugher, Leah, for Rachel. (Jacob gets his wives' two maids, as well, but that is another story.)

This story not only reminds us of the complexity of our human relationships, it also contains some interesting detail about wedding traditions. The concept of the week after the wedding as a time for the couple has no doubt influenced our concept of the "honeymoon." And it is the custom in Judaism today that the groom gets to see the bride right before the ceremony. In fact, there is a ritual act of looking under her veil so that he can be sure he is marrying the right bride. Because biblical laws that probably come from a later time than the origins of this story, such as Leviticus 18:18, prohibit a man from marrying his wife's sister while his wife is still alive, this story of Jacob, Leah and Rachel has its origins in an earlier time. Typically, the biblical text does not try to smooth out contradictions and discrepancies but includes them all as a part of the inheritance of tradition.

Laban is a clever scoundrel. He has tricked the trickster Jacob, the one who masqueraded as his own brother (see Genesis 27, not included in this part of the lectionary).

In the Old Testament texts – the narrative passages as well as the prophetic, poetic ones – we encounter such human, flawed, frail characters. These scoundrels are our ancestors in the faith. God chooses Jacob in spite of himself. We live in families and human relationships that are complicated and sometimes less than ideal, and yet God chooses us.

And the winner is …?

Most of us have wrestled with experiences that, difficult as they seemed at the time, turned out to be in some way a blessing. The ongoing bitter conflict between Esau and Jacob, the twin sons of Isaac, has reached a new yet still uncertain place. Jacob is coming home after years of serving his uncle Laban. Tensions between Jacob and Esau caused Jacob to leave his homeland in the first place; now, tensions between Jacob and Laban are prompting Jacob's return. There have been drama and deceit all around.

Jacob is filled with fear and trembling: he hears that Esau is on his way to meet him with a big force. Jacob assumes and fears the worst.

In the dead of night, Jacob is alone. A man appears; Jacob wrestles with him until daybreak. It is not Esau. In ancient pagan traditions it would be a river demon; although the biblical texts show traces of such ancient traditions, this man is in some way divine. The process and intensity of the struggle result in a name change for Jacob. He will now be called "Israel," which means either "the one who strives with God" or "God strives." Jacob/Israel has striven with God and with humans and has prevailed. As one commentary says, the name "Israel" is associated with struggle and triumph in the face of overwhelming odds.[34]

Jacob/Israel calls the place where he struggled "Peniel," which means "face of God." The phrase "face to face" in the next sentence is used in the biblical text only for encounters between God and humans, whether this is an adversarial confrontation or an experience of tremendous intimacy. "Yet my life has been preserved" is another phrase of tremendous power. The idea being expressed is also part of the Moses saga. Moses hides his face at the burning bush, when God tells him that it is impossible for a human to look on the divine visage and live. As the JPS commentary puts it, "This is the biblical way of

---

34   *The Jewish Publication Society Torah Commentary: Genesis*, 227.

expressing the intensity of the experience of the individual encounter with the Divine Presence – the utterly overwhelming nature of the mysterious contact with the awesome majesty of the transcendent but immanent God."[35]

Our God is not a comfortable God. Comforting, sometimes. Challenging, sometimes. Our God of justice and relationship, always. How have we, are we, transformed by our encounters with the divine? Be very specific.

---

35   *The Jewish Publication Society Torah Commentary: Genesis*, 228.

Joseph and his amazing technicolour dreamcoat

"Mind the gap" is the phrase used in the London, England, tube system to remind people to watch out for the space between the subway train and the platform. In this lectionary passage, the gap between verses 4 and 12 is a crucial one. On Sunday, read the entire text, from verses 1 to 28. These extra seven verses will add no more than a minute to the liturgy.

The Joseph saga is the longest saga in the Bible. It runs from chapters 37 to 50 of Genesis. This story may be connected in literary terms to the Wisdom literature, such as Proverbs. It depicts a young man who has a few character flaws but ends up overcoming them. He also overcomes some dramatic circumstances that are beyond his control. He rises through his own ability and prudence to a senior position of authority. In a manner very typical of Wisdom literature, there is very little mention of God in the whole saga. The exceptions are chapter 38, a text that the church tends to neglect or misuse, and the sections on blessing and Joseph's forgiving of his brothers for selling him into slavery in Egypt. Genesis 50:20 offers a message often found in Wisdom literature: "Even though you intended to do harm to me, God intended it for good, in order to preserve a numerous people, as he is doing today."

A difficulty for preachers is that although the saga is long and detailed, it appears in the lectionary only twice: this week and next week. Seize the opportunity and tell the story with its difficult theology of Providence: many Christians have seen the musical version of this story but lost the deeper meanings. In this story, God, in effect, creates good out of evil. We all know examples of difficulties being transformed, but we also all know times and places where that does not happen. Do as the Bible as a whole does: wrestle with this reality.

Joseph wept

Reread the entry for last Sunday (Proper 14) for some background on the Joseph story. One could preach about family reconciliation or forgiveness, but that theme stands out clearly and powerfully in the text and really does not need interpretation. Try letting the power of the story speak for itself.

Recap the plot of the Joseph saga for people who missed last week's service and, since this is the second and last reading of the Joseph texts, tell them where the story goes from this point on. Use a light touch with well-chosen words and phrases. It is God's story, after all.

Joseph is presented in this text as ever so human. He clearly has outstanding leadership skills or he could never have risen to the position of Pharaoh's second-in-command. But the meeting with his brothers, who have come to buy food in order to stave off starvation in Israel, and the talk about his youngest brother, Benjamin, moves him to the point where Joseph could no longer "control himself before all those who stood by him … and he wept so loudly …" (Genesis 45:1-2).

We proclaim in our Judeo-Christian tradition that we human beings are made in the image of God. Such emotion as is portrayed here, such depth of feeling, standing side by side with such strength, gives us a biblical model of leadership. We are to care, and care deeply, for each other. We are to be strong and do the things that need to be done. We are to hold both together. Thanks be to God!

Five women and a baby

With this week's reading, the lectionary begins nine sequential weeks of reading from the Book of Exodus, the second book of the Old Testament. Its name in Hebrew consists of the opening words of the book: "These are the names."

This passage, about the birth of Moses, explains the change in the Israelite people's circumstances in Egypt, their response to those changes, as well as the Egyptians' reactions to the Israelites. The oppression of the Israelites is not working. Pharaoh calls in the Hebrew midwives and instructs them to kill any baby boys that are born. (We hear the names of the midwives, but the Pharaoh's name is not given. According to the text, the midwives are more significant than he is.) The midwives obey God, not Pharaoh, who represents the earthly powers of empire. They make up a story for Pharaoh, which he believes. The midwives survive Pharaoh's power play. The context is now set and the passage shifts to the birth of Moses.

Moses' mother, sister and adoptive mother all conspire to save his life. Like the midwives, Shiphrah and Puah, these three women defy the earthly powers that be. Pharaoh's daughter, although not a worshipper of the God of Israel, has pity and compassion. She willingly accepts the challenge to preserve life.

This is a particularly helpful passage for inter-faith dialogue and for church/state relationship conversations. It gives a biblical model for the fact that defiance of the state, actual civil disobedience, can be our calling in the faith.

The preservation of life is the be-all and end-all. Because Christianity so early in its history (313 BCE) entered into relationship with the state, this is a biblical story of which we need to be constantly reminded. Our words and acts are to be about life, not death.

This passage also reminds us that while we are to be bearers of life, we are not the only bearers of life. Those who know God differently from how we know God can also be called to God's divine imperative for life.

"Who am I?"

Moses is acting in a shepherd-like capacity when an angel of the Lord appears to him in a bush that is on fire without being consumed. No need to dwell on what the angel is doing there: it is common in the Bible for the lines between God and an angel of God to be blurred. Moses is to be God's instrument in freeing the people from slavery in Egypt, and he needs to be told of that fact. His attention is caught by the bush; then God calls him. God's presence makes this place holy. In Genesis, we encountered sacred time: the Sabbath. This is an instance of a sacred place.

After identifying himself, God declares that he has seen, heard and known the plight of the people and is going to do something about it. God will send Moses to Pharaoh. Moses, as an instrument of God, will free the people. Verse 8, which lists the residents of the land to which the people of Israel are returning, reveals the complex makeup of the land. Geographically, the region was and is one of the most diverse in the world. Its almost constant scarcity of natural resources and its placement near major trade routes have resulted in frequent movement and upheaval of peoples.

Like all prophets, Moses protests that he is not worthy of the task. But God is not to be deterred. God promises to be with Moses; this is the sign that God indeed is the one who sent him. Again, names are important. The name that God gives can be translated as "I Am Who I Am," "I Am That I Am" or "I Will Be What I Will Be." The specific, proper name for God can be called the Tetragrammaton (the four consonants). (See the Introduction for more on this name.)

As we can see, the grammatical form of God's name is a verb. God is active in the world!

God has seen oppression and is going to bring an end to it, using a human instrument, as God so often does. God is going to use Moses to bring freedom and liberation. Moses is not so sure, not so sure at all.

He has lots of protests, all of which God parries. Armed with God's assurances, Moses will go forth.

Time to search ourselves. Have there been times in our lives when God has called us to do something really difficult and we have come up with too many excuses to do it? Not next time …

Reprise

See Year A, Maundy/Holy Thursday

This passage reminds us that the whole community is to be involved in the regular and ritual sharing of a meal that is intimately associated with God's divine action in liberation and salvation. It is to be celebrated as an institution, a festival with God throughout the ages.

Time out for Charlton Heston

It is difficult to hear this passage on the parting of the Red Sea without calling to mind the vivid scene from *The Ten Commandments* where Charlton Heston stands with his staff waving and his hair blowing in the wind. But let us set him aside today.

This text is about God's sovereign control over history and nature. We may love and appreciate this text as a proclamation of God's unparalleled and unstoppable will for freedom (and the text does contain great visual images!), along with a deep discomfort at the fate of the Egyptians. This text made a huge impression on subsequent Hebrew literature, and became the paradigm for the future redemption of Israel from the exile in Babylon.[36] In all those retellings of it, interestingly, the fate of the Egyptians is rarely mentioned. Perhaps others felt the same discomfort. A reference in the Talmud says, "On seeing the destruction of the Egyptians the angels wanted to break forth in song. But God silenced them saying: 'The work of My hands is drowning in the sea, and you desire to sing songs!'"[37]

Did this miraculous escape through the sea really happen? Did it look like a scene from *The Ten Commandments*? We'll never know, and it is not important in the end. What is important is that the people of Israel believed, and subsequent generations of believers believe, that God is the Lord of History and is active in the events that are a part of our human reality.

So where in our world, right now, is God acting to bring oppression to an end? And how are we to act in concert with God in that circumstance?

In what ways do we act like the Egyptians in this biblical saga, oppressing others? It is a human tendency to always want to see ourselves as the hero in stories, biblical or not, but we are capable of being the oppressor, too.

---

36 *The Jewish Publication Society Torah Commentary: Exodus*, 70.
37 Talmud 34.

Grumble, grumble, grumble

As the JPS Exodus Commentary says, simply and succinctly,

> It is now six weeks after the Exodus. With the oasis at Elim now behind them and the provisions brought from Egypt exhausted, the people face a severe shortage of food. The wilderness conditions offer little possibility of securing fresh supplies. Popular discontent flares, and harsh accusations are hurled against Moses and Aaron. God responds to Israel's material and spiritual needs: He supplies manna and quail and institutes the weekly Sabbath rest day.[38]

Again we need to discuss the point of "miracles" in the biblical text. And this is not idle grumbling that the people are indulging in. It's not the type of grumbling we do when traffic is terrible and we are late for an important meeting. The people of Israel were grumbling because they knew they were on the brink of death. There would have been no pasture for the flocks and herds they brought from Egypt, so the animals would have to be eaten. If the people eat up all the flocks and herds, then the people ultimately cannot survive. Their will to live was so strong, they would have rather gone back to slavery in Egypt than die in freedom in the desert.

God hears grumbling. This is a point that, in pastoral contexts, I have often made. The Psalms make that point over and over again. Yet somehow we still think we have to present God with nice, tidy, well-articulated, polite prayers. As if God did not know about the grumbling already! God responds with what will sustain life. Manna rains down from the sky, but the people are to gather only enough for one day at a time. They are to trust and not be greedy. Their grumbling is against God, but God responds with both physical sustenance and the holy presence to supply the spiritual need. By both, the people shall know that God is their God.

---

38 *The Jewish Publication Society Torah Commentary: Exodus*, 85. Note that according to this commentary, verses 16 to 20 are a part of the unit that then flows on through the rest of the chapter.

God wills us to have what we need – not necessarily what we want, but what we need; there can be a big difference between the two! We are incarnate human beings. Our physical being matters. It is a channel by which we respond in relationship to God and others. God wills us to have what we need. This is our reality as well. God was present. God is present. God will be present. In spite of our grumbling. Perhaps, sometimes, because of our grumbling. Thanks be to God!

A canon within the canon

Like Exodus 12, this passage from Exodus 17 shows up twice: here and in Lent 3. (See what was said in Year A, Lent 3.) To the depths of the text …

Scripture often refers to other parts of itself. The New Testament is full of quotations or paraphrases or allusions to other parts of scripture, particularly the Psalms and the Book of the prophet Isaiah. Some of these we may recognize, while others are not familiar to us. This passage from Exodus is referred to over and over again, in a variety of ways, in other parts of the Old Testament. How and why?

According to the JPS Exodus commentary,

For the third time the people grumble against Moses. Their rhetoric grows stronger and more threatening; they even question God's providence. The seriousness of the episode left an indelible impression on the national historical memory, and its locale was called by a derogatory, symbolic name: Massah-Meribah. The frequent mention of this narrative in the Bible indicates that it had become a favorite subject of homiletic and didactic interpretation in ancient Israel.[39]

Some biblical texts point to this passage as an example of the people of Israel provoking God. Others use it to witness to God's active presence in sustaining Israel in times of great need. Still others use it to portray God as provoking or trying the people of Israel.[40]

Clearly, this passage was formative for the faith of the people. Their situation was serious: a life-and-death thirst for water. Their grumbling is a sign of the intimacy between the people and their God. Moses cries out and God provides the life-giving water. The people's faith that God was truly with them was tested beyond their limits.

Note that there are no negative repercussions for the people's behaviour. They believe that when the situation is desperate, they can complain and they will be heard. And that is so.

---

39 *The Jewish Publication Society Torah Commentary: Exodus*, 93.
40 *The Jewish Publication Society Torah Commentary: Exodus*, 93.

You shall, you shall not

The lectionary omits several verses (and commandments) in this week's reading. Read it straight through, from verses 1 to 20, to include the verses dealing with the nature of God being expressed in these commandments and the deep meaning of the institution of the Sabbath.

This is the first instance in the Torah of the ten commandments, which are also described in Exodus 34 and Deuteronomy 5. Churches almost always use the Exodus 20 version. (When I used to teach the "Religion and Life" course for the Scouting movement, I would have the Cubs [ages 8 to 10] look at the three versions and find their similarities and differences. Those Cubs were very astute!)

For the people of Israel and our modern-day Jewish sisters and brothers, the ten commandments – and, for that matter, all of the Old Testament rules and injunctions – are gifts of God. These have been primary revelatory texts down through the centuries. The Exodus was a supreme act of God's grace that freed the people from slavery and oppression into a new life of independence and relationship with their God. The ten commandments are a further gift from God, an awesome guide for how to live that new life in a way that respects the people's relationship with God and with each other. They are a blueprint, one might say, for right relationship in every facet of life, because God cares about every facet of life. And God always will.

The ten commandments are often very concrete: they are detailed and, in their place in the biblical text, fall in the midst of talking about the vibrancy of the relationship between the people and God. God cares about how we live our lives. The details of how we live our lives witness to what we believe about our relationship with God.

Some time ago, there was a slightly off-the-wall Christian campaign whose purpose was to witness to our Christian calling to be faithful stewards of the environment. Called "What would Jesus drive?", its purpose was to call us to reject such gas-intensive vehicles as SUVs. Off the wall? Maybe. Or maybe not.

Carpe diem

The church believes that the Old Testament reveals God to us in our time and place. This week's text is full of preaching opportunities. Rabbi Gunther Plaut says about this passage,

> ... the Torah now tells a story of human dimensions, a story of anxiety and restlessness over the absence of visible leadership, of incomprehension over the true meaning of theophany. Moses' mysterious connection with the unseen God must have been a source of constant discussion and doubt among the people ... and now, to cap it all, the man has vanished completely. He said that he is going aloft to God up there, when we need God down here just where we are; but he has not come back, and it must be supposed that that God of his made away with him ... We have to take matters into our own hands. An image has to be made, and then the power of the God will enter the image and there will be proper guidance.[41]

In addition, the text describes God's tremendous anger against the people, Moses' plea to God, God's change of heart, and Moses' smashing of the sacred tablets.

Perhaps the most crucial theme is the people's anxiety over the lack of visible leadership, and the result of that anxiety. Even though two incredible acts have happened – the freedom from slavery and the giving of the ten commandments – the people are still anxious. They turn to the visible and the material for proper guidance. We do the same. God has given us awesome gifts: as a community, we are to remind each other of God's generous presence and to act in that truth.

At church meetings, I often hear that overused phrase "That's not the way we've always done it," whatever "it" is. I heard it recently from a social justice colleague who would have considered himself on the cutting edge of both change and resisting anxiety based on the lack of institutional structures. Golden calves can spring up anywhere, it seems!

---

41   Plaut, *The Torah*, 664.

Proper 24 – Exodus 33:12-23

Context matters

It is always a good idea to link the day's reading with what has come before and with what comes after, especially since we know that many people are not in worship Sunday after Sunday. Context is particularly important in dealing with today's passage. The making of the golden calf, which resonates through the history of the people of Israel, has just happened. The renewal of the covenant and the giving of a new version of the tablets of the ten commandments (which were smashed during the golden calf event) is about to happen.

In between those two texts is a revealing story. One of the reasons why I find such depth in the Old Testament – why it speaks so deeply to my faith, why I often hear God's voice and experience God's presence through its texts – is that it is painfully honest about the complexities of relationship: among human beings, and between human beings and our God. Moses has been up on Mount Sinai, very close to the presence of God. He seems to converse directly with God and be answered. This passage shows his uncertainty, his need to be sustained. Moses wants God to lead the people. He needs, longs, prays to know God's favour and God's ways. God agrees to lead the people onward in their journey from the Exodus to the promised land.

But now Moses wants more! Even Moses, who has been closer to the presence of God than any other biblical personage so far, and closer than most to come, wants more. Moses wants to behold God's very presence! In an intriguing passage, God agrees. God can be seen and yet not entirely seen. The overwhelming nature of the divine holiness is more than human beings can be exposed to, but what can be seen is enough for Moses. It enables him to carry on with his calling, to carve the new tablets of the ten commandments, and to be present with God again on the mountain for 40 days. This passage resonates with the New Testament texts of resurrection stories where Jesus is both recognizable and not recognizable; can be known by voice but not appearance; can eat fish and pass through doors; can be touched sometimes but not all the time. God connects with our lives, but we cannot confine God to our limited understanding!

The last act

Here are the last verses of the last book of the Torah. We hear of the death of Moses as the people are poised on the very edge of re-entering the land of Israel. It has been 40 years of wandering in the wilderness after the Exodus from Egypt, 40 years of trials and of complaining, but also 40 years of wondrous revelation and experience of God's great love, care and compassion. The generation that left Egypt, and that includes Moses, will not enter the homeland. It will be a new generation, with new leadership. Deuteronomy is set up as a speech Moses gives to the people of Israel as they gather by the Jordan River. Moses reminds the people of all that God has done for them. He reiterates God's gracious gift of the laws of divine-human, human-human relationship, including the ten commandments.

God reminds Moses of the promises that have been made down through the generations. God tells Moses that he himself will not cross over, but God shows him the entire land to which the people are about to return. Then Moses dies. The Pentateuch/the Torah/the Five Books of Moses concludes with statements about Moses' leadership, which is without equal. He did wondrous things indeed, and he did them all wrapped in his call from God. He did them as one who knew God face to face.

Scripture interprets Scripture. As the Book of Deuteronomy tells the story of the up-and-down relationship between God and the people, much is the same as what we have heard in Genesis to Numbers, but some things are different. (Compare the ten commandments of Deuteronomy 5 with those in Exodus 20 and 34.)

From our standpoint, in our time and place, we cannot always explain those differences exactly to our rational satisfaction. The point is that the circumstances and context of the people have changed, and therefore so must some of the details of the guidelines of grace. Our faithful task is in the discernment of living our dynamic relationship with God in our time and place.

The God of life?

The Book of Joshua takes up the story of the people of Israel where Deuteronomy left off. Having been freed from slavery in Egypt, having wandered for a whole generation in the desert, having received the great gift of the laws of life (the ten commandments and all the rest), having done some complaining along the way and Moses having died, the people are now about to re-enter the land that they believe God has promised to them through their ancestors. Verse 10 says, "By this you shall know that among you is the living God who without fail will drive out from before you the Canaanites, Hittites, Hivites, Perizites, Girgashites, Amorites and Jebusites."

When I was in theological college, we spent too much time trying to identify those peoples and not enough time dealing theologically with this passage. How will we treat this passage now? Avoid taking it literally. The biblical text itself speaks against a literal interpretation of this passage. The Book of Joshua describes the people's own efforts to establish themselves in the land again. The Book of Judges shows a somewhat different process of assimilation.

In terms of some of the other specific details of this troublesome text, the detail around the ark of the covenant is significant. The ark is the sacred space in which the laws of life, the tablets of the ten commandments, are contained. On the ark, between the wings of the cherubim, God resides – at least some of the time. God is not to be pinned down or contained.

What to say about the holding back of the waters of the Jordan? We have seen waters held back before, in the crossing of the Red Sea. It is not necessary to search high and low for a natural, scientific explanation. It is necessary to say what it means: the ark is sacred. It accompanies the people and it sustains them. The sacred is present in the lives of the people and in our lives. But just because it is sacred does not make it easy to live with. Resist both easy explanations and easy rejections.

No entry

The lectionary does not include an Old Testament reading for All Saints Day in Year A or Year B. But you can connect the Old Testament with the saints. The two New Testament genealogies, one in Matthew – placed at the very beginning of the New Testament to set the context and connection for what is to be told to us – and one in Luke, list our ancestors in the faith. Some we know well; others are unfamiliar. Matthew in particular challenges our understanding with those listed in his genealogy. Try preaching from one genealogy, either from the Old – particularly those in the Book of Genesis – or New Testament, this Sunday.

Emphasize how important the people thought it to see the continuity of their story, to detail the ongoing nature of their faith in and relationships with their God.

And it is not always obvious why those named in the genealogies are those named. Even in genealogies, creativity abounds!

Consult a genealogist in your congregation – most congregations have several, professional or amateur.

The rubber hits the road

Today's reading is missing important chunks of the story. Verses 3b to 13 contain some of the difficult issues with which to wrestle. Verses 26 to 28 give us details about the making and marking of a covenant, traditions that recall what we read in Genesis about Jacob's encounter at the Jabbok River. This is a great opportunity for a dramatic reading, with different voices taking the roles of Joshua, God and the people.

The general theme of Joshua is the establishment of the nation of Israel, now that the people have returned from the Exodus. The book may have been written, at least in an early form, around 1000 BCE, the time of King David. During this time, as the kingdom was being set up, the history and traditions of the people began to be gathered. Towards the end of the book, Joshua, who is the successor to Moses, reminds the people of God's covenant promises to them. He instructs them to remain in a loving and obedient relationship with God .

Shechem was a holy place at that time. Joshua gathers all the tribes, elders, judges and officers of Israel there. To gather there is to present themselves to God, because it is a holy place. Joshua reminds them all of their history and relationship with God, emphasizing that the people have not always worshipped the Lord as their God. Their ancestors served other gods. While in Egypt, the people worshipped various gods. The land into which they have now come has its own gods, gods of materialism and fertility. Monotheism was not the norm. Early Israelite traditions squarely faced the fact that people gave their allegiances to other deities, but they, and in later Israelite tradition all peoples, were to give their allegiance to God alone. This is what was revealed to Abraham and carried through the ancestors.

Then there is a test. Joshua declares for his family that they will serve the Lord. All the people say the same, remembering as a community all that God had done for them. God asks for our full allegiance.

Although God is a "jealous" God, God does forgive.[42] The test is this: are the people ready, in the face of the temptation of materialistic and fertility gods, to give their total allegiance to the Lord? They say yes. Would we be able to say the same?

---

42 Forgiveness is not just a New Testament revelation. The Old Testament is full of references to God's forgiveness and constant love (e.g., Psalm 103:8: "The Lord is merciful and gracious, slow to anger and abounding in steadfast love.").

Not again!

The history of the people's relationship with God is linear. This is a major difference in understanding from the ways that other ancient peoples perceived their relationship with their gods.[43] But in Judges we see a cyclical pattern in the midst of that linear history. Over and over again, the people slip into doing things that are evil in the sight of God, though the exact nature of the evil is not always specified. Most often, the evil has something to do with worshipping other gods. Over and over again, God then puts the people in the power of an oppressive political regime. The people cry out to the Lord, and the Lord sends a judge to deliver them.

The term "judge" in the Bible is not synonymous with the term as we use it today. In the Bible, these figures make judgments among the people. They are also leaders who fulfill a variety of roles, many of them military. They lead the people into battle, as happens in this story. They have colourful adventures, like Samson. Long stories are told about them. They even make horrific mistakes, as Jephthah does, but always, they remain loyal to God.

Judges 4 and Judges 5 (there is much more to this story than the lectionary gives us) contain the story of the judge Deborah, the woman Jael, the Israelite commander Barak, and the Canaanite commander Sisera. The Israelites had once again done evil. They had once again come into the power of an oppressive enemy – in this case, King Jabin of Canaan. They had again cried out to God, who sent them Deborah, one of the few Old Testament women whose stories we hear in the lectionary texts.[44]

Deborah was a prophet and a judge in Israel. Having been empowered by God, Deborah calls out the Israelite general, Barak, to

---

43 See Cahill, *The Gifts of the Jews*, a generally helpful and readable book, for more detail on this topic.

44 Two helpful books that examine the women of the Old and New Testaments and that do not hesitate to deal with the difficult and painful stories are *Miriam, Mary and Me*

lead the people in battle for their freedom with the Canaanites. The assurance is that the Israelites will prevail and thus obtain their freedom. Reading to at least verse 10 would enhance the vibrancy of the story. (While few preachers will want to tackle verses 17 to 22, this is part of the story.) The stories of the Judges told in this book show in colourful detail God's connection with the details of human lives. God continues to love the people. There are consequences for sin and evil, to be sure, but there is always the chance of starting again. Thank God for that!

(Northstone Publications, 2000) and *Stories Seldom Told* (Northstone Publications, 2000), both by Lois M. Wilson.

Priest and prophet

This passage has been chosen for Reign of Christ or Christ the King Sunday, that Sunday on which we close the Christian year. Today, we try to define who Christ is for us.

Ezekiel, one of those who were taken away from the southern part of the land of Israel into exile in Babylon in 586 BCE, received his call to become a priest/prophet there. (There is little dichotomy between prophets and priests in biblical writings.) Ezekiel is called to minister to the exiled. He is to remind them of God's love for them – a love that is the grounds and foundation of hope. Because he is a priest as well, much of his message has to do with the Temple and its ritual. In this text, however, Ezekiel gives another message.

Using an image that we know well from the gospels and, of course, Psalm 23, Ezekiel reminds us that God is like a shepherd. Since Christians believe that God is in Christ, this image is appropriate on this day of the church year. As a shepherd, God actively seeks out the sheep, the people. The Shepherd brings them out of all the places where they have been scattered in dark times and into their own land, where they will be nourished and refreshed. Like other prophets do, Ezekiel points out that God has particular concern for the lost, the strays, the injured and the weak. Those who are fat and strong have, by implication, become so through unjust means. It is time to bring justice to bear. It is Israel's darkest hour, historically, and yet Ezekiel proclaims a message that speaks deeply and vibrantly of God's justice and intimate caring for the people.

Vines, fig trees and pomegranates

When you read the Book of Deuteronomy, which is frequently, I hope, remember the pivotal role it plays in the canon of Holy Scripture. Deuteronomy is the transition between the first four books of the Torah and what follows – what our Jewish sisters and brothers call Prophets and Writings. Deuteronomy sums up the history and relationship of the people with their God so far, and then retells some of that history and relationship, sometimes with different emphases and priorities, to empower the people for the next stage of their lives. We have heard the early stories of Creation and of the patriarchs and matriarchs. We have heard the stories of the Exodus, the wandering in the wilderness, and the giving of the grace-filled instructions for how to live in relationship with God and with other people. Now the people are poised to re-enter the land. Deuteronomy is to be heard as a final speech by Moses telling the people everything they need to know to go forward without him.

This lectionary passage is a typically Deuteronomic passage. It reminds the people that it is not by their own efforts that they are going home. The bounties of the land are noted in great detail. There will be enough of everything. The words "wealth" and "prosperity" speak of a much more basic level of life than many of us in the West are used to.

The passage goes on to remind the people that it will be tempting, when they are living comfortably in the land, to exalt themselves and to forget the Lord their God. A rehearsal of the great deeds of God on behalf of the people follows, making this an obvious passage for Thanksgiving. As we celebrate the plentiful harvest, focus on the great and wondrous acts of God in our lives and in the world. Find ways to share with the many in our communities and the larger world who do not have enough for their basic, human needs. It seems pretty obvious. It seems to be the best way to remember and give thanks to the Lord. Bless the Lord our God indeed!

Year B

The power of prayer

Here, at the beginning of Year B, we start a three-week series of Isaiah passages. (There are a lot of Isaiah passages in Advent in Year A as well.) Today's passage comes from a late context in the book of the prophet – what some scholars refer to as Third Isaiah. The exile in Babylon is over. People have returned to the land. Now is the time for rebuilding the community in Jerusalem. It is an awkward settling-in period, probably between the rebuilding of the Temple and the revival of temple worship and the leadership of Ezra and Nehemiah: sometime after 520 BCE and before 444 BCE.

It is a kind of in-between time in the life of the people, which resonates with the kind of in-between time that Advent is for us. This passage, like many later chapters of Isaiah, reaffirms the wondrous and salvific promises of God, but declares that things are not exactly wondrous and salvific yet. In Advent, we reaffirm that God is coming to us in Jesus Christ, that the wise men are on the move, that the angelic chorus is warming up, that the shepherds are feeling restless without knowing why, and that Mary is wondering, wondering. But we are waiting still.

In this lectionary passage, there is no minimizing the fact that things are not yet as they should be with the people. There is sin and transgression. But God is called to a dramatic action of coming down in the situation of need. An action so dramatic that we would think twice or three times before wanting to witness it. The people believe that God can and will come down. Verse 8 makes the key point. Hope is possible no matter what: the wonderful and salvific promises are true. The people's shady response is real, but so is God's foundational commitment.

And as we wait, as the wise men mount their camels, as the angels find their notes, as the shepherds respond to the new feeling in the air, as Mary wonders, worries and waits, we are called to whisper and to shout. To whisper and to shout not that we have run out of wrapping paper and cannot think what to buy crabby great-uncle, but that we know what we are waiting for.

God's coming is expected and unexpected, and nothing like tame. It shines the spotlight of starlight on our failures of nerve, but reverberates through and through with the continual hope that defies all fear.

We wait and we know that there will be good news for all people. Life is Real. God is Real Life.

Both/and

The times they are a changin'. Well, sort of.

Chapter 40 marks a major transition in the Book of the Prophet Isaiah. Some scholars call it the beginning of Second Isaiah. It certainly shows a different historical context from much of the first 39 chapters of Isaiah. The superpower Assyria has fallen; the superpower Babylon has arisen. The latter has taken some of the people, possibly the leaders, into exile in Babylon. In that dire situation, the prophet is proclaiming a message of supreme hope and comfort.

But the transition is perhaps not so major as it is sometimes made out to be, and that is a good thing theologically. It is not true, as is popularly said, that the first 39 chapters of Isaiah are chapters of judgment, and those from 40 onwards are chapters of hope. The themes of judgment and hope are intertwined through both (or all three) parts of the book. It is just that the emphasis on each is weighted somewhat differently. The first 39 chapters also contain hope. In chapter 40 and onwards, we also find judgment. Hope and comfort are proclaimed with wonderfully poetic imagery there, but the comfort is not a kind of "teddy bear" comfort that is all fluffy and cuddly.[45] It is a comfort that holds to the original covenant of God with the people: a covenant of grace and just response to that grace, which can mean judgment. The covenant will judge bad behaviour but will also always hold to God's foundational love and grace: grace-filled liberation from slavery in the

---

45 One of the women in my congregation was asked to do a presentation at her children's school on the meaning of Christmas. We talked about the presentation as we packed up the church crèche for her to take with her, agreeing on how important it was to relate the power of the story, to move away from the "sweetness and light," "Rudolph the Red-Nosed Reindeer" kind of perception of the Christmas story to the radical justice of a story that includes disreputable shepherds and privileged, powerful magi. She confessed later that she thought I was overstating the need to do so, until she heard the questions and comments before she began her presentation!

exile, and grace-filled "rules of engagement" with life in relationship to God and to others in the ten commandments.

Walter Brueggemann says that this passage generally speaks of "a powerful intervention that creates new possibilities."[46] Verse 9 summarizes the good news of this passage. "The gospel makes the God of Israel visible and effective in a setting from which [God] had seemed to be expelled."[47] This is why this book of prophecy is the part of the Old Testament that is the second-most frequently quoted in the New Testament, second only to the Psalms. This passage defies both the imperial arrogance of Babylon, which thinks it has dominated the people of Israel and made their God irrelevant, and any propensity for exilic despair that the people might be feeling. This defiance is a powerful message for people today in the face of imperial, material, consumer power and a society and context that sometimes, in some places, try to push faith into irrelevancy. This tendency is perhaps particularly visible in the contemporary season of Advent, as elevator Christmas music strives to make us feel trite. God is present, and our calling is not a passive one. In the assurance of that presence, however, that makes God visible and effective, we are called to defy both the powers of the world and our own tendencies to despair. Emmanuel.

---

46   Brueggemann, *Isaiah 40–66*, 16.

47   Brueggemann, *Isaiah 40–66*, 20.

Scripture within Scripture

The Gospel according to Luke, chapter 4, verses 18-19, is a direct quote of the Book of the Prophet Isaiah, chapter 61, verses 1-2a. It would be a deep and thought-provoking bible study possibility, for Advent or for anytime of the year, to have people reflect on biblical passages, of which these are but one example, that are identical to each other but appear in different parts of Scripture. Jesus uses this passage from Isaiah in declaring who he is and what he has come to do, which makes it an obvious choice for Advent. Jesus read from the scroll of the Prophet Isaiah in the synagogue; then his hearers heard him say that in him this Scripture had been fulfilled. Consequences followed.

How might the Isaiah passage have been heard by the people of Jesus' time and place before Jesus read it and expounded on it, though?[48] The passage as we have it begins with the voice of a human agent, who recognizes the divine calling to do God's work of justice and mercy among the people of God. Although Christians understand this human agent to be God in Jesus, in the original setting of the passage in Isaiah, the speaker is not identified. The tasks of the speaker are specific and concrete, though. There is widespread agreement among scholars that the phrase "the year of the Lord's favour" refers to the concept of the Jubilee year, which is set out in chapter 25 of the book of Leviticus. The Jubilee year was a time "when all properties lost in economic transactions will be restored and returned in order to permit a stable, functioning community."[49] This passage proclaims a theological vision of a human agent, acting according to the divine energy and will for justice and mercy, covenant and compassion, in

---

48 Brueggemann, *Isaiah* 40–66, 212. Note that this lectionary reading omits the middle verses, 5 to 7, which breaks up the alternation of speakers. The intimate connection between God's resolve and human vocation is broken when these verses are omitted.

49 Brueggemann, *Isaiah* 40–66, 214

ways that will make concrete, physically discernable differences for how the vulnerable and marginalized in society will live. No "pie in the sky when you die" here, but rather someone sent by God to make a difference in the suffering of the here and now. That is the message of Advent, and it reverberates through such Advent carols as "All Earth Is Waiting" (Alberto Toulé, 1972), "Hope Is a Star" (Brian Wren, 1985), "O Ancient Israel" (Michael Joncas, 1994), and "Tomorrow Christ Is Coming" (Fred Kaan, 1966).

Moving to the second part of the passage, as the lectionary lists it, we hear that the Lord God will "recompense" the people. Israel is not to be rewarded because the people or the nation have earned it. Rather, Israel is to be rewarded because that is the nature of God's covenant and relationship with people. The exile could never be the end because God is a God of faithful covenant, continually loving and forgiving the people and calling for the kinds of concrete justice that the human speaker is proclaiming. God is calling to the people of Israel and calling to us. In Advent and in every other time! And so we sing "Hark the Glad Sound" (Philip Doddridge, 1738) and "Hail to God's Own Anointed" (James Montgomery, 1821).

To build or not to build

Once upon a time I was leaving a service in an urban, downtown, very visually prominent church. A person who was without a home came up to me and asked, pointing to the church, "Is God in there?"

"Yes," I answered, "and also out here."

"Well, that's good. " the man responded, "because I want to talk to him!"

In many congregations the pressure of busyness, shopping, parties and the desire to sing Christmas carols can be rather feverish by this fourth Sunday of Advent. But today's passage is about tension, and tension is a common feature of Advent. This could be a tension between wanting a simple, faith-filled Advent and Christmas and not being able or willing to let go of all the details that are built up around the season. In the case of this passage, the tension is one of trying to contain or assure God's presence and knowing God as a God of complete freedom. Is God indeed inside our buildings and all the details with which we try and fill this season, and/or outside them and all around?

King David is settling into the work of ruling a nation state. He has been anointed king over all Israel, he has brought the ark of the Lord to his capital, Jerusalem, and now he wants to build a Temple or house for the Lord. An act of piety, nation-building and trying to keep God contained and close at hand, no doubt. Nathan the prophet agrees with David's plan – until the Lord comes to him by night and declares that a permanent dwelling is out of the question, because it would violate God's freedom. God has done great and faithful things for the people, taken care of them, given them leaders, and established them in a land, but in doing all that has never asked for a house. God has been going to and fro in tent and tabernacle and will continue to do so for the time being.

Verse 16 gives us a précis of the message of the omitted verses. David and his lineage do and will have permanent pre-eminence through the will and acts of God. This situation is not because of any particular merits on the part of David and his successors, but because they are God's choice forever. After all the detail about how God has not needed or asked for a Temple, it seems that David's successor will build one with God's approval. So what gives? Well, that's where tension comes in. There were very real tensions in Israel about whether there was a need for a permanent royal line, about whether the leadership was conditionally or unconditionally given. There were very real tensions in Israel about the relationship of God to the political powers. The Bible never tries to whitewash over these tensions or to deny the complexity of the questions the tensions raise. They remain in the text for us to see and to struggle with in our own time and place.

This passage became a messianic one for Jews and Christians, in spite of the tension, because of the absolute assurance of the sustaining and eternal quality of God's promise to make the world a just and righteous reality "within the historical process through a historical agent."[50]

---

50   Brueggemann, *Isaiah 40–66*, 258)

Christmas Eve – *Isaiah 9:2-7*

See the entry for Christmas Eve, Year A.

We cannot have too much of a good thing – this is also the passage for Christmas Eve in Year A, so please look at that entry. This is one of those very few Old Testament passages that are repeated. In preaching from it, think about the effect there might be, could be, should be from that fact. For people who attend church less often, this may be one of the few Old Testament passages they ever hear.

Christmas Day 1 – *Isaiah 62:6-12*

See the entry for Christmas Day 1, Year A.

Christmas Day 2 – *Isaiah 52:7-10*

See the entry for Christmas Day 2, Year A.

I've got the joy, joy, joy, joy ...

It is a foundational premise of this book that we are trying, when we look at these Old Testament passages, to get at least a glimmer of what they meant in their original context. Of course, we read these passages, always, through the reality of the life, ministry, death and resurrection of Jesus Christ. And the lectionary is set up accordingly; it moves through the first three Gospels canonically, matching up Old Testament passages with the Gospel readings, for the most part. (There are exceptions, in which a few Old Testament narratives are read continuously for a few weeks, and the Gospel of John does show up here and there according to the rhythm of the church year.) I usually discuss only the Old Testament passage for the week. Here I also explore the gospel reading of the day: Luke 2:22-40, the presentation of Jesus in the Temple, which is one of my favourite biblical passages. (See page 172 for a comment on "favourite" biblical passages.)

It may well be that the lectionary editors saw in this passage from Luke the details of the "consolation of Israel," the "salvation" and the "light for revelation to the Gentiles and for glory to your people Israel." It seems possible, at least to some, that Simeon's words hearken back to Isaiah 61–62.

This passage from Isaiah is in that part of the book that may be addressed specifically to those who have returned to the land after the exile. Life there is new and often far from easy. Yet this is a hymn of rejoicing! The phrase "greatly rejoice" is an intensive phrase in Hebrew, which repeats the word "joy," "joy." We just cannot translate that easily into contemporary English. We hear, though, that the speaker of the hymn is exultant and decked out in the salvation, righteousness, fireworks and Te Deums that are glorious and celebratory. Nature is, as always, connected to this salvation and righteousness, and can be seen as a model for it. The point, however, is not the joy of the individual. It is the community that is the recipient of God's salvation and righteousness. The poetry is lovely, but the context is crucial! This passage comes very shortly after Isaiah 61:1-2, the passage that Jesus uses as his concrete proclamation of his mandate of justice and Jubilee. Verses 5 to 9 of this chapter of Isaiah also reflect the joy-filled proclamation of economic justice. No more despair for the people: life is now transformed in real and sustaining ways.

What if we saw this Sunday after Christmas, one on which, unfortunately, few people tend to show up in church, not as a time of rest and recuperation from the excesses of turkey and ribbon, but as the joyful launch of our living the good news to those oppressed in any way? With fewer distractions of presents and parties, your congregation could be a "crown of beauty" that starts organizing visits to local politicians on behalf of the homeless people of the community. Joy, joy indeed.

For an alternative to this entry, see Christmas 2, Year A.

Thus says the Lord, or telling the end of the story

When the seventh Harry Potter book was released, my son was the first person in our family to finish reading it. It was mighty tempting for him to tell the dramatic end of the story. But he did not give in to this temptation. He knew that to do so would take away from the reading experience of the rest of the family. This lectionary passage from the Book of the Prophet Jeremiah, on the other hand, does not keep the end of the story under wraps. It means to and does tell us the end of the story from God's perspective. It is up to us to listen.

The balance of power of empires was shifting. Jeremiah saw it coming. He prophesied in the southern part of the kingdom of Israel in the years after it had divided in two, and he witnessed the destruction of Jerusalem and the exile of some of the people to Babylon. It was not just Judah, the southern part of Israel, that was in trouble and turmoil: much of the world was experiencing unrest at that time. The power balance between or among empires was shifting. That shift created chaos, with no let-up in sight for the oppression, economic or otherwise, that came then and comes still with the power of empires. The dates of Jeremiah's ministry of prophecy were about 626 BCE to sometime after 586 BCE, the year Jerusalem fell to the Babylonians.

His message was not well-received. Most of the powers of his own country, with the exception of King Josiah, did not want to hear what he had to say. At times, he found himself in jail.

Judgment as a cause for the disaster to come was one of Jeremiah's main themes. The judgment was always, however, interwoven with both the great and wondrous possibilities that repentance could bring, and with God's great concern for individuals, who were both graciously loved and, at the same time, accountable to God.

The biblical scholar Brevard Childs points out that this Scripture passage is one of numerous "promise oracles," written poetically and manifesting eschatological hope, and found throughout the Book of the Prophet, but particularly clustered in chapters 30 to 33. According to Childs, "The prophetic book bears witness to the belief that, regardless of the severity of the divine judgment on Israel, the ultimate goal in the divine economy was redemption."[51] So this lectionary passage, is, in effect, telling the end of the story. It comes before the devastating fall of the city and the southern part of the country, but it declares in no uncertain terms that God will "turn their mourning into joy, … and give them gladness for sorrow" (verse 13). God knows how the story will end. Thanks to Jeremiah, we can, should and do know, too. Thanks be to God!

51   Brevard Childs, *Introduction to the Old Testament as Scripture* (Philadelphia: Fortress Press, 1979), 351.

Epiphany – *Isaiah 60:1-6*

See the entry for Epiphany, Year A.

How? and Why?

In the beginning, or when God began to create, or in the beginning God created – all these phrases being possible translations from the Hebrew – there was water everywhere, these verses from Genesis tell us. A wind from God, or the Spirit of God, or a mighty wind – all these phrases being possible translations of the Hebrew – swept over the face of the waters. English, and, in fact, most modern languages, have many more words than Hebrew does, hence a wondrous variety of translation possibilities. When we differentiate in English between "wind" and "Spirit" and "breath" in the biblical text, doing the very best we can to translate the context and meaning of the passage into context and meaning in English, we need to remain aware that all three of those English words are exactly the same word in Hebrew, each and every time. (This is only one example of the issue; other Hebrew words have multiple translations as well.) Therefore, the "wind" the NRSV translation uses here in these first five verses from Genesis may be the same as the Spirit who descended like a dove on Jesus at his baptism.

Another issue that this passage raises for preaching is the relationship between faith and science. The biblical text is not anti-science or anti-Darwinism. My son has been a museum addict since his early days. One summer he went to a program on dinosaurs being held at the museum in our city. Upon returning home he told me what he had learned about dinosaurs, but then said that he feared I would be disappointed with the program. When I asked why, the answer was that they had talked about the beginning of the world and the universe, but, "Mom, they didn't mention the Bible!" He was young then and somewhat surprised when I responded that I would not expect the museum program, which is based in science, to talk about the Bible. Science tells us *how* things came to be; the Bible tells us *why*.[52]

In this passage, the Bible tells us that God is the Creator; that the wind, breath, Spirit of God is moving in the created universe; that it is God's will and good purpose to bring order out of chaos (in the ancient world, the deep, the waters, were often representative of chaos); that God creates in an active mode of word; and that God names the Creation "good." In the beginning, indeed.

---

52 There are many excellent authors writing on the relationship between faith and science – John Polkinghorne is my first choice, but Ian Barbour and Stephen Jay Gould are also worth reading. This is an ever-growing field. Find time to read one over the summer holidays.

Here I am

In the beginning was a woman named Hannah who could not have a child. She prayed for one so intensely that the priest thought she was drunk. Eventually she had the child of her dreams. In thanksgiving, she offered him as a servant of the Lord in the Lord's sanctuary at Shiloh. And so it came to be that the boy Samuel was "lent" to the service of the Lord for as long as he lived. And so it came to be that the boy Samuel was sleeping in the sanctuary when he heard a voice call his name. He responded, "Here I am," thinking it was the elderly priest, Eli. Three times Samuel heard the voice call him, and three times he answered to Eli. The priest had sons who were, in the words of the NRSV, "scoundrels," but he himself was a faithful servant of the Lord. He recognized that it was the Lord who was calling Samuel. He told Samuel to answer accordingly the next time he heard the voice. What Samuel heard from the Lord was bad and dire news. There were to be severe repercussions for the behaviour of Eli's scoundrel sons. Samuel did not want to tell, but Eli, being a faithful servant of the Lord, encouraged him to tell. Eli knew the words were true and accepted them. From that time, it was Samuel who was the prophet of the Lord to Israel.

This vibrant and dramatic story simply stands in its power. One way to illustrate something of that power is to read it dramatically, with members of the congregation primed to be the voice of God – perhaps a different person for each time Samuel is called. (Be sure to include female voices.)

This is a story of the beginning of a new time in the history and faith of the people of Israel. The former leadership line can no longer continue: a new leadership is called into being by God, through a dream theophany or encounter with the divine, which is a common device in biblical stories.

Eli and Samuel are both obedient servants of the Lord. They stand together in hearing the news that shifts the balance of prophetic power. God uses whom God chooses: both Eli and Samuel, in their very different roles in the story, understand this and move forward. Eli's sons had acted unjustly towards God and towards God's people, and injustice cannot be allowed to stand.

Who we are in this story? In an affluent North American context, many of us act as Eli's sons did, taking the best for ourselves. What about us? How do our actions harm the environment? How many people around us live in poverty? Who lacks adequate housing? How many are unemployed? Who does not receive proper health care? These are questions to ask ourselves. It may be hard news for us to hear, as it was hard news for Eli to hear, that there are repercussions for taking more than our share. Yet would we want anything but a God of justice who can make new beginnings?

The reluctant prophet

One of the current problems in looking at the book of the prophet Jonah is that all too often an examination of the text gets weighed down by arguments such as whether there really are fish with throats big enough to swallow a person whole. To get weighed down in such arguments from any perspective is to miss the point of the book.

Another problem is that the book of Jonah appears only once in the three-year lectionary cycle. This only reinforces any tendency to omit discussion of chapter 4, which is the key to the book. Chapter 4 is God's lesson to Jonah about what being "a gracious God and merciful, slow to anger and abounding in steadfast love" really looks like in the lives of individual prophets and entire peoples.

The prophet Jonah is not a nice guy. When God tells Jonah to go to Nineveh and tell the people of their great wickedness and call them to repentance, he immediately goes … in the opposite direction! Many adventures later – adventures involving not only a great fish (the text never uses the term "whale") but also "pagan" sailors who are far more just and compassionate than Jonah – he ends up in Nineveh anyway. God is not to be denied. Jonah does not want to preach repentance to Nineveh because he does not want the Ninevites to repent and be spared by God.

This is a very tough thing that God has asked of him. Nineveh is the capital city of Assyria, the nation that had enslaved and oppressed the northern part of Israel, yet they are to repent and be forgiven. They are also, obviously, cherished by God. This book of the prophet Jonah, whose name in Hebrew means "dove," was probably written in the eighth century, at a time when Assyria was a bitter, oppressive and enslaving enemy of the historical Israel. No wonder Jonah doesn't want them to be saved.

The Book ends with a reference to the animals of Nineveh. The verses that are skipped in the passage for this Sunday (verses 6-9) refer to the role of the animals of Nineveh in the repentance. Clearly, they are a part of the corporate repentance. There are many biblical references to the connections between people and nature in the healing of the world, but few have been included in the lectionary. This is one that has not quite made it in, but can be used if the whole book is dealt with more broadly. Note that the King of Nineveh can proclaim repentance for the whole city – women, men, children and animals. This seems to be in tension with other places in the biblical text, where individual responsibility, in combination with collective responsibility, is held up highly. That is one of the wondrous things about the Old Testament; it cannot be pinned down to a single stream of thought that always supports our own thinking. Rather, it continually challenges us!

Like Jonah, we can be very reluctant to forgive those who have done us great wrong.

A prophet is as a prophet does?

The trouble with prophets is that one cannot always know if they are legitimate until after the fact. In this passage, as is the case in much of the Book of Deuteronomy, Moses is the speaker. The book as a whole is his sort of "farewell" address, his recapitulation of the people's relationship to their God before some of them enter the promised land – an event that does not include Moses and all those of his generation. This specific passage on the nature of prophets is a part of a larger section of laws dealing with the welfare of the community and cultic and judicial matters. There is no separation of these various matters in the life of the people; these kinds of rules and guidelines for just and right living are part of relationship to God. In this kind of complicated context, it is very important to know who speaks legitimately and who does not.

In the verses immediately preceding this passage, the people are not to associate with or through the "soothsayers and augurs" who are part of the local community in the land they are to enter. Child sacrifice – a common practice in many places in that time, occasionally done by the people of Israel as they accommodated themselves to the social context around them rather than their living relationship with their God – was not to be a part of the new way of life in the land after Exodus and wanderings, nor was magic. It is the prophet of Israel who, on the Lord's authority, is to be the one the people will heed. Verse 16 refers to a human tendency to want the presence of the divine to be somehow mediated. The direct and intimate presence of God could be too overwhelming. The new prophet, who will take on Moses' role in the life of the community, will truly speak the words of God to the people. The people are to heed those words or be called to account for it. There are dire repercussions for speaking in the name of God something that God has not called to have said.

The big question for the people – and for us, biblically, theologically, homiletically – is how one discerns if a word of prophecy comes from the Lord or not. Looking at verse 20, it is clear, in more graphic terms than we want to hear, that false prophets speak an oracle God did not command them to speak, or speak in the name of other gods. How to tell this now, in the 21st century? It is not easy. Grounding ourselves in Scripture is one way. Discerning the calling of Scripture in community to be sure, listening carefully and prayerfully to both the signs of the times and the voice of God are others. Interfaith dialogue, by which we engage in the depth and fullness of our own faith tradition with the depth and fullness of another's faith tradition, is also helpful. But we have made mistakes even so, and we know it. Hindsight is indeed 20/20, and there are no guarantees. Are the current leaders of the environmental movement prophets who speak in the name of the One who is the Lord of all Creation?

In one Sunday sermon in my congregation, I asked those gathered for worship to name out loud those whom they considered prophets. Different Christian traditions may provide different names, but this is one way to deepen reflection on a very difficult question.

To comment or not to comment

The Book of the Prophet Isaiah is often composed of words of great and wondrous poetic imagery. It feels, and probably is, somewhat inappropriate to try and dissect those words too vigorously. How many people have felt that Shakespeare or the works of some other great writer were ruined for them by the dissections of a high school English class? So, it is with fear and trepidation that I venture any comments at all on this passage. One of the best things to do with this passage in liturgy is to have it read with great emphasis and power.

The poet/prophet speaks words that resonate with parts of the Book of Job and that are intended to speak to the reality of the Lord as the God of Creation, who is both totally other and totally engaged in the world of his creation. Earthly princes and rulers are dismissed, as are the gods of the oppressor state in the verses immediately preceding these ones. (Isaiah 40 is in the section of the book addressed to the people of Israel in exile in Babylon. The intention was to bring comfort and assure them of the complete and eternal promises of God at a time when those promises were hard to remember.) The point of verses 21 to 24 is clear: God's power is the complete opposite of the transitoriness of all the rest of the world, particularly of those considered to have earthly power and influence. Nothing and no one can rival God. In verse 26, even the stars are witnesses to the power of God. The imagery of the language is revelation.

In verses 27 to 31, the language gets more specific. The exile in Babylon was feeling too long. It was too hard to remember that God's power and promises were ultimate. The response was then, and is now, that God is always attentive and responsive to those who are faint and weary and without power. God's work as Creator is always ongoing, a statement that in that time and place was both political and pastoral.[53]

---

53 A simple response to those who say that Christians should not be political, is that they have not been reading their bibles. The Bible deals continuously and

God is the source of strength for the exiled. The people are not to let themselves be defined by the Babylonian exile; they are the people of God above and beyond all. We, too, are the people of God above and beyond all secular boundaries and boxes and empires, be they political or consumer or material. We, too, will rise up with wings like eagles, but we are called to wait on the Lord for our strength, for that rising. How hard to hear when the waiting seems endless, painful and stressful and we are sick, depressed or having things go badly at work. At such times, glory in some part of God's Creation, repeat over and over that you are a beloved child of God, and read this passage from Isaiah until you know it by heart.

Your strength will be renewed.

thoroughly with issues of politics. We are to remember that and live it, always with prayer and discernment, in our current context.

Happily ever after?

Tell the story. Tell the story. Tell the story.

There are so few narratives in the lectionary's choice of Old Testament passages. This one is intriguing, detailed and mystifying. It pushes us, in our time and place, in some difficult directions. It is a healing story; it is a miracle story. It makes us ponder what we think about healing and miracles, and remember meanwhile that the Bible neither understands nor believes in literalism, nor is it completely metaphorical. It is a story that is full of rich (and I do not refer to the talents, shekels and garments) detail – detail that the biblical writers and editors wanted to be sure that we knew in our own quest to discern its meaning.

The text comes from the cycle of Prophet Elisha stories, from the Book of 2 Kings. It is one of those books that are sometimes called "historical," but this term is not used in a literal, chronological way. The Books of Kings and Samuel tell the stories of the interactions between God and the people in the time of settlement and development in the land. The stories stretch from the birth of the Prophet Samuel until the fall of Jerusalem and Judah, the southern part of Israel, to Babylon (the north fell earlier to the Assyrians). The actions of both the Israelites and others are judged in accordance with how they proclaim God's will and purposes. This is especially obvious with the stories of the reigns of the various kings. Some that we know from extra-biblical records to be kings who brought economic prosperity and stability to the land, for example, are judged negatively by the text because they did not follow in the ways of God. Others that we know from extra-biblical records, although much less successful in the worldly sense, are judged positively by the text because they walked in the ways of God.

The Prophet Elisha is the clear successor to the Prophet Elijah. Elisha's reputation included, among other things, the power to heal leprosy. Note that in any exposition of this text, the one who is healed, Namaan, is not of the people of Israel. He is an outsider, but is someone through whom God had given victory to the king and people of Aram. Apparently, God heals whom God chooses. After some political anxiety on the part of the king of Israel, Elisha deals with the situation. If Namaan had been more co-operative, the situation would have been settled even more quickly. It is the common sense of his servants that brings the desired resolution. God always wants all of us to be thinking!

Reading on in the story, which is essential with this text, Namaan comes to an understanding of the God of Israel, but Elisha does not require it of him before invoking the healing. All ends happily ever after, except for Elisha's servant, whose greed gets the better of him. This is another key text to use as we explore what we believe God's relationship is with persons who do not belong to our faith tradition, what we believe about healing and miracles, and what we believe about the nature of God – all crucial questions of faith. Ask them!

Behold, I make all things new

Verse 18 is rather an odd place to begin a biblical reading when both verse 14 and verse 16 begin with that frequent biblical prophetic phrase "Thus says the Lord." This phrase often marks the beginning of a section or prophecy. It is also an odd beginning for a text since verses 14 to 17 rehearse the history of the people of Israel with their God. This sets the context for all that is to follow. A Christian interpretation of the Old Testament, however (and the lectionary reinforces this), is often drawn by such language as begins verse 18 and goes on into verse 19: "Do not remember the former things, or consider the things of old. I am about to do a new thing; now it springs forth, do you not perceive it?" The reason that so many of the Old Testament lectionary texts are drawn from Isaiah, as John Sawyer says in his book *The Fifth Gospel*, is that the Book of the Prophet Isaiah has spoken, more than other Old Testament books, to what Christians have, in the light of their resurrection faith, seen in Jesus Christ.[54]

What is this "new thing" from the point of view of the original hearers and readers of this text? A very plausible idea is that it is about a release from exile. Such a new thing, such a release from exile, such a return to the homeland is not, however, an isolated event. It brings about transformation in all kinds of areas. Nature is changed, too. The former things referred to in the passage might be Creation or the Exodus from Egypt or both, as in those events nature was profoundly affected. Note that in a desert context, water is always central to life-giving transformation.

A further possible interpretation, put forward by the biblical scholar Brevard Childs, is that the "former things" are the prophecies of judgment and doom that might be called First Isaiah. These are now to be disregarded, since the "new things," what might be called

---

54   John Sawyer, *The Fifth Gospel: Isaiah in the History of Christianity* (Cambridge: Cambridge University Press, 1996), 1–7.

the prophecies of Second Isaiah, the prophecies of restoration and healing and hope, are now in the ascendancy.[55] Whichever interpretation is followed, the "former things" and the "new things" are clearly in tension with each other. The "former things" both set the context for the "newer things" and are to be disregarded at one and the same time. This tension is common in the Bible and in our lives.

Verses 22 to 24 paint a clear picture of the people's lack of faithfulness to their God while in exile. They have not praised their God through the particularities of human existence, and they have fallen into sin and iniquity. But "I AM" is one who blots out iniquities and forgets sins. And this is both a "former thing," as the biblical text has witnessed to many times before, and a "new thing" that is present, active, real and transforming both the people and the cosmos in their time and place. A "new thing" that Christians proclaim is in the ministry, death and resurrection of Jesus Christ and the sustaining presence of the Holy Spirit.

Know that we live in the midst of tensions in our time and place, as did the prophets. Name these tensions in terms of the specifics of your congregational life: tensions such as whether parents should sit on more committees at their children's school, or have more family time; tensions such as whether to dip into the congregational capital fund or continue without designated community outreach ministry. Proclaim that God's ultimate answer of love does not obliterate those tensions, but enables us to live with and through them.

---

55   Childs, *Introduction to the Old Testament as Scripture*, 328–29.

The personal is political

In the early days of feminism, an oft-quoted phrase or mantra was that "the personal is political." Such a phrase did not come out of a vacuum. This passage from the Book of the Prophet Hosea clearly shows the interconnections of the various themes and realities of life. God is wooing the people as a loving, forgiving, incredibly magnanimous husband would woo a straying wife. The people have pursued other gods, but God is always forgiving and drawing them and inviting them back into relationship. And doing it tenderly, at that. All the people's needs will be supplied; the time of the Exodus from Egypt, a time when Israel really understood her complete relationship with her God, is invoked. It is a personal relationship; it is also one that involves covenant with nature and abolishes war from the land. Love and justice are completely intertwined. Love is justice and justice is love. What else could our hearts ever crave?

This is also an ideal passage for debunking the unbiblical but frequently believed and promoted notion that the Old Testament God is a God of vengeance and the New Testament God is a God of love. The New Testament contains endless examples of Jesus' proclamation of himself and his ministry being in line with the faith of his people, but this is a book about the Old Testament. Previous verses in Hosea never minimize the cost of unfaithfulness to God; Jesus never does either. This week's passage is overflowing with graciousness and warmth and love and tenderness and the constancy of God, which will continually, no matter what, keep chasing after and alluring the people.

This is not an abstract debunking that needs to be done by preachers and biblical scholars to keep us in faithful relationship to the text. Down through the ages of Christian history, lines of expression, faith and ecclesiology have been drawn through peoples' lives because of an unfaithful distinction between the portrayal of God in the Old and New Testaments. Much anti-Semitism, sometimes carried to the extremes of pogroms and other acts of murder, has been visited upon our Jewish sisters and brothers because they are thought to worship a different God, or to worship a God of violence and vengeance. Christians, who supposedly worship a God of love, have inflicted violence and vengeance upon Jews for their beliefs. The irony does not escape God's attention.

This situation is not just a thing of the past. Every time you hear the phrase "an eye for an eye," used in a way that implies revenge, that is what is going on. That text, in its context, is actually pushing the people forward – away from violence, not towards it. Anti-Semitism is very real in most corners of our world. In speaking out against it, we shall, as this passage states, "know the Lord."

For the third time

This is the third time in the first five books of the Old Testament that the ten commandments are given. They are given first in Exodus 20, and then again in Exodus 34 after the golden calf catastrophe and the smashing of the first set of tablets. It is no surprise that they show up again in the Book of Deuteronomy, since the purpose of the book is to remind the people of the key elements of their history. The people of Israel are about to enter back into the land. Deuteronomy is, in almost its entirety, a speech of Moses, who will not be going with them. Moses reminds them of all the things they need to know as they move forward into this next phase of their life in community and in relationship to their God. The very name, Deuteronomy, is a Greek word meaning "second law." The Hebrew name of the book, following the usual tradition of Hebrew naming, is *Devarim*, which means "words." The book begins with "These are the words that Moses spoke ...."

Those words Moses spoke reminded the people of God's goodness to them from the time of the Exodus, through their journey of years in the wilderness, and the promise of a homeland. Moses summarized the grace-filled laws of God, including the ten commandments. The theme of the whole book is love – the love of God in relationship to the people, and the love of the people in relationship to their God.

That love is clearly seen in the commandment to observe the Sabbath day. Only part of the ten commandments is included in this lectionary passage: the part about the Sabbath. On the seventh day, the people are not to work; neither are their children, their slaves or their animals. The people are reminded of their past suffering as slaves in Egypt, and therefore are commanded to be just to all. In the Exodus version of this commandment, the Sabbath is proclaimed as sanctified time, a time for rest because God rested at that point in Creation. On the Sabbath, the people "re-enact the creative process and thus renew their own creative power."[56] In Deuteronomy, the Sabbath is linked not so much to God's creative role but rather to God's redemptive role. The Sabbath is founded not so much on cosmic time but on historical time. Reality, social justice and a form of equality are being proclaimed. Both ways of understanding the Sabbath proclaim God. Taken together, they proclaim God as active and alive and dynamic, both outside and inside history. Creation and redemption can thus be seen together: the focus is on both self and other. The various recitations of the ten commandments are not in any way in opposition to each other; rather, they come together. As Plaut says, "... in Exodus the day's observance is aimed at rekindling human awe before the miracle of existence, in Deuteronomy the quality of gratitude is the focus and out of this gratitude arises the obligation to safeguard the humanity of others."[57] Creation and redemption are joined together by revelation. Try to see both in your own personal living of the Sabbath.

56   Plaut, *The Torah*, 1360.
57   Plaut, *The Torah*, 1360.

Chariots of fire

The story of the Transfiguration in the Gospel according to Mark mentions the Prophet Elijah as it relates that awesome sight of Jesus on the high mountain. Today's Old Testament passage seems to be the obvious choice to accompany it. It is the hope of this book that more and more preachers will preach on this 2 Kings passage on Transfiguration Sunday.

Moses and Elijah are prophets number one and number two in the history of the people of Israel.[58] The Book of 2 Kings relates the stories of the prophets Elijah and Elisha, along with the history of the northern and southern kingdoms after the kingdom of Israel was divided. The Books of 1 and 2 Kings as a whole, together with the Books of 1 and 2 Samuel, relate the entire history of the nation of Israel, from its beginning during the period of the prophecy of Samuel to the fall of the southern part of the kingdom to the Babylonians. All of that history is described in terms of the covenant of God with the people. Stories are told and judgments and perspectives are given, according to that template of covenant. Throughout all four of the books, prophets abound!

As for this story, it is a pretty strange one. Stories about prophets are always rather strange; we do not need to try and smooth over their disconcerting qualities. If we think a story is straightforward and easy to understand, we have probably missed the point. Because we believe that God acts in history, and that God has acted and does act in the lives and times of particular people, because we believe that God came directly and incarnationally into the world in the person of Jesus, a human being, a Jewish man in a particular nation, in a particular time, it should never surprise us that the details of stories that come from times and places far away might be a bit perplexing. How will refer-

---

58   Ask a Jewish friend or colleague about the ritual tradition about the Prophet Elijah that is enacted in the Passover seder. Or just google it.

ences to "Mother Teresa" or "Bono" resonate 2,000 years from now? But, more important, the overwhelming love and justice of God is always disconcerting if we allow ourselves to be even a little open to it.

The faithfulness of Elisha, in the face of Elijah's direct orders; the numerous companies of prophets centred in certain holy places or shrines; the nature of prophetic miracle acts; the desire of Elisha to have the strength and purpose of Elijah; Elijah's ascent to God – all these could be part of a sermon on this passage. But no matter how much exegesis one does, it still remains a mysterious passage, and so it should. We dare not put God into a box; prophets can rarely be contained by our tidy and rational thinking either. The presence of prophets in life, the fact that they both speak and act, the challenge they present, and our own call to faithfulness are all parts of this passage. Any New Testament story of the Transfiguration must connect Jesus with the prophets of his people: the messengers and spokespersons of the Creator God.

Signed, sealed, delivered

At the beginning of Lent we start the journey with Jesus into darkness nigh unto death, a death that is ultimately and forever overcome by the resurrection, but that is real death nonetheless. The lectionary thus starts the Lenten season by reminding us of the eternal covenant of life that God has with us. "Covenant" is used seven times in this passage: there is no missing that this text is about covenant, even if the lector should mumble. The passage comes from the closing parts of the Noah story, after the ark has settled on dry land. The people and the animals have emerged from the somewhat travel-stained vessel, and Noah has ritually praised God. The verses right before this passage (9:1-7) are the very important Noachide covenant. This covenant is thought by the Jewish people, specifically in rabbinic theology, to apply to all the peoples of the earth. It includes not partaking of the blood from an animal's body. This origin of Jewish kosher food laws reflects the belief that blood is life, and since life is sacred to God, it is not to be consumed.

Covenant is about relationship: the relationship between God and the people. And, as verse 10 shows, it is also between God and animals. God's love and care are everlasting: never again will a flood be the consequence of people's failure to uphold the covenant. The rainbow – the sign of the covenant God is making with all living creatures for all generations –has become an indispensable part of every telling and every children's toy about Noah's ark. The rainbow already exists in nature, but it now has a new meaning: it is a symbol of relationship like no other natural phenomenon.[59] The text is also, however, clear in its use of the Hebrew word that signifies a bow as a weapon. Bows (and arrows) figure frequently in both biblical texts and other texts of the Ancient Near East. In this story, a sign of the power and might of war and fighting is transformed into a sign of reconciliation.

---

59   *The Jewish Publication Society Torah Commentary: Genesis* (New York: The Jewish Publication Society, 1989), 63.

Note that it is God, not the people, who seems to need the reminder about the everlasting covenant between divinity and all living creatures. This is a difficult detail in a story that is full of difficult details. (Once, when I was telling the Noah story as a children's story, my then four-year-old son piped up, "This is not a nice story!") The point is that the repercussions of sin are real. They affect all relationships of the created order. And yet, God's covenant of relationship is everlasting. In the slightly broader context of this passage it is clear that the divine covenant is with *all* peoples. This is certainly a biblical text of inclusivity.

Covenant, Act II

The curtain rises on another reiteration of the covenant, a reminder of life in our Lenten journey of darkness, this time with some details about naming. It is very important in the reading and preaching of this text to make it clear that "Abram" becomes "Abraham" and "Sarai" becomes "Sarah." A name change has always signified, and still does signify, greatly for human beings. It is only within recent memory that the members of the British royal family did not change their names upon assuming the throne; in the Roman Catholic tradition, popes still do assume a new name. A name change marks a new beginning, and the new name means something, either literally, or because of associations with someone who has gone before. Biblical names always mean something: here, "Abram" (exalted father) becomes "Abraham" (father of a multitude). Nations – plural – will come from Abram and Sarai. This is a great text, therefore, for interfaith discussions. Currently, there is much discussion, in literature and in seminars and presentations, of the nature of Abraham as the father/ancestor of Judaism, Christianity and Islam.[60]

A particular family in a particular time and place is to be the bearer of the covenant for the sake of all the nations. Up until the Abraham saga begins in the Book of Genesis, the stories deal with humanity in general. With Abraham, God is in covenant with a particular person, revealing that God's love and relationship with all peoples are real and individual. It is a covenant that will endure for generations. What a gift of grace that God declares such love for generations yet unborn! Future generations, with their behaviour and faithfulness as yet unknown, are assured of relationship with the Divine.

In the renaming of Abraham and Sarah, it is stated that they will be the ancestors of kings. In our democratic, 21st-century context,

---

60   The author Bruce Feiler provides but one example of this kind of discussion. See Bruce Feiler, *Abraham: A Journey to the Heart of Three Faiths* (San Francisco: Harper Perennial, 2004).

the notion of monarchy is not always positive. In Abraham's time and place, however, regardless of how kings behaved, monarchy meant stability and identity as a people. It meant existence and a structure for being in relationship with the neighbouring peoples. It could even mean the difference between death and life as a people.

The ten words

We think of this passage as the ten commandments, and yet nowhere in it is the term "ten commandments" used. According to the JPS commentary on Exodus, this term is but one way of rendering into English the Hebrew phrase that appears in Exodus 34:28 and Deuteronomy 4:13.[61] The Hebrew is better expressed by the phrase "the ten words." One of the anti-Judaic tendencies in the church, a tendency that misrepresents the faith of Jesus and the faith of our Jewish sisters and brothers past and present, is the tendency to talk, preach and pray as if there is a major gulf between "law" and "gospel." The word "commandment" is often associated with the concept of "law." However, both the Old and the New Testaments contain passages about judgment and passages about grace. Furthermore, as is stated elsewhere in this book, for the people of Israel and for Jews today, "law" generally and the "ten words" specifically are considered great gifts of grace from God. So whatever we say about this passage, which certainly lends itself to a whole series of sermons, we must set it in that context.[62]

It is worthwhile exploring verse 5 of today's text. The standard English translations use the term "jealous" to refer to God here. That is not an incorrect translation, but neither is it totally correct. The original meaning of the Hebrew word is "to become intensely red." It came to be used to describe ardour, zeal, rage and jealousy. (Because there are many fewer Hebrew words than English words, translation is truly an art as well as a science.) The Hebrew word is also used in the Bible only for God – never for a human being. It carries the understanding of the marriage bond as an implied metaphor for the

---

61   *The Jewish Publication Society Torah Commentary: Exodus*, 107.

62   Christians always retain this passage, even though they tend to dismiss other Old Testament laws or commandments, such as those in Leviticus, as having been superseded by Jesus. This raises the very crucial interpretation question of how we choose which parts of Scripture have which kind of standing for us.

covenant between God and the people.[63] It is equally possible, therefore, to translate the word by "impassioned." In preaching from this passage, underline that what is meant is not the kind of petty jealousy we might see in a human being. Rather, it shows that God cannot be indifferent to the people and is indeed deeply involved in how we live and move and have our being.

Staying with this verse, we must understand what is being said in the language of visiting the guilt of the parents on children and subsequent generations. In Israelite theology, being bound in covenant with God meant that the society was collectively responsible for its actions, and that individuals, too, were accountable for doing or not doing things that affected the life of the community. It was recognized that the behaviour of a community could have impact on succeeding generations. (Current discussion around our environmental crisis makes this point easy to relate to.) The text believes in and proclaims the relationship between responsibility and consequences. Throughout the Bible, the balance between collective and individual responsibility and consequences shifts back and forth, but both are always present.

---

63   *The Jewish Publication Society Torah Commentary: Exodus*, 110.

You've got to be kidding!

This is the kind of Old Testament passage that causes preachers to become reluctant to preach from the Old Testament. Take a deep breath and let us plunge in ...

The people of Israel are reaching the end of their wanderings in the wilderness. This story is but one of the colourful adventures in the last part of their journey back to the land. They are skirting the land of Edom because they are in conflict with the people of Edom, a conflict reflected in the stories of Jacob and Esau in Genesis. (Esau is the ancestor of Edom and Jacob is the ancestor of Israel.) As has happened many times before in this wandering story, the people get impatient, tired and cranky. The journey has been very long – a whole generation, according to the text – and there have been many serious hardships along the way. Food and water are scarce, and the people are getting sick of eating manna day after day after day. Of course, we can understand their complaining. On the other hand, we can imagine that God might be getting a little irritated with the frequent whining. But are the poisonous serpents really necessary?

The language is difficult here. The Hebrew adjective "poisonous" can also easily mean "burn," with the idea that the bite of the serpents inflamed the skin, to the point of death. Even more challenging is that the Hebrew word is the very same as the one for the winged celestial beings: the Seraphim. Walter Brueggemann, in his writings, reminds us not to try and put God in a box, not to try and make either God or the biblical text conform too tightly to our particular and dearly held interpretation. The people realize that somehow, the serpents are a consequence of their lack of faith and trust in the covenant relationship. They cry to Moses, Moses prays and God provides the remedy.

This story has been used by Christians for centuries to speak about Jesus. The bronze serpent set up on the pole is Jesus set up on the cross. To "see" Jesus is to be granted life. The story also has meaning, however, in its original context, although that meaning may be difficult to discern. For many of the ancient cultures in the time and place of the people of Israel, the serpent was a symbol of fertility. The people of Israel were constantly trying, with mixed results, to resist being drawn into the worship practices of those around them. The serpent image was a particularly slippery one because the biblical text tells us (2 Kings 18:3-4) that the image of a bronze serpent on a pole (recalling this very incident) was in the Temple in Jerusalem at the time of King Hezekiah in the eighth century BCE. Unlike Moses, however, King Hezekiah, whom the Old Testament portrays as a very good and faithful king, sees the serpent image as being completely out of line with the worship of the God of Israel. Under his watch, in an action for which he is commended in the Bible, out of the Temple it goes. So what gives?

This story may be told as a way of justifying that presence of the bronze serpent on a pole in the Temple. In the Kings text, Hezekiah is clearly right get rid of it, but an explanation was needed for why it got there in the first place. Also bound up in the story (and this is not a comment one way or the other on the historicity of the event, but rather on its place in the text) may be a reclaiming of the serpent symbol. Many cultures – the Greeks being the best known for it – took on the serpent as a symbol for healing. It still appears on the caduceus that is so familiar to us as a symbol of the healing profession.

In preaching, tell the story as the journey of a people that is trying to work out their relationship with their God. As for God sending the serpents, well, in that time and place, everything was attributed to God as a way of proclaiming that God is indeed the Lord of Creation and *the* God. The God of Israel is not for a moment to be confused with those other gods that other peoples worshipped. Those other gods were thought to have power over only certain parts of Creation. It may not seem to be an entirely satisfactory explanation, but when were we ever promised that the Bible would be entirely satisfactory according to our definition of that term?

A New Covenant – sort of

God does not break covenant! The people have broken the covenant: that is clear. God, who loves the people as a husband loves a wife, is making a new covenant. That is not the same thing as a divine breaking of covenant. This may seem like a fine point, but the whole context of Scripture bears it out.[64] And it is definitely not a semantic or theological fine point in preaching, because it has so often been said that this passage speaks to what God's covenant with Christians looks like. This covenant could, it is said, do away with most of what are considered "laws" (see the comments in Lent 3, Year B, on Exodus 20) because everything is internal and individual in our new relationship in Christ. As Christians, we can most certainly say that we have a new relationship, a new covenant, with God in Christ. We do. This remaking of covenant – written on the hearts of the people of Israel, as we hear in this Jeremiah text – this individual, interior knowing of the presence and reality of God, is real. It is a new form of covenant, too, though not in any way abrogating the gift of grace that such "laws" as the ten commandments are. In our preaching, however, we cannot dismiss the "Old Covenant" as having been completely replaced by the "New Covenant." These kinds of statements, which say that God is unfaithful and breaks covenant, can lead to anti-Semitism.

Jeremiah writes at a time when things are becoming very hard, catastrophic even, for the people of Israel. The destruction of the nation and the exile to Babylon are imminent. At this point in his book, he speaks and acts words that acknowledge the people's past sins and the grim aspect of the current situation. He also proclaims, however, that God's ultimate reality and will for the people is love. In the

---

64 The Apostle Paul, for instance, in Romans 9–11, clearly states that God's relationship with the people of Israel, whether they become those who accept Jesus as the Messiah or not, is never broken by God. For further reading, see "Bearing Faithful Witness" on The United Church of Canada website (http://www.united-church.ca/partners/interfaith/bfw; accessed June 11, 2008).

next chapter, chapter 32, in the face of dire times and destruction and seeming hopelessness, Jeremiah goes out to buy a field. He buys land as a sign of hope and future, knowing God's promise (32:15) of hope and future.

As you move into the week ahead, think about what unlikely, unexpected proclamations of hope you can make.

Palm/Passion Sunday – Isaiah 50:4-9a

See the entry for Palm/Passion Sunday, Year A.

Holy Thursday – *Exodus 12:1-4, (5-10), 11-14*

See the entry for Holy Thursday, Year A.

Good Friday – Isaiah 52:13–53:12

See the entry for Good Friday, Year A.

Which comes first?

A quick read through this passage should make it very clear why it was chosen for Easter Sunday. It contains the imagery of a feast, a time of celebration with all the best rich food and wine. For the people of Isaiah's time, such a text would have provided a sharp contrast to their frequently subsistence-level farming and the resultant poor diet. We also find the imagery of the shroud that is cast over the people who are being destroyed, and the statement that death is no more. God has saved the people on that day, wiping away their tears. The people are to rejoice and be glad in their salvation. In this time, many centuries before the Resurrection, this passage resonates with ways in which Christians experience the wondrous reality of the change in life and world wrought by the Resurrection. The imagery of the passage may in fact have helped Christians to express their post-Resurrection experience of life and the world that way.

In its original context, however, this passage also had deep meaning for the people of Israel. The Book of the Prophet Isaiah (or perhaps the editorial school of the prophet Isaiah, as some scholars, including the late Gerald T. Shepherd, would maintain) contains texts from before, during and after the Babylonian exile. Those texts speak the word of God to their particular contexts. Many texts in Isaiah come from the time before the Babylonian exile, and many are texts of judgment that call the people to right and faithful behaviour. The difficult time of the exile is seen as a consequence of not answering that call. Texts from the actual time of the exile, on the other hand, are mostly (but not completely) texts of comfort. And texts from the post-Exilic period reflect the joys and challenges of the time of rebuilding and resettling.

Today's text comes from the early part of the book, but in spite of the generalization above, it is most definitely not a judgment text. In the midst of judgment texts and calls to faithful worship, this text serves as a reminder of what the ultimate reality of God looks like.

It is the wondrous, generous, very real reign of God that is being described. Mountains are always important as possible places of encounter between humanity and the divine. This is true of both the Old and New Testaments. And God will actually swallow up death (see 1 Corinthians 15:54).

Walter Brueggemann reminds us that biblical faith "is an act of yielding in the present … to the assurances given for God's future."[65] In 2007, I attended the Religious Leaders' Summit that convened in Germany to challenge, for the sake of God's people, the G8 Summit being held there. The Religious Leaders issued a powerful statement, "Just Participation," for the sake of Africa and all peoples of the globe. We met in the context of the famous German tradition of the Kirchentag. At the opening service of the Kirchentag, a service attended by 10,000 people in one location alone, the preacher proclaimed the Gospel in a simple and short way: "Do not fear. He is risen. You are witnesses." May we so proclaim the Gospel this Easter Day and every day.

65   Walter Brueggemann, *Isaiah 1–39*, 200.

Bones, bones and more bones

The lectionary suggests this passage as an alternate to the Acts 2 passage of the tongues of fire, rush of wind, coming of the Holy Spirit. Why not do both?

The prophet Ezekiel went with the people into exile in Babylon after the fall of the southern part of the country, Judah and Jerusalem, to the Babylonians in 586 BCE. Just note along the edges of a sermon through this passage that because the book contains many dates, it is easy to date its prophecies with some precision. Also, because of the distance of the people from the Temple and temple worship, many of Ezekiel's prophecies and images focus on the Temple, trying to keep it real in the minds and hearts of the people. Ezekiel's main point, however, and he states it very clearly, is that God is the sovereign and must be acknowledged as such by all people. God's initiative and control over all Creation are held up by Ezekiel over and over again. This is a God on the move. It would have been very comforting for this people that had focused its worship on God as resident in the Temple in Jerusalem, but who were no longer in Jerusalem and whose Temple had been destroyed, to know that God was God anywhere and everywhere.

Try to have some fun with this passage. God has a great sense of humour, as we see throughout the Bible. There are a number of possible thematic ways to go with this text: the power of the Holy Spirit, our connectedness with one another, God's ability to do anything and everything, God as a God of life. All of them are all good and important biblical themes. A fun way to go, however, is to designate different people in the congregation to be the different parts of the body. With a few chairs set up in the chancel of the church, and the congregation singing "Dem Bones" (by James Weldon Johnson and J. Rosamund Johnson), each of those people takes on the role of one of the kinds of bones the song illustrates, then connect to the others with their hands. Preaching the Word can feature a visual component!

Seraphs abound!

Preachers should perhaps not have favourites among biblical passages, but I suspect we all do. This Isaiah passage is one of mine.

The Book of the Prophet Isaiah details the call of the prophet to his vocation and ministry. It does so in a way that is formulaic; it resembles in structure and tone other prophetic calls. This call passage, which appears early on in the book, legitimates both the prophet and the book itself. It also makes clear that Isaiah did not condemn the existence of the Temple or its worship, systems and structures. He might even have been a priest serving there.

Amid an overwhelming sense of the presence and holiness of God, Isaiah praises the Lord, confesses unworthiness, receives forgiveness and then is commissioned to a prophetic vocation. All of this happens in a physical context that speaks of both the Temple and a heavenly throne room. I have the privilege of worshipping frequently in the traditions of our Orthodox sisters and brothers. This setting in Isaiah 6, which speaks of Temple and heavenly throne room, thus seems very familiar to me.

Note, too, what this passage describes about the very nature and being of God. The God who is completely to be praised, who is high and lofty, is the same God in whose presence and reality human beings experience the depths of their unworthiness, their unclean lips. Still and forever, the very same God, with a methodology that could be painful, makes it clear that guilt is blotted out, that sin is departed. Cleansed, a human being can then experience and answer the call to God's ministry, a call to engage with the world and the people.

To the question "Whom shall I send?" we can respond, "Send me."

God's call: Persistence personified

See the entry for Epiphany 2, Year B.

Keeping up with the "Joneses"

"Well, everyone else has one! How come we can't?" Parents are pretty used to that kind of whining. This passage from First Samuel contains a lot of whining, too. Instead of omitting verses as the lectionary does, read verses 4 to 20, and think about adding the passage from chapter 11 as well. The people of Israel are whining to the Prophet Samuel, and he is passing on their message to God. They want a king because all the other nations around them have a king. The leadership of Samuel as a judge was going really well in the chapter before this one, but here, in chapter 8, everything changes – and quickly. The elders who approach Samuel note right off the bat that Samuel's sons have not been following Samuel's model. (Remember Eli's sons, whose behaviour led to Samuel becoming the judge and leader in Israel.) Samuel does not defend his sons, but he is not pleased with the people's request. He understands that this request indicates a crisis, a rejection of the "foundational social community" and a rejection of theocratic authority. This is indeed a crisis in Israel's life and faith.[66]

Samuel informs God immediately, through prayer. God, in deep and no doubt sad wisdom, understands that the request is more a rejection of divine authority than of Samuel. Whether the cause is the poor leadership of Samuel's sons, or the belief that a king and centralized human authority will offer more protection against the surrounding nations, or both, God tells Samuel to agree to the people's request – the request that is a rejection of God in order to be like the other peoples. Once again, the people have turned from the God who gave them life and sustained them. Once again, the people are unwilling to have God "as the source and rule of life."[67]

But they will, at least, be warned about what they are in for. Beginning with verse 10, Samuel, at God's command, tells them "the

---

66 Walter Brueggemann, *First and Second Samuel* (Louisville, KY: John Knox Press, 1990), 61.

67 Brueggemann, *First and Second Samuel*, 62.

ways of the king who shall reign over them" (verse 9). It is not a pretty sight. Samuel paints a picture of centralized authority that requires forced service in all areas of life. It assumes and takes the best of everything for the king; in effect, the people are slaves. That word "slaves" is a dire one, indeed. It means a return to all that the people had escaped in the Exodus. The request for a king is, in fact, a rejection of the liberation and grace that were writ large for the people in the Exodus. The stakes here are enormous, but God is not a God of coercion, and so the people get their king. The entire biblical text remains ambivalent about the notion of kingship, and never tries to obliterate that ambivalence. King David (though not always his deeds) is held up as a model and son of God. Jesus is referred to as a king. But passages like this one in 1 Samuel 8, which proclaim that God should be and wants to be the only King, are very real, too. Tension in our human reality and tension in our relationship with our God are things we know all too well.

Proper 6 – 1 Samuel 15:34-16:13

See the entry for Lent 4, Year A.

Note the addition of 1 Samuel 15:34-35 to this reading of the passage. Both Samuel and God grieve, even though Samuel had done exactly what God told him to do.

Proper 7 – 1 Samuel 17 (1a, 4-11, 19-23), 32-49

Five smooth stones

David and Goliath. Such a familiar story – though probably more familiar chopped up in bits, as the lectionary does, than with all the detail of chapter 17 of 1 Samuel. This is another one of those Old Testament texts where it is best to just tell the story. Note a few things along the way, but let the power of the narrative stand. God is the God of history; the stories of that history are meant to detail for us the living relationship between God and the people. God works with and through particularity and cares about the details of human life.[68] The story of chapter 17 was deliberately crafted as a whole for a reason. When read all the way through, the suspense builds towards the resolution that the reader was meant to hear and experience.

The Philistines were Greeks. They migrated from Greece and ended up settling along the coast of the land of Israel. They were a sea-faring people, highly militarized and technologically advanced. There was much conflict between them and the people of Israel, conflict that was complicated by the fact that the Philistines had iron for better weapon technology at a time when the people of Israel had only the much softer bronze. The Philistines also had the technology for chariots, which could be used effectively on the plains of the coast, but less effectively in the hill country further in, where the people of Israel tended to be.

It is from "Philistine" that the name "Palestine" comes. For many of us, our ancient origins have roots in the Greek world, which places us in some kind of relationship to the Philistines. The biblical text, taken as a whole, resists stereotyping and pigeon-holing. It carries ambiguity and diversity, as we saw in the reading in Proper 5.

---

68   For background and broadstroke reading on this topic, see Cahill, *The Gifts of the Jews*.

How the mighty have fallen!

David says this phrase three times in the course of this reading, and he means it each time. David has been informed, before this text begins, of the deaths of Saul and Jonathan – Saul's son and David's beloved friend. David grieves their deaths in poetic lament. King David is known for many things in the life of the people of Israel, in the faith of Judaism and in the faith of Christianity. One of those things is his poetry.

The Bible contains numerous examples of David's poetry, especially the many Psalms attributed to him. Whether everything which is attributed to David was actually written by him word for word is immaterial. The point is that he was renowned as a great poet in Israel, that poetic texts were considered to be important expressions of faith and relationship with God, and that we are to so regard and pray them now.[69]

"How the mighty have fallen!" says David. David praises Saul and Jonathan in this lament poetry, truly and publicly lamenting their deaths. He grieves for what is lost: for the death of a king and prince of Israel. He also speaks plainly about the cost and pain of war. As you preach consider setting the context and the story, but letting the words of the poetry stand without analyzing them too much. Then point to our contemporary society's need for public lament and grief. Name examples of events that were openly grieved. Which situations would perhaps be better acknowledged, better healed from and better overcome if they were truly and well grieved and lamented by us all?

---

69   In verse 18 of this passage, it is said that David ordered that "The Song of the Bow" be taught to the people. This order had some connection with the lament and public grieving in which he is about to engage. The verse goes on to tell us that the song is written in the Book of Jashar. It is fascinating that the biblical text refers to other texts. This is a particularly common thing in the books of 1 and 2 Kings. Most of those texts referred to are no longer extant, as is the case with the Book of Jashar.

The Lord is my shepherd

The south of the land of Israel has already accepted David as king. In this passage, we hear about the tribes of the north coming to him at Hebron in the south and making a covenant with him before the Lord. Only then does he become king of the whole people and the whole land. He is a shepherd kind of king. As Walter Brueggemann reminds us, "The term 'shepherd' is a conventional metaphor in the ancient world for king, indicating the responsibility of the king to guard, nurture and protect the flock; that is, the community over which he presides."[70] David, we were told in the Goliath story, was a shepherd boy who was able to keep his flock safe from harm by the power and might of God. Now he is a shepherd king. It is no accident that the prophet Nathan, when confronting David for his sins with Bathsheba later in this extended narrative, uses a lamb/sheep analogy. Christians believe that in Jesus, the shepherd metaphor reaches wondrous heights – the shepherd goes so far in guarding, nurturing and protecting the flock that he lays down his life for it.

Although David at other times and places acts rather autocratically, we are told here that his kingship of the north is established by means of a negotiated covenant. That covenant is made before the Lord. Everything, including political ways of governance – even the institution of kingship, which is regarded so ambiguously in the biblical text – is grounded in the reality of God. The anointing, which is liturgical, indicates approval by God.

The lectionary omits verses 6 to 8, which Brueggemann calls "among the most difficult in the books of Samuel."[71]

Perhaps the city of the Jebusites, which was to become the city of David, seemed so impregnable that people believed even the blind and lame could hold it against an attacker. Perhaps David is said to

---

70 Brueggemann, *First and Second Samuel*, 237.
71 Brueggemann, *First and Second Samuel*, 239.

hate the blind and the lame because they are holding the city against him. Perhaps, then, the blind and lame are said to not be allowed to come into the house, a phrase later interpreted in more exclusionary ways, because they held out against David. We cannot know for sure. But these verses were included in the text for a reason. Struggle with what that might be. And remember the overall thrust of the biblical text that moves from human realities of exclusion to God's vision of complete inclusion for all.

With the sound of the trumpet

The Samuel narratives continue. This is one of the longest series of narratives in the lectionary, even though the lectionary leaves out more stories from First and Second Samuel than it includes.

King David is continuing to consolidate his reign. The next thing on the agenda is to bring the ark into Jerusalem, the city of David. The ark has been in "storage," so to speak, since its return from the Philistines. Now, after 20 years, it is time to bring it to the new capital. The symbol of the former way of being in relationship with God, the ark, is now intended to legitimate the new way of being and the future. David dances before the ark in a liturgical way, with reminiscences of pagan rituals, perhaps, but with great pageantry and gratitude to God and also with great political calculation. His wife Michal, however, the daughter of his predecessor, whom David displaced, depises him in her heart when she sees David leaping and dancing before the Lord. The text does not tell us why she feels this way; it more likely had to do with political reasons than with whatever David was wearing or not wearing. The dancing is a good reminder that our God is a God of all the senses. God is Word, most surely. We see this in the beginning of Genesis and the beginning of the Gospel according to John, as well as in many other parts of the Bible, but God is God of the whole person, and we are to express that truth in all of physical reality. The body is a temple, after all.

Let's turn now, as we did in Proper 9, to the part of the text that is omitted by the lectionary. It is clear why it was left out. As the ark is transported into Jerusalem, it teeters on the ox cart. Sensibly, someone reaches out a hand to steady this sacred vehicle of the Lord so that it will not fall. What happens next seems not only illogical but also disturbing: the person who steadies the ark, Uzzah, is struck dead by God for touching its holiness. David's reaction is both anger at God and fear of God; he is reluctant to continue taking the ark to his city. So back it goes into storage for another three months, until it is clear that the Lord has blessed the person guarding it and it is safe to continue the journey. The trumpets abound again.

The message in the disturbing story of the touching of the ark is that God is not to be contained or presumed upon. The ark is indeed the symbol of God and a place where God has been said to dwell, but it is not something that David or the people can "own." It may be a symbol of both an older way and a newer way of being in relationship with God, but to touch it is to presume too much: it implies that God's holiness can be accessed at will. This is a vital reminder to all powers of governance that the divine will be done, not our will be done, and is an important message in preaching.

Offspring after you

See the entry for Advent 4, Year B.

The difference between these two renderings of the passage is that this one includes reference to David's son, Solomon. Solomon's kingdom and throne God will establish forever, and Solomon will be the one to build the Temple of the Lord. If you stop reading at 14a, as the lectionary would have you do, it all sounds rosy and promising. But the biblical text always deals in reality and consequence, deeply surrounded in everlasting love. Reading verses 14b to at least 17 shows that reality and consequence.

In the spring of the year

"In the letter [David] wrote, 'Set Uriah in the forefront of the hardest fighting, and then draw back from him, so that he may be struck down and die.'" So ends the reading of the Old Testament lesson for Proper 12. If your liturgical tradition is one that ends such lessons with "The Word of the Lord," there are going to be a few raised eyebrows, to put it mildly, in the congregation.

This is part of the story of David and Bathsheba, one of those biblical stories that congregation and preacher often think they know, but some of the details of which prove to be less than familiar. The story continues, without its biblical conclusion, next week in Proper 13. When preaching, therefore – especially when preaching in the summer, which is when this passage appears – it is essential to give the congregation some sense of how the story began, in case they were away in previous weeks, and how the story is going forward, in case they are away in following weeks. That will help with the questioning of how exactly this text is the Word of the Lord, but more also needs to be said.

Note that this passage is even more disturbing than you might think. It begins with this simple but no doubt accurate statement: "In the spring of the year, the time when kings go out to battle ...." Every year, springtime apparently equals war time. Any student of history knows this to be so, but we sometimes overlook this point. It is in the context of that time when kings regularly go out to war that David sees Bathsheba, wants her and gets her. Did she have any choice in the matter? Probably not. Is she the whore or loose woman that church tradition has often made her out to be? Highly unlikely. The king summons, and one obeys whether one wants to or not. Once Bathsheba is pregnant, David must cover up his actions. There is no chance that she is pregnant by her husband, Uriah, since he was away at those springtime wars. David attempts the cover-up by using not only Uriah, in this case to the death, but also by using his own people.

Uriah, faithful and loyal to David and to his soldiers as he is, cannot be persuaded, even under the influence, to go home to comfort when war is afoot and others are uncomfortable. The ark of the Lord is even out and about in the field. Therefore, plan B is to ensure, through the springtime war, the death of an innocent man. Joab, who is David's to command, ensures that it is so.

This passage must be explained not only as part of this particular story, but as part of the wide, deep and broad story of the relationship of God with the people: a relationship that is honest about the failings of the people, a relationship that reveals in its holy scriptures, in colour, all the sins of the people, including some truly dreadful ones. The good news – and there is good news – is that there are always consequences, immediate or long term. In the overall context of Scripture, God keeps on calling for life, not only in the spring of the year but each and every day. Sometimes the people get the point. Sometimes *we* get the point, too.

Speak truth to power

Caught red-handed! This passage begins by telling us several key parts of the story. The wife of Uriah (note that she is most commonly referred to in that way, emphasizing the line David crossed, rather than by her name, Bathsheba) hears that her husband is dead and mourns for him. Did she know that David arranged for his death? The text does not tell us. It is also useless to speculate about whether she truly loved Uriah or whether theirs was an arranged marriage, as were the vast majority of marriages in the history of the world until the last century or so. The point is that she did what was right and appropriate in the circumstances. Then David took her to wife and she bore his child.

David may have thought that he had gotten away with the crime. After all, who among his people would dare to comment or criticize? God, however, saw what David had done and was displeased. God sent the prophet, Nathan, bearing the word of divine power, to speak to secular power run amok. The parable Nathan tells shocks David, but he cannot, at first, see that like all parables, Nathan's has one point, and that one point is directed at the hearers. In verse 7, Nathan the prophet moves from telling a parable to direct prophetic speech. Even kings must listen to prophets who carry in their speech and in their beings the phrase "Thus says the Lord!" David is reminded in no uncertain terms that everything he is and has is from God. He has responded to such grace with an act that violates the covenant. He has coveted, committed adultery and killed. The sin, as it is made clear in verse 10, is a sin against Uriah, to be sure, but is also clearly against God. And there will be consequences.

Verses 11 and 12 refer to a further part of the story, in which one of David's sons rebels against him. As was customary of such a rebellion in that time and place, the son takes David's wives publicly. The point of this episode is what David is able to say and confess in verse 13: "I have sinned against the Lord." He didn't have to confess. As king, he could have ignored the prophet Nathan or done away with him. But there were enough traces of the divine relationship still present in him that when he was caught red-handed, he could see that his behaviour was reprehensible.

The chapter goes on to detail the specific consequences. Although the lectionary does not include these, several points need to be made homiletically from this reading. Sin, covenant breaking, does not escape God's notice. Also, because we are all in relationship with God and with each other, and because God is the Lord of Creation and of Life, sins that we commit against others, or against Creation, are also committed against God. Further, there are consequences for behaviour that is contrary to the best interests of our neighbours and the will of God. And further still, in spite of ourselves, because of ourselves, God continually works to set us back on the right path and continually maintains relationship with us.

The king was deeply moved

The rebellion of one of David's sons that was referred to in verses 11 and 12 of the previous lectionary reading has indeed come. Absalom rebelled against his father, David, and the result was war. According to the politics of that time and place, in light of the long-term need for peace in the country, and in light of David's military skills, war is unavoidable. But David is more than a politician and military commander. He is a father. In a very touching line in the first verse of this passage, though David does not refer to Absalom as his son, he says to his commanders, "Deal gently for my sake with the young man Absalom." In a battle between the "men of Israel," who were apparently supporting Absalom (a divided country to be sure – this really sounds like civil war!), and the "servants of David," the "men of Israel" were defeated, "… and the forest claimed more victims that day than the sword." An odd statement, one that sets us up for what is going to happen in the next act, but also says something somewhat puzzling about the nature of forests in that place and time.

Absalom meets with a bizarre fate. Perhaps it is because of his wonderful hair, for which he is famous, but his mule rides on and leaves him hanging in "the thick branches of a great oak." He is "left hanging between heaven and earth." It may simply be describing the physical reality of Absalom's situation, but it is an unusual phrase to use. Perhaps it also referrs to the fact that he hangs between life and death, between the natural outcome of being a defeated rebel and the natural reality of being the king's son. He is caught, the end is in sight, but it is not yet.

In spite of the fact that David had said, "Deal gently," his military commander, Joab (the same Joab who had Uriah killed under David's orders) makes a military, strategic decision. He thrusts three spears into Absalom's heart. That action is omitted in this Sunday's passage. We hear that it was ten young armour-bearers of Joab who finish off

Absalom, but it was Joab's doing, and it went against the words of King David.

In a scene reminiscent of the one in which Uriah's death was announced to David, the messenger brings what he thinks will be good news for the king: the leader of the rebellion has been killed. David does not act on the fact that his orders were disobeyed. What is done is done. He does not shoot the messenger, as he did in 2 Samuel 1:15-16. Instead, he weeps for his son. The biblical text gives us several instances of David's grieving. He grieved for Saul and Jonathan, and for his newborn son. And he often grieved in wondrous poetry. Here, he simply grieves in deep pain. He no longer refers to the young man by name, but to his son.

Real people, real emotions, real complexity in life. David is father, commander and king, and must play all those parts, even when they come into conflict with each other. Relationship with God, in God, does not take away complexity and pain in our lives. We are in relationship with God always, to be sure, but also with others in a difficult and hurting and complex world. That is exactly why these stories speak to us and of the situations we face in our lives.

Door number three

After an update on the death and reign of King David, we are launched into the story of his son Solomon, who is the new king. In this passage, Solomon is the good guy. In fact, he is very much the good guy, though that is not always the case in the biblical record. We are told that he sacrificed and offered incense at the "high places" – places associated with the Canaanite religion, which were often incorporated into the worship of the God of Israel and were viewed with some ambivalence. The text tells us that such worship is fine at this point, because Solomon had not yet built the Temple. Solomon loved the Lord, in the model of his father, David. (Despite his transgression against God through Bathsheba and Uriah the Hittite, which we have heard about in recent weeks, David loved the Lord.) It is, as I said above, in the very complexity of the biblical text and its characters that the Gospel is proclaimed. David is, in a number of ways, appallingly human. God always points out sin and its consequences, but God continues to use David for divine purposes. The biblical record, while detailing the places of dire failure, also describes what God can and will do with flawed human beings.

When Solomon goes to sacrifice and offer incense to God, God appears to him in a dream, telling him to ask for what he wants God to give him. Solomon asks, "Give your servant therefore an understanding mind to govern your people, able to discern between good and evil; for who can govern this your great people?" God is pleased. Solomon did not ask for anything for himself, not long life nor riches nor victory over his enemies, but "understanding to discern what is right." Because Solomon chose door number three, which was the right answer for the sake of the people whom he is now to govern, God will give him "a wise and discerning mind" and the riches and honour for which he did not ask. And if he keeps God's statutes and commandments as David usually did, Solomon will get the long life, too.

The wisdom for which Solomon becomes renowned is a gift from God, given for the sake of the people. Obviously, wisdom is the most important thing to ask for. This is a great biblical text to use, as I once did, when a colleague or friend is about to embark on a new adventure, especially a new adventure in the name of God. It is not personal success that we are to strive for; it is not fame or honour or glory. Those things might happen along the way, but they are not the goal. The goal is wisdom for the sake of God's people. The goal is to be able to discern (we hear echoes from the story of the Garden of Eden) between good and evil. Solomon was given that gift in the context of worship and prayer. And we must not discount our dreams. The biblical text believes firmly and proclaims often that God sometimes speaks to us through that medium, too, as God spoke to Solomon.

Opening day

I have tried to be patient with the fact that the lectionary often breaks up biblical passages, but the breaking up of this wonderful, detailed passage is really too much. Solomon's Prayer of Dedication for the newly finished Temple begins in verse 22. One could start reading there, with a verbal introduction to the whole chapter that summarizes the previous 21 verses and gives some indication of the context in which verses 41 to 43 are set. But much of the vivid detail of the opening verses of the chapter would be lost that way, including the realistic description of verse 8. There we hear that the poles of the Ark of the Covenant, in which resided the two tablets of the law placed in there by Moses, "were so long that the ends of the poles were seen from the holy place in front of the inner sanctuary; but they could not be seen from outside; they are there to this day."

It is problematic to skip the descriptions and details of the Temple and of the sacrificial worship system. The implication is that these details are irrelevant to our Christian faith. That implication has led us down the slippery slope to anti-Judaism and even anti-Semitism. It is faithful to speak about the concrete details of our human reality, and how our Christian faith in an incarnate God who so loved the world points to God's care for such concrete details. Finite human beings use holy vessels, arks and sanctuaries to proclaim their connection with the holy. To give in sacrifice is to proclaim the source for all that we have.

So Solomon dedicates the house of the Lord in the presence of the people of the Lord, and with praise of the Lord. He speaks of God's covenant with the people and of God's steadfast love for them. This covenant requires that they walk before God in justice and faithfulness; it promises ongoing succession to the royal line of David and Solomon. Solomon's words also show some of the biblical tensions between a conditional covenant and an unconditional covenant. Biblical scholars have gone back and forth trying to decide whether

the conditional or the unconditional covenant is the core of the biblical witness; the text carries both in some tension, and lets that be so.

Then we have that great question of whether God can dwell on
earth – in this house of the Lord that Solomon has just made. The answer is both yes and no. God cannot be contained in a box or a house;
God cannot be contained in the highest, broadest, deepest heaven we
can imagine; but God can, will and does connect with us in times and
places of our earthly existence. Verses 41 to 43 show that the prayers
of those outside the community count, too, since God cannot be contained or owned by any particular people either.

Gazelles abound

The Song of Songs is not a book of prophecy, not a book of law or instruction, not a book of history or narrative. In this text we are dealing with a very different kind of biblical literature than most of what has been chosen for the lectionary. The Hebrew title of this book is "Solomon's Song of Songs." Since prepositions are used in wondrously varied and diverse ways in the Hebrew language, this could mean that it is a song by, for or about Solomon. The Bible of our Jewish sisters and brothers, known as the TaNaKh – for the three divisions of the text, Torah, Nevi'im (prophets) and Kethubim (writings) – places this Song of Songs/Song of Solomon book in the writings section.

It is a book of erotic love poetry, though it has been and can be interpreted as a book expressing the detailed and passionate love between God and the people. Medieval mystics often expressed their relationship to God in sexual, erotic terms; there are some beautiful representations of that expression in art. This was a way to express intimacy and desire for deep relationship, a way to express the reality that for the mystic, God could and did completely possess and encompass them. Such an interpretation can be seen to resonate with other biblical passages of expressed intimacy between God and the people, such as in parts of the Book of the Prophet Hosea. That is a legitimate reading of the text, but the text is, nonetheless, erotic love poetry.

Throughout the book, the voices of a man and a woman (or possibly sometimes choruses of multiple singers) speak to each other and about each other. The details of their context and their relationship are given to us in vivid images. At times, the Hebrew words are so graphic that the English translators have chosen euphemisms or listed in a note that the meaning of the Hebrew word is "uncertain." (It may or may not be.) The details of the context and the relationship of the lovers is very closely bound up with details of nature, both flora and fauna. God is love, and God's love encompasses the details of our human existence, all of which are intertwined. The actions of humanity affect the natural world. The biblical text can and does use natural events to point to what is happening on a human and on a cosmic scale. (The darkness covering the earth at the time of the crucifixion is another key example of that connection.) Here in Song of Songs we see this link and convergence, with things being as they should between humans, between God and humans, and in the natural world. In the love of the man and the woman for each other, the winter is past, indeed, and flowers have appeared on the earth.

The art of living

Wisdom literature is a particular kind of biblical literature. While there are features of it in biblical books that we do not commonly consider to be Wisdom literature themselves, such as the Joseph story in the Book of Genesis, entire books do fall into the Wisdom category. Proverbs is one of those books. The Prologue of the Book of Proverbs defines Wisdom literature. "For learning about wisdom and instruction, for understanding words of insight, for gaining instruction in wise dealing, righteousness, justice and equity ..." (Proverbs 1:2-3). Wisdom literature is about our day-to-day lives. It offers practical advice on the art of living eons before the rash of self-help books. As the Introduction to Proverbs in the NRSV says, "Acquiring wisdom and knowing how to avoid the pitfalls of folly lead to health and success." Some Christians find an uncomfortable emphasis on material success in Wisdom literature; it is important to remember that this kind of literature was written in the context of a frequently subsistence-level Eastern society, where water and meat were often scarce for many, except the very wealthy. Material success could be a life-or-death issue.

Although the words and phrases of Wisdom literature such as the Book of Proverbs can sound "secular" to 21st-century Western Christian ears, Wisdom was always seen as based solidly on the "fear of the Lord." "Fear of the Lord" is a common biblical phrase that is closer in meaning to what we might term "awe" than "fear." Although the Book of Proverbs rarely mentions God, in 1:7 it says, "The fear of the Lord is the beginning of knowledge." The beginnings and endings of biblical books are very important for setting theme and tone. Wisdom literature is always completely grounded in the reality and presence of God.

Solomon, with his reputation for wisdom, was an obvious and natural patron for the tradition of Wisdom literature. Whether he actually wrote any of the proverbs in the Book of Proverbs is unknown, but the book was certainly thought to be in line with his tradition.

And so we turn to this Sunday's reading from Proverbs. The Introduction to Proverbs in the NRSV says, "Most proverbs are short, compact statements that express a truth about human behaviour." So it is with the selected verses from chapter 22. A good name is considered better than riches; the Lord is the maker of all; injustice will be its own reward; and we are to share with the poor. God pleads the very cause of the poor. While a social justice theme is apparent in this choice of verses, that theme, like many others, including a good name and table manners, weaves its way through this book and through Wisdom literature as a whole. Surrounding and encompassing this Wisdom literature is the belief that all wisdom, however secular it may sound to our ears, is centred in God. God so loves the world that God cares for it in all its particular and concrete detail. We in turn are to manifest and magnify that love.

Wisdom calling

For some background on Wisdom literature, see the entry for Proper 18, Year B.

The Book of Proverbs, in a number of places, depicts Wisdom as an active, dynamic woman calling the people to her. The passage for Proper 19 is the first such example in the book. (Another is chapter 8.) Wisdom, in the biblical tradition, has been present with God since, during and even before Creation. The Hebrew word for wisdom, *hokmah*, is feminine, as is its translation into the Greek, *sophia*.

There she is on the busiest corner of the city, speaking at the entrance gates, crying out in streets and squares. It is a side note, but not an unimportant one, to mention the detail that this passage gives us about the physical makeup of cities in that time and place. The entire biblical tradition, from Genesis through Revelation, refers to cities frequently. While many biblical stories and traditions are also set in rural, pastoral contexts, this does not mean that idyllic, pastoral scenes are somehow truer to the context of faithful witness.

There is Wisdom, personified as an active, vibrant woman calling out to all and sundry as she moves through the city. She is more than willing to share of her wisdom, but the people remain in their simplicity, scoffing and foolishness. Since they have ignored the call and the gift of wisdom, Wisdom personified will not respond when the inevitable happens and calamity strikes. Line after line details how she will not listen now that the people, who would not listen when times were good, finally turn to her when times are bad. It sounds harsh to us, but the passage is making the point that there are consequences for not living in the light and knowledge of God. This brings us to the question of the relationship between God and Wisdom. Monotheism is a given for Christianity, though the Old Testament text does reflect earlier traditions in many places that allow for the presence in the universe of other gods. They are not *the* God – they are the gods of other peoples, and they are clearly not to be worshipped. It is in the later stages of the biblical tradition that the reality of the One God, who is the God of all peoples, is firmly set out.

Wisdom is a creation of God, present with God from the beginning and delighting in all else that God creates. She calls the people to the kind of knowledge that is contained within the Book of Proverbs, not the kind in the self-help books found in airport bookstores, and always makes it very clear that choices should be grounded in the "fear" of the Lord – that is, awareness of the holy, other, awesome, creative, redemptive, salvific, sustaining reality of God. Wisdom is both a gift of God to the people and something to be sought after. In this passage, the gift is clearly present, waiting and indeed actively seeking to be received. The problem is that it is not being sought. The essential knowledge for the art of living is available but being ignored. There will be consequences, but wisdom will always remain an available gift.

"A capable wife?"

I have to confess to having ambivalent feelings about this Sunday's Old Testament passage. This well known passage in the Book of Proverbs turns up at weddings, funerals and events where women are being elegized. The woman in the passage is a superwoman. She can do everything – she can leap household chores in a single bound, she is faster than a speeding bullet at buying appropriate land, she opens her hand to the poor and reaches out to the needy, and she speaks with the voice of wisdom. She is everything that the personified Wisdom who calls in chapter one of Proverbs would have hoped and wanted all the people to be. This super-capable woman grounds all in "fear" (deep consciousness of the power, might, holiness and all-encompassing awesomeness) of the Lord. She also does all that she does so well for the sake of her husband and children and household. There is so much about her to be admired and emulated. But we need to set such a passage in the context of its time and place.

This portrait of a capable wife reflects an urban setting of wealth and privilege, of city gates and crimson and purple and fine linen. There is money to buy land. This portrait is also set in a time and place where women's whole purpose and being was to be given for the sake of husband and household. Such wealth, privilege and resources were not, however, the lot of most of the women of that time and place, just as they are not the lot of most women of our time and place. Also, the time, at least in most Western societies, in which women were seen primarily as domestic support for men is long gone. In preaching through this passage, keep those kinds of things in mind, rather than simply painting a glowing picture of a superwoman of another time and place that most people today cannot hope to emulate, even if they wished to.

Yet in the context of the themes of the Book of Proverbs, in the context of Wisdom literature, this capable wife is a model for us all. She is resourceful and practical; she takes the initiative; she sees what is needed and follows through on it. She has strength and dignity and good humour and kindness. Her actions of justice towards the poor are completely integrated into the details of her everyday life. She does all in her knowledge of and desire for the God who is the Lord of Life and Creation, and who cares about the concrete ways we live our lives. In Christian tradition and theology, we say that God has so loved the world, so loved it in all its complex and sometimes messy reality, that God entered into it to live the life that we know. Thanks be to God!

Pretty is as pretty does

A wonderful opportunity to really delve into this story in a very real way is to enter into dialogue and conversation with a neighbouring synagogue and join with Jewish sisters and brothers in the celebration of Purim, a celebration of costumes, certain traditional foods, and general riotous festivity. That is what the Book of Esther is about: recording the institution of the annual Jewish feast of Purim.

For the purposes of preaching in Sunday liturgy, focus on telling the story. Much of the story is not given to us in the lectionary passage, obviously for issues of length. But since this is one of the few times that the Book of Esther surfaces in the Christian tradition, tell the story so that the people in your pews will know the stories of our faith tradition.

In telling the story, pick up some of the vivid detail of the descriptions, and outline the historical and political setting.[72] Vashti was the Persian king's first queen. She has often been somewhat scorned in both the Christian and the Jewish traditions, but a close reading of chapter one gives a broader picture. The king gets angry at Vashti because she refuses to come at his command to be shown off to the gathered male notables as an object of beauty. The men feared that other women of the Persian kingdom would be inspired by her example of courage and resistance and would also not respond to menial and demeaning commands by their husbands!

Esther, a Jew, succeeds Vashti as the next queen. When the king's official, Haman, devises a plot to destroy all the Jews in the provinces of the kingdom, and the king agrees, Esther must act. With the encouragement and inspiration of her Uncle Mordecai, she takes a risk. She concocts a clever plan to foil the plot. Mordecai said to her earlier, in chapter 4, verse 14, "Perhaps you have come to royal dignity

---

72   Persia was an empire in the Ancient Near East where a number of Jews lived. It fell to Greece in 331 BCE.

for just such a time as this." She believes and acts accordingly, with no assurance of success or even of her own survival. I find this biblical phrase to be particularly inspiring in terms of the way in which I am called to live and move and have my being in ministry in my particular time and place. "For [just] such a time as this" is the refrain of a popular Christian soft rock song that I like to listen to on my car sound system. It calls to mind and heart and spirit Esther 4:14 and the centring in God that is found in this kind of biblical literature. It is a phrase that can spur us on to action and justice.[73]

73   For example, this phrase has become the title of the current initiative on the part of the Canadian Council of Churches and other church and faith bodies in Canada to educate and inspire our people to challenge the powerful G8 countries of the world to fulfill the promises they have made for the sake of the poor and vulnerable. It is also the title of the momentum to host the Interfaith Religious Leaders' summit in 2010, when the G8 meets in Canada and needs to be reminded that our sisters and brothers are dying around the globe every day and that the G8 can take steps to alleviate their suffering.

Have you considered ...?

Following on the heels of the Book of Esther is the Book of Job. It also is considered part of the canon of Wisdom literature – sort of. The Book of Job shares many features with Wisdom literature, or, rather, it does not share many features with Torah and Prophetic literature. The Book of Job is a unique book of Holy Scripture. And does it ever raise questions! Difficult questions. "There was once a man in the land of Uz whose name was Job. That man was blameless and upright, one who feared God and turned away from evil." So goes Job 1:1, the first verse of the book and the first verse of this lectionary reading. The lectionary then skips over all the detail about Job's family and his possessions, and the really disturbing story in which the satan (best translated as "the adversary") taunts God. Job loves and fears God and is so blameless and upright, the adversary says, because God has given him so much. Let it all be taken away from him and then see where he stands. How disturbing is that, that God agrees to such a test?

Then the lectionary skips over the destruction of Job's children and all his possessions and Job's famous statement, "Naked I came from my mother's womb, and naked shall I return there; the Lord gave, and the Lord has taken away; blessed be the name of the Lord." Since, after all he has suffered, Job still does not curse God, the satan decides to up the ante and taunts God to send Job physical suffering. This Sunday's passage picks up the story here. God clearly says that Job "still persists in his integrity, although you incited me against him, to destroy him for no reason." And so God gives Job and his health into the adversary's power, with the command only to spare Job's life. Why does God agree to this?

I wish I could set down a neat and tidy answer to the many questions that have surfaced so far. But there are none. Theories about getting at this book and its disturbing story theologically exist, but satisfying answers to the disturbing questions are elusive.

Job's own wife urges him to "Curse God, and die." Job responds with an answer to some of the questions we have raised so far, but it is far from comforting or satisfying. In verse 10, he points to the idea that both good and bad come from God. One way to approach preaching the next four weeks, when the Old Testament lectionary selections are from Job, is to delve into some small bits of the massive amount of extra-biblical literature, ancient and modern, that revolves around the book. The questions that have been troubling us here have troubled faithful believers down through the millennia. Instead of spending a lot of time on theories that the book reflects and is framed by an old folktale, and that that is why the first chapter and the second seem repetitive, explore the deep questions raised in the book that surface every day in our contemporary context. Rabbi Harold Kushner's best-selling book *When Bad Things Happen to Good People* it is an excellent lens through which to prayerfully reflect on Job.

And remember that one of the great gifts of the biblical witness is that it faithfully records the stories of the people's doubts and struggles. It does not provide quick fixes or facile answers. As we know, those do not exist in the real world. Rather, the text claims and proclaims that God is the Lord of all things, all people, all time, all places. God will not be contained even by our questions.

Hide and seek

The plot thickens. After losing almost everything, including his family and possessions, and after being stricken with a dreadful physical condition, all perhaps to prove a point among the heavenly beings, Job has a further affliction: the company of three so-called friends. (Note that Job gets to keep the wife who urged him to curse God and die. Even in the midst of a difficult and dire episode, God's sense of humour is evident!) Much has been written about the long speeches of the three friends. To be sure, there are differences among them in terms of how they approach the question of suffering, and how they urge Job to deal with it. One simplified way of categorizing a major theme in their long conversations is that they say Job cannot be as innocent and undeserving of suffering as he claims. He must have done something to deserve what is happening to him, they believe, even if his punishment seems out of proportion.

This kind of argument, espoused by at least some of the friends, sounds familiar in our time and place. One can find it in the news media, for example, almost every day. When we think about those who depend on financial support from the government to live, or those infected by HIV/AIDS, do we think in our heart of hearts that they must not have tried hard enough, must not have been careful enough? Do we think they are blameless?

Job maintains his innocence. That is the focus of this passage. Job wants to encounter God, to call God to a sort of courtroom setting. He wants, as verse 4 of this passage says, to lay his case before God and argue his innocence in a kind of legal framework.[74] Job wants to hear what God will say in the face of his protestations of innocence, and is confident that when confronted by the justice of his case, God

---

74 Walter Brueggemann, in his *Theology of the Old Testament: Testimony, Dispute, Advocacy* (Minneapolis, MN: Augsburg Fortress Publishers, 1997) and other books, describes the entire Old Testament as set in a kind of legal dispute framework; this passage from Job is but one example.

will acquit him of any wrongdoing. The friends will then be proved wrong. Job is summoning God to appear and answer to charges, but God cannot to be summoned. Job cannot find God. And yet, when we read straight through the passage from verse 9 to verse 17, including verses 10 to 15, we discover something amazing. Although Job is feeling terrified by God, he is confident that he "shall come out like gold." A deep and firm faith indeed!

Where were you?

This is another one of those parts of the Bible that lends itself to being read as a larger section than we seem to think we have time for in liturgy. The whole of chapter 38 of the Book of Job is a wondrous piece of poetry, full of images of creation and of wisdom that clearly establish belief in God as the Lord of Creation and the Source of all wisdom. This style flows through all of chapter 39 as well, but even I think that it might be overwhelming to read two whole chapters! It is a misunderstanding of the nature of biblical poetry, or any poetry for that matter, to try and pick away at specific words and phrases or take any kind of literalist approach to the text.[75]

The point of chapters 38 and 39 is to proclaim the wonder, majesty and awesomeness and complete power of God, and to point out that Job is asking the wrong questions. God is so much more than Job's questions and assumptions. God, who laid the foundation of the earth, who shut in the sea with doors, who comprehends the expanse of the earth and has seen the gates of death and deep darkness, is not to be summoned by Job. In asking his self-serving questions, Job has missed the big picture. God is not accountable to us human, created beings. God laid the cornerstone for the foundation of the earth, "when the morning stars sang together and all the heavenly beings shouted for joy." God is in relationship with human beings and with Creation, and that is enough. It is hard to remember when the things we pray so hard for do not happen, but we are called to let ourselves go into the truth that God is enough.

---

75   Lest we forget, literalism is a form of interpretation that rose to particular prominence in the past few hundred years, encouraged by the empirical, factual methodology of the Enlightenment, a time when image, symbols, metaphor, etc. seemed less important.

Told you so

Job is right and his friends are wrong.

Job has begged and longed for God to appear. Job has maintained his innocence in the face of the seemingly endless verbal battering of his friends, who have been determined, for about 35 chapters of this book, to prove that he must have done something wrong to be suffering as he is. In chapter 38, God, who is not to be summoned by human beings, finally appears in a whirlwind and points out, through glorious examples of the natural world, that Job has been asking the wrong questions. It is not about Job's human protestations of innocence or even, much as we might long for an answer, about why bad things happen to good people. It is about God as the Lord of Life and Creation and History. It is about God's awesome power and "otherness." The Bible never deals in neat, tidy, comfortable answers to our questions; it was never intended to do so. Rather, the Bible deals in the awesome, mysterious and intimate details of the life of people with their God. The Book of Job is even less about neat and tidy and psychologically satisfying answers than other parts of the Bible.[76]

The first six verses of this lectionary passage give us, in magnificent and dramatic language, Job's realization that he has been asking the wrong questions, that he has been demanding satisfaction for something that he had no right to demand satisfaction. He has uttered what he did not understand. He submits to the awesomeness of God. His eyes see God and he repents in dust and ashes. But – and we need to read through verses 7 to 9, which are not included in the lectionary even though they are essential to the story – Job is also right, and his friends are wrong. In verses 7 to 9, we hear, in the Lord's words, that Job's friends have been wrong all along. Job has not suffered because of anything he did. Job is indeed innocent.

---

76   See Frederick Buechner's book *The Magnificent Defeat* (New York: HarperOne, 1985) for more insights on this point.

Now, that may not feel like a satisfying denouement. In a sense, it takes us back to the beginning of the Book of Job, where it seems that God brings disaster on Job on a whim. But the Bible is not a comfortable book and was never intended to be so. What the Book of Job does is speak to us and for us about the reality of evil in our world. Two thousand years of biblical reading and theological development in Christianity mean that we may not say in our time and place that God directly causes evil. But the question of why God, who is all powerful, does not prevent tragedy and disaster remains, and will remain, I believe, until the eschaton.[77] The final verses of this Sunday's text describe how Job possessions are restored to him, and he is given a new family. But that is not satisfying, either, because it seems to devalue his previous family. The testing of Job seems even more like a heavenly game. The bottom line is that there are many parts of our human reality that we do not understand, and the presence of suffering and evil is definitely one of those. In spite of it all, our God is indeed present to us and ultimately wills healing and health and wholeness for all Creation.

77   Sir John Polkinghorne's book *Searching for Truth* offers a helpful exploration of the painful depths of this question.

Wait for me!

Certain verses from the Book of Ruth are often read at weddings. Whenever parts of the book were read at a wedding I was conducting, I challenged the congregation to read the rest of the book after they recovered from the reception the next day. After all, I told them, it is only four chapters, and it makes for a very good, dramatic read. Sometimes the congregation thought it a little strange that the minister was giving them homework at a wedding! But why not?

It is a great story – one that, if we read it deeply, pushes at our human boundaries. The story, set in the time of the judges of Israel, reflects one of the limited periods of peace between the nation and people of Israel and the nation and people of Moab, who were considered both related and "other." There was a famine in the land.[78]

Because of the famine, an Israelite went with his wife, Naomi, and two sons to the land of Moab, where there was food enough to survive. The Israelite died, then later the two sons died. The widow was left with her two Moabite daughters-in-law, Orpah and Ruth. The famine in Israel had ended, so Naomi wanted to return home. But first, she implored Orpah and Ruth to stay behind with their own people. Orpah finally agreed to do so. Years of biblical interpretation have denigrated her for her actions, but Orpah was the obedient one. She simply did what her mother-in-law asked. It was a difficult choice. Israel was not her home, and Naomi had no visible means of support.

---

78 Note to the congregation that famine was a regular event in the history of the people of Israel and, indeed, of all peoples of the region. Famine affected much of the people's lives and movements and behaviour. The common reality of famine coloured many biblical details, such as many of the instructions in the Book of Leviticus, and included the entire sacrifice system.

On the other hand, she would be another mouth to feed for her family in Moab. Starvation could have lurked in either direction.[79]

Ruth's lovely words in verses 16 and 17 – "Where you go, I will go … where you die, I will die …" – resonate through our tradition. Not just our wedding traditions – after all, they are words spoken by a daughter-in-law to her mother-in-law – but our Christian tradition as a whole. These words of loyalty and love go far beyond what is expected. Ruth even takes the God of Israel as her God, in the place of the gods of Moab.[80]

In her origins, Ruth is not of the people of Israel. She is of a people with whom the people of Israel are in frequent conflict. And yet it is this very Ruth who is clearly named as an ancestor of King David, and as an ancestor of Jesus in the opening verses of the Gospel of Matthew, the opening verses of the whole New Testament. Regrettably, this genealogy from Matthew is not included in the Protestant lectionary, perhaps because we judge genealogies to be boring, and thus is rarely preached from.[81] Still, Ruth's example of selfless love and commitment speaks to us across time and cultures and inspires us today.

---

79 Naomi's talk about being too old to have another husband and bear other sons for Orpah and Ruth to marry reflects the common practice of Levirate marriage in that time and place. We see this practice in several other places in the biblical text, most notably Genesis 38 and Jesus' confrontation with the Sadducees in Luke 20. In the case of the death of a husband, the wife was then to marry the nearest male relative. In a subsistence-farming culture, this practice addressed the patriarchal need to hold on to property, and provided a means of support and life to women and their children who might otherwise starve.

80 In such places as verse 15 and many other biblical texts, the existence of other gods is accepted in this early time in the history of the people of Israel. It is only later that the God of Israel is understood to be the only God and the God of all peoples.

81 It is in the Roman Catholic lectionary, on the Vigil of Christmas.

Blessed be the Lord!

Naomi's plan, which centres on the custom of Levirate marriage (see the entry for Proper 26), now unfolds. She is determined to secure a future for her daughter-in-law Ruth; Boaz is the second-closest kin and a wealthy man by the standards of the time and place. This story is even more vivid and engaging than appears on the surface. In verse 4 of chapter 3, Naomi tells Ruth to observe where Boaz is lying on the threshing floor and then to uncover his feet, perhaps an action in line with an ancient tradition. In verse 7, Ruth does just that. In a context dealing with life and generations, it is a euphemism to say that it is Boaz's feet that Ruth uncovers. (The Bible is often more detailed and graphic, if we allow ourselves to see it, than our religious sensibilities seem to want us to be. For biblical faith, God is the Lord of all Life and all the details of life. There is no taboo subject or imagery, especially when the details of what brings life are concerned.)

It is difficult to understand why such stealth is needed to ensure a further and future relationship between Ruth and Boaz. Naomi makes clear in verse 3 that Ruth is not to reveal herself until the eating and drinking after a hard day of work are over and all have settled in for the night, sleeping on the threshing floor itself so that work may begin quickly the next day. Verse 14 tells us that Ruth got up and left before it was light enough for people to recognize each other, because Boaz said it must not be known that a woman had come to the threshing floor. Perhaps the discretion was necessary because there was a closer next-of-kin. Whatever the reason, chapter 4 then gives us a very detailed accounting of the practice of Levirate marriage, including its dimension of land ownership.

The details of the Levirate marriage procedure (exchanging a sandal) that chapter 4 gives us in verses 7 and onward may explain the origins of that wedding custom of tying shoes to the back of the couple's car. What is certain is that all those details make it clear that Ruth is now part of the family. The Moabite woman is, as verse 11 says, "… like Rachel and Leah, who together built up the house of Israel." Bethlehem, which will be called "the city of David," is mentioned, and Tamar, who is also a participant in the tradition of Levirate marriage but also not an Israelite, is invoked. The very same Tamar shows up in the genealogy of Jesus in the first verses of the Gospel of Matthew – one of the four women counted as significant ancestors of Jesus (The others are Ruth, Bathsheba and Rahab.) Sarah, Miriam, Deborah, and others, meanwhile, are not mentioned in those early verses of Matthew. Perhaps a point is being made in these references to the lineages of David and then Jesus about the inclusion of those who were seen as outsiders.

My soul magnifies the Lord

With the Books of 1 and 2 Samuel and then 1 and 2 Kings, the Bible begins a long narrative, most of which is not included in the lectionary, detailing the realities of the life of the people of Israel as a burgeoning nation in complex, challenging, comforting relationship with God. The narrative flows from the stories of outstanding (though sometimes flawed, as the text honestly proclaims) male leaders – Samuel, Saul, David, Nathan, Solomon, Elijah and Elisha, and then the numerous kings who followed Solomon until the subjection of the nation kingdom to Assyria and Babylonia. The first book of this series, 1 Samuel, begins by establishing that the leadership of these prominent men comes from God. The story, however, starts with a woman.

Hannah wants a son. Her husband, whose impeccable lineage is set out in the opening verses of the book, loves her. (Always pay attention to the beginnings and endings of books.) His other wife, however, has children, and throws that in Hannah's face. Hannah decides to make a deal with God. She prays, she vows, that if God will give her a son, she will dedicate him to God as one consecrated or set apart. She prays so fervently that the priest at the sanctuary thinks she is drunk.[82] (The Temple in Jerusalem is not yet built, so the people worship at various places around the land, many of which had their roots in the native fertility worship of the local peoples.)

Once he learns that she is sober and her prayers are sincere, the priest Eli tells Hannah to go in peace and in the hope that God will grant her petition for a son. "In due time Hannah conceived and bore a son. She named him Samuel, for she said, 'I have asked him of the Lord.'" As we have seen, biblical names are often stuffed full of meaning. Hannah names her child Samuel because the word means something like "God hears," for she believes that her prayer has been heard.

---

82 We will see such a misunderstanding again in the Acts story of Pentecost. I wonder how often in our time and context we pray so fervently that those around us mistake us for ones who have had much wine? Not often, I suspect!

This Samuel, who is so clearly established as being who he is and where he is through the activity of God, will one day move the nation and the people forward in their development. This Samuel clearly has the authority to consecrate kings and speak God's word.

Hannah's prayer in chapter 2 might sound familiar to us. Mary's Magnificat in chapter 2 of the Gospel of Luke is based on it: "The bows of the mighty are broken ... those who were hungry are fat with spoil ... He raises up the poor from the dust; he lifts the needy from the ash heap." Hannah's prayer ends with what is the very purpose of these early chapters in the Samuel/Kings narratives: to set up the king to come. "The Lord will judge the ends of the earth; he will give strength to his king, and exalt the power of his anointed." Christians, of course, see this king to come as being in the line of David, to be sure: the king is Jesus, the Messiah.

The end is the beginning

Christ the King Sunday, the Reign of Christ Sunday, the end of the Church's liturgical year, declares what and who Jesus is for us before launching into the anticipation of his coming that is Advent.

So, on this last Sunday of the church year, we hear the last words of the chosen king of Israel. David was chosen by God to be king for the sake of the people. David's last words sum up the ideal of kingship, if not the reality as David lived it. First, as Walter Brueggemann says, the ideal king is one who is king by virtue of God's sovereign power. Such a king, who is indisputably set in place by God, is therefore accountable to God.[83] A second characteristic of an ideal king, as given to us in this lectionary passage, is that the king "… rules over people justly, ruling in the fear of God." The fact that David frequently fell short of the ideal is not the point. The text outlines what a king should be; Christians believe that the text speaks to our understanding of Jesus as the king of kings. Third, this passage reflects the conviction that an unconditional covenant has been made with the line of David. God is abidingly faithful. For Christians, Christ the king perfectly fulfills all three of the characteristics of leadership and calling that these words of David proclaim.

We who are "little Christs," which is what the term "Christian" means, now bring one liturgical year to an end. We stand poised on the brink of the new church year, certain that our Messiah and king is in deep, complete connection with God the Father; certain that our Messiah and king can, does and will rule justly; certain that God's covenant is faithful and constant and sure.

How do we, as people who live in a broken and hurting world, proclaim and show those truths in all that we say and do? For each congregation and parish, the answers to that question will be both unique and universal. As their preacher, offer specific insights based

---

83   Brueggemann, *First and Second Samuel*, 346–47.

on your faith, your studies, and your deep knowledge of the people and your context as a community, remembering as you do so that we, too, are accountable to God, that we are to act justly, and that God is always faithful in loving relationships. How will your congregation make that obvious to the world so loved by God, as obvious as the coloured lights that are starting to appear? How much more are we called to defy the darkness?

Year C

Emmanuel is coming! Really!

Jeremiah is in trouble. He is waiting it out in jail, with no personal "Get out of jail free" card for the near future.

This passage comes more than halfway through the Book of the Prophet Jeremiah. The end of the city and the end of whatever independence the southern part of the nation had is in sight. Jeremiah is held in captivity by his own people for daring to speak plainly. Right before this Advent 1 lectionary passage, the prophet speaks again about the coming destruction of Jerusalem. Then, without even time for a breath, he goes on to prophesy its restoration in great detail. In the chapter before, in one of those signs/actions that the prophets are famous (or infamous) for, Jeremiah has taken action: he will wait out the coming destruction by buying a field. This act is a sure sign that he believes in restoration, stability and the hope of God. This action is rather like waving a "Get out of jail free" card for the people long term.

The Book of the Prophet Jeremiah as a whole records difficult times in the life of the nation and people of Israel. Whether they know it or admit it or listen to Jeremiah or not, the people and the nation of the south wait for the destruction of the city of Jerusalem and the subsequent exile of some of them to Babylon. Jeremiah was often unpopular, because he prophesied the destruction that was to come as a result of the people's and the nation's unfaithful behaviour. This passage can be unpopular to preach at the beginning of Advent, when people might prefer a more saccharine-sweet message.

Judgment – often a judgment of the power structures of his society and always judgment of the people's corruption, injustice and lack of response to God – was one of Jeremiah's major themes. However, Jeremiah always believed and proclaimed that repentance – the turning in another direction, turning to God – was possible. He also always held together both the collective responsibility and the individual responsibility that people had for their behaviour. He believed and proclaimed that God is in charge, and that we are responsible to God, that justice is both the divine will and our faithful response, and that God is abidingly faithful. Emmanuel indeed!

Then comes the certain good news of the Gospel of the Lord, for which we all wait. The promise will be fulfilled, a righteous branch of the lineage of David will spring up and "... he shall execute justice and righteousness in the land." At this time of year, for many people in the West, the focus is slipping and sliding into parties, presents and frantic busyness. The call of this passage, the call of Emmanuel, is to remember that the Prophet Jeremiah knows what it means to be unpopular. He knows the imperative of justice; he knows the judgment of corruption and the people's lack of response to God. Jeremiah knows what it means to wait for fulfillment and restoration, and that in spite of the darkness and the waiting, joy comes in the morning. Advent is so much more for us than just waiting to unwrap the presents and carve the turkey. Being willing to be unpopular, calling for the imperative of justice, both individually and corporately, speaking out against corruption and lack of response to God and at the same time waiting for God's fulfillment and restoration are all part of the season for us, too. That is part of the active waiting.

My messenger

Beginnings and endings of biblical books are important. These verses from Malachi are found in the last two chapters of the Old Testament; from the Christian perspective, they clearly anticipate the New Testament. In fact, Christians rearranged the Jewish Scriptures; the Book of the Prophet Malachi, whose name means "my messenger," is actually found near the middle of the Jewish TaNaKh. The Christian Old Testament, then, is the writings of our Hebrew/Jewish ancestors in the faith, rearranged for Christological purposes, to point to Christ, whose coming we proclaim in this Advent season.

The Book of the Prophet Malachi reflects a late period in the history of the people of Israel. The return from exile in Babylon was long past. The Temple in Jerusalem, or at least a smaller, less lovely version of it, had been rebuilt. But prosperity had not come. The people were suffering physically but also spiritually. They were not in what Malachi considered to be right relationship with God. His message, therefore, was full of rebuke and warning. Scandalized that the people seemed to have forgotten the depth and meaning of their relationship with God, Malachi called them to repentance, as the prophets always do, certain that they can experience God's blessing once again. His is not a message filled with sweetness and light, as the messages of the prophets never are. The messenger coming to prepare the way – and, in the traditions of Israel, both prophets and priests were often called messengers of the Lord – is going to refine and purify the people. The day of the messenger's coming will be one of judgment, in which people will not be able to stand or endure. But the purification and refining will result in the people becoming truly righteous, and their relationship with their God will be restored. This is a hard and challenging message in this season in which our congregations do not want to hear hard and challenging messages.[84]

---

84 For some vivid theological commentary on this kind of message of purification and refining, see Dante's *Purgatory*, a key piece of Christian literature that we all should read.

It may be too late already for this Advent season, but try setting your people up for a different kind of Advent next year. Early next fall, put forth some suggestions or encouragements, perhaps one a week in the bulletin or congregational newsletter for a simpler Advent/pre-Christmas season. Picking single names for gift-giving in large families, rather than giving to everyone, and, dare I say it, fewer parties and decorations. And be sure that congregational life models simplicity, depth and a priority for justice.

Same time, same channel

Well, not exactly. The prophet Zephaniah wrote in an earlier period of the history of the people of Israel than did the prophet Malachi, whom we read last week. Do note, though, that both of them (plus ten other prophets, including Micah, whom we will read next week) make up the part of the Old Testament called the "Book of the Twelve" or the "Twelve Minor Prophets." They are called "minor" not because their message is any less important than that of the major prophets, Isaiah, Jeremiah and Ezekiel, but simply because their books are shorter. In the days when scriptures were written on scrolls, the average length of a scroll meant that Isaiah and Jeremiah and Ezekiel all had their own scrolls, while the other twelve prophets could all fit together on the same scroll. Although, canonically, the twelve minor prophets are just as important as Isaiah, Jeremiah and Ezekiel, they are included in the lectionary less often. Make the most of these readings in this Advent season for Year C because we will not encounter these prophets often.

The prophet Zephaniah wrote at a time when the nation of Israel was in some decline. He wrote as one who held together in his person, as the prophet Isaiah always did, too, the roles of prophet and leader in the society and circles of power of the time. It is unbiblical to insist that the prophets are always on the outside of their society and are somehow against established, institutional religion. What they always call for is righteous religion and the justice that flows from it.

The good "reform and righteousness" king Hezekiah had died, and things had gone downhill. The usual suspects were the problems: injustice and unfaithfulness in terms of worship and right relationship with their God. Good king Josiah had launched reforms in both those areas, but to Zephaniah, the people were not hearing the call for reform and repentance.

Zephaniah believed that the day of the Lord was coming – a common prophetic theme and phrase – with severe consequences for the behaviour of the people. Take a quick look at chapter 1 for some of the dramatic and harsh language of the consequences. It is not just the people of Israel who are being called to account, but all the nations, all the peoples. The Moabites, the Ammonites, the Cherethites, the Philistines of Canaan and the Ethiopians are all also under judgment and are all also accountable to God. God is the God of all nations and all peoples, whether they recognize that fact or not.

But the lectionary reading for this third Sunday in Advent takes us to the place to which the prophets always take us. The judgment is real. The consequences are real. But the opportunity and encouragement and inspiration for repentance and renewal are also real. In fact, these are God's will. And so these glorious verses at the end of the book: "The king of Israel, the Lord [for the Lord is always the true king of Israel] is in your midst."

The third Sunday in Advent is not really about the Advent carol versus Christmas carol debate. Name with your congregation an area of congregational repentance and renewal – more volunteers for the food bank, a re-institution of the monthly Amnesty International letter-writing campaign, a study/dialogue series with sisters and brothers of other faith traditions. How will your congregation act as a messenger of God?

O Little Town of Bethlehem

It is obvious why this text was chosen for Advent 4: the reference to "Bethlehem of Ephrathah."

Micah is our third minor prophet in a row in Year C. All three of these readings might be more of a challenge to preach from than the Advent readings of Years A and B, because these passages of Scripture are less well-known. On the other hand, that could be an advantage: we may see with fresh eyes, and the congregation may hear with fresh ears. Micah's name means "Who is like the Lord?" Contrary to the time of the previous two minor prophets, Micah's time was one of comparative economic prosperity. However (and this is an all too familiar situation in many areas of the world today), the fruits of the economic prosperity were in the hands of the wealthy. There was much injustice. Micah clearly stated that God hates both injustice and worship that is continually just going through the motions. It is not true that the prophets condemned the sacrificial format of the worship of that time and place. Worship, which was rooted in the biblical imperatives for sacrifice, was a way of expressing and entering into the sacred and holy relationship with God. Micah called for depth, meaning and authentic worship that led to justice.

Back to Bethlehem. Micah declares that a ruler will come forth from this town in the south of the country. He will care for the people, like a shepherd, in the strength of the Lord. The image is one of a more political ruler than Jesus our Messiah, which is why the lectionary cuts off the passage at verse 5a and leaves us with the message that "he shall be the one of peace" rather than moving on into what the text says about the Assyrians. Bethlehem is said to be of one of the little clans of Judah, but remember that it is the city of David.

The lead-up to Christmas is one in which those who have wealth can, should, must use it to show forth their love. Simply remember that God has so loved the world, and we are called to do likewise.

Christmas Eve – *Isaiah 9:2-7*

See the entry for Christmas Eve, Year A

Christmas Day 1 – *Isaiah 62:6-12*

See the entry for Christmas Day 1, Year A.

Christmas Day 2 – Isaiah 52:7-10

See the entry for Christmas Day 2, Year A.

Another year, another robe

Such a little snippet of Scripture, but one that, when taken in context, says so very much. It said much to the people of Israel, it says much to our Jewish sisters and brothers, and it says much to us. This passage continues the story of the child Samuel, Hannah his mother, and Eli the priest – a story we encounter in Year B, Proper 28. Hannah, childless but married to an Israelite man whose lineage is clearly set out in the text for purposes of credibility, prays fervently for a son and in a sense, plays "Let's Make a Deal" with God. She promises that if God will give her a son, she will dedicate him to God's service forever and ever, amen. Her prayer is granted and, with no reluctance that the text records, Hannah, with proper ritual and form, takes her son, Samuel, to the priest Eli in the sanctuary at Shiloh to serve God throughout his life.[85]

This reading gives us details about Hannah and her husband's yearly visit to Samuel when they went to offer the proper sacrifice. Eli, the priest at Shiloh, knows that Samuel is a great gift to the Lord. Eli blesses Hannah and her husband for such a gift. Verse 26 establishes the meaning of this story, though reading verses 21 to 25, which are not included in the lectionary, adds to the understanding of that meaning. We need to know that Eli's sons, who would normally have been his successors in the priesthood at Shiloh, were guilty of very bad behaviour, which is, in a sense, the fulcrum of the story.

Because of this bad behaviour (we also hear about it in verses 12 to 17, which are also omitted in the lectionary), God is making a new start: with Samuel. It is Samuel who grows in favour with the Lord. It is Samuel, as we will see in the call narrative of chapter 3, who carries the authority of the Lord. Indeed, he will ultimately anoint the first kings of Israel. It is also crucial to know what the sons of Eli are guilty

---

85   The existence of the Temple in Jerusalem was still many years away. The people were worshipping at different shrines around the country, shrines that had sometimes been holy to the other inhabitants of the land, the Canaanites.

of doing; this tells us what the new start in Samuel aims to correct. The sons of Eli are corrupt in the practice of their priesthood, and they are unjust. Their sins are not only against other people, but against God. Samuel is God's new beginning, a new beginning of faithful priesthood and of just and right relationships with the people, which means being in just and right relationship with God. Samuel has the authority and credibility to be, in God's name, the leader of the people in a way that, in the biblical tradition, combines the priestly, political and prophetic functions, holds tight the relationship between the people and their God.

Christians believe the same of Jesus. That is why this passage, a narrative passage in the midst of many passages of poetic prophecy, was chosen for the first Sunday after Christmas, after the proclamation of the incarnate leadership of Jesus in our lives and the life of the world as priest, prophet and incarnate justice.

And now for something completely different

Jeremiah, prophet of the south, Judah, through good times and bad (very bad), declares in this text that good news will be the ultimate outcome. Exile to Babylon is not the final answer. God will ensure that the people return home. This text vividly describes what that return home will look like. I once studied homiletics with Paul Wilson at Emmanuel College in Toronto. Professor Wilson would say, "Don't just talk about the Reign of God, show me what it looks like!" Well, that is exactly what the prophet Jeremiah is doing in this passage: painting in glorious living colour what the return from exile will look like.

So preach a different kind of sermon today. Reformulate the images and words of Jeremiah for his time and place into words and images for our time and place.

Something like this ...

For God says:

Shout out from the rooftops for God's people,

And call from the apartment balconies;

Inscribe billboards, advertise and say,

"Save your people, O God, the diehard ones."

I am going to bring them from isolation and despair,

And gather them from their fear and loneliness,

Among them the unemployed and the depressed,

The single mothers and the refugees, together;

With fear and desperation they come,

But I hug them tight

And bring them home safe and sound.

I will be sure that they have food and drink,

And a life of dignity and purpose;

For I am mother and father to my children,

And my Church is my witness.

You can keep going with something like this, or make it more specific to your context. Those of you who have the gift of poetry or rhythm, or know a creative soul in your congregation, or have the desire to try something new, could even set a paraphrase of the words of Jeremiah to a rap beat. Reading *The Gospel of Dr. Seuss* inspired me to think that most of us can be more creative than we think. And fortunately, God has a sense of humour!

Epiphany – Isaiah 60:1-6

See the entry for Epiphany, Year A.

Do not be afraid

In June 2007, I had the privilege, as a religious leader, of participating in an Interfaith summit held in parallel with the G8 meeting in Germany. Fifty-eight leaders from a variety of faith traditions around the globe, including Archbishop Desmond Tutu, gathered to create, publish and promote a statement called "Just Participation." The ongoing purpose of the statement is to speak to the G8 leaders and heads of state out of the divine imperative. We speak and act on behalf of the poor and vulnerable, to encourage, challenge, push and inspire the G8 leaders and heads of state to act in ways that are more just for all God's people, particularly our sisters and brothers in Africa. I received a good hearing from the Canadian G8 office on this "Just Participation" statement, and was encouraged to continue engagement with them for future meetings of the Interfaith religious leaders and its subsequent statements.[86]

During this gathering, I attended the opening service of the German Kirchentag. Ten thousand people heard the message of the sermon at that opening service, a message that proclaimed the Gospel summed up in three phrases: "Do not be afraid. He is risen. You are my witnesses." As a Christian, I find great sustenance and sustaining power in those three powerful phrases. As Christians, we find great sustenance and sustaining power in the sacrament of Baptism and in the remembrance of Jesus' baptism – the remembrance of going down into the waters and then rising into new life. Turn to the Isaiah passage for this Sunday and see how the baptism we proclaim is so much in

---

86   Feel free to google the statement "Just Participation" and use it in all times and places possible. Each year from 2007 onwards, there will be Interfaith leaders' summits in whichever country is hosting the G8 meeting, and statements will be issued to continue to challenge, push and inspire the G8 to do justice. The statements from the 2008 Interfaith leaders' summit are on the website of The Canadian Council of Churches: www.ccc-cce.ca. In 2010, Canada will host both the G8 summit and the Interfaith leaders' summit. It is not too soon to begin raising our voices!

line with the witness of the Old Testament. The statements from the 2008 Interfaith leaders' summit are on the website of The Canadian Council of Churches: www.ccc-cce.ca. In 2010, Canada will host both the G8 summit and the Interfaith leaders' summit. It is not too soon to begin raising our voices!

Verse 1 proclaims, "Do not fear." These three words are repeated over and over again in the Old Testament – often in this Book of the Prophet Isaiah, but in many other places, too. The words move into the New Testament in the Angel Gabriel's words to Mary, the angel's words to the shepherds, and many other places. "Do not fear" is a foundational statement of faith for us. This Isaiah passage makes clear that the people are not to fear, because God has redeemed them, has called them by name (another reason why this passage was chosen to sit alongside of the one about the Baptism of Jesus). When the people pass through even such great difficulties as water and fire, they will be held safe by God. "Do not fear" is repeated in verse 5, in the context of the gathering together of all God's beloved children. In the original historical context of this passage, the people were in exile. They were being promised the glorious love and restoration of God. The imperative not to fear echoes down through the eons to us, living in a world where there is much to fear, too.

Verses 3 and 4 might sound as if the people of Israel have somehow a greater value than other peoples. It does sound that way on the surface, but taken alongside the witness of the entire Old Testament, especially the Book of the Prophet Isaiah, in which all peoples are deeply cherished by God and used as witnesses by God, these verses make a point about the depth of God's care and how precious people are to the Holy One.

My God, my God, why have you forsaken me?

These verses from the Book of the Prophet Isaiah begin with the implication that God has been silent and distant for some time. Much as we find this scenario difficult, it is a reality for people of faith. One can pick up writings by almost any writer of faith – Frederick Buechner and C. S. Lewis spring instantly to mind – and read their experiences of isolation and distance from God. The biblical text, particularly the Book of Job and the Psalms, also witnesses to this reality. We hear it and feel it, too, in Jesus' cry of desolation from the cross.

This silence and distance from God that we sometimes experience is real. But it is never God's final word. In this passage in the Book of the Prophet Isaiah, a passage speaking, in its original context, to the people of Israel returned from exile, the people are trying to settle into the homeland and finding it rather hard going. The glorious vision of restoration and inclusion remains glorious, but there are lots of disputes and contentions to deal with as the people try to rebuild their lives in the land. They do not agree on priorities and forms of worship. All those disputes and contentions are in the background in this lectionary passage, though. The passage pushes past silence and distance from God, and conflict. The passage proclaims and carries forward the vision of the vindication and salvation of the people, which will be such that all the world will see it. This event will be marked by the giving of new names. The people will no longer be called "Forsaken" but "My Delight Is in Her." What a great name for a congregation to call itself, especially one that is either an amalgamation or living some kind of transformed new reality!

Walter Brueggemann reminds us that "a change of name signals a new identity, a new relation, a new chance for life in the world."[87] God does not deny that there have been silence and distance, nor that there are difficult realities in the life of the people. But God pro-

---

87   Walter Brueggemann, *Isaiah 40–66*, 220–21.

claims and acts the message of salvation. God rejoices over the people. The marriage imagery of that rejoicing speaks deeply to the realities of that time and place. It speaks of covenant and relationship. In talking about the land being "married," the concept of covenant and relationship is carried over to the land as well. In biblical theology, the people and the land are bound together. Salvation and rejoicing abound. God's delight is real and is forever.

From this day forward

The introduction to the book of Ezra in the New Revised Standard Version of the Bible reminds us that in the earliest Hebrew manuscripts, the books of Ezra and Nehemiah were one book. The story that they tell is in line with what we have been hearing in recent lectionary texts from Isaiah and Jeremiah. The people of Israel, now more commonly referred to in the text as the Jews, have returned from exile in Babylonia. They have been set free – sent home, in several waves, by Cyrus the Persian after his conquest of Babylon and as a result of his foreign policy. Back home, the Jews have been engaged in rebuilding the city of Jerusalem and the Temple. The work is slow and discouraging. At least in the minds of some, the finished products fell short of the glories of city and Temple before the exile. Yet it is not only the physical details of the people's lives that must be rebuilt, but also the practice of their religion – the ways they relate to each other in their relationship with God and their understanding of their Scriptures. This is the context for this Sunday's verses from the book of Nehemiah.[88]

The passage deals with reading the book of the law and instruction, the Torah. Now that the exiled people are back (Ezra having come with one wave and Nehemiah with another), the city walls are restored and the Temple stands again, though in a much smaller and more basic form, it is time to remind the people who they are and whose they are. The people, both women and men, listen attentively and respond to God's great love and grace for them with worship and praise.

This late text in the history of the Jews includes some details about their worship. Verse 8 tells us that the reading from the law of God was done with "interpretation" so that the people could understand

---

88 It seems that this reading is chopped up the way it is because it appears too difficult for a liturgical reading. There are many Hebrew names, which seem hard for English speakers to pronounce. Feel free to insert the omitted verses!

it. And although the people seem tempted to weep and mourn after hearing the reading, perhaps because it is then clearer to them how they have been falling short in responding to God's great and grace-filled love for them, they are told not to weep. They are to respond with thanksgiving, eating and drinking, enjoying the gifts of God, and making sure that those who do not have food of their own are also fed. God's care for the poor and vulnerable is always present and is always a divine imperative for us.

Who, me?

Prophets are often reluctant to be prophets, and Jeremiah is no exception. It is a thankless job. To be a prophet is to be someone who speaks for God, who carries God's word in their own words and actions, often in the midst of a hostile crowd. To be a biblical prophet is not to be a fortune-teller. Rather, the biblical prophets proclaim the word of God to their time and place. They say dire things to be sure. They can see with more clarity than the rest of us where people are falling short of God's will for them and what the consequences of that falling short will be. They use tough language and can use graphic terms to describe the consequences of people's unfaithfulness to God. This unfaithfulness usually takes one of the following forms, or a combination of them – worshipping other gods, worshipping God in a mechanistic or meaningless way, or acting unjustly towards others, particularly the poor and vulnerable.

The biblical prophets also lived very much among their people. They spoke with kings and advised them to follow in God's way and path; sometimes that advice was followed, and sometimes it was not. Some prophets were priests in the Temple; others were mystics, speaking in wondrous images; still others used everyday objects and actions to make their point. Their message was always to turn the people – and often the leaders, the rulers, the wealthy and the powerful – back to faithful worship of God and to the faithful response of justice that issues directly from that worship. Prophets were often persecuted or ignored.

So who would want the job? Certainly not Jeremiah. God's call to him is clear and arrives early in Jeremiah's life. God called him before he was even formed in the womb! God called him and consecrated him, set him apart to be, in God's name, a prophet to the nations. Note that the call is not just to be a prophet to the people of Israel, but to the nations. Though people do not always remember it, God is the God of all peoples, all nations. Jeremiah understands that God has called, and called early, but he sees himself as still young and not knowing how to speak. This is a typical response to the call to be a prophet. Moses says the same; next week we will see Isaiah having his "unclean lips" cleansed so he can be God's prophet.

God's call is not to be denied, however. Jeremiah will go to all those to whom God sends him, and he will speak what God tells him to speak. That phrase we saw in the lectionary reading for the Baptism of Jesus appears again here: Jeremiah is not to be afraid. God is with him completely, always, and that is enough. Through that presence anything and everything can be accomplished. With God's very touch, the divine words are put into the mouth of Jeremiah. These words are not merely uttered and then forgotten. There is power in the words, power both to destroy and to build. To be appointed by God is to carry in some way, in one's very being, the powerful and effective and judging and redemptive word of God. There is no choice but to take the job.

How unpopular are we really willing to be in our vocation to witness to the living God?

Here I am, Lord; send me

At every ordination service in the Toronto Conference (roughly equivalent, administratively, to an archdiocese) of The United Church of Canada, two banners are prominently displayed. The words on those two banners are a paraphrase of part of verse 8 of this passage from the Book of the Prophet Isaiah. One banner says, "Here I am, Lord" and the other says, "Send me." The call of the prophet Isaiah has echoed down the centuries in the call of people to ministry in the Body of Christ.

Isaiah's call has much in common with the call of Jeremiah, discussed in the entry for last Sunday, but there are also definite differences. In the call of Isaiah, we are given much more detail about the setting in which it occurs. Isaiah has a vision of God while in the Temple. Isaiah may have been a priest in the Temple in Jerusalem. It was possible to be both a priest and a prophet.

Too often, we are told that prophets are always on the fringes of their society. Such statements are biblically unfaithful. That attitude can lead to a kind of anti-Judaism or anti-Semitism that equates Jewish tradition and the Temple with an old, empty ritual sacrificial worship system and equates the prophets with the restoration or initiation of a more "pure" spiritual and justice-proclaiming worship in the line of Jesus. Isaiah had access to the kings of his day, although they didn't always listen to him. In his vision, he saw God and the glorious atmosphere surrounding God, and survived, in spite of the declaration by some parts of the biblical witness that God is so wondrously other that mortals cannot see him and live. The incense filled the Temple and he knew what the vision meant. Although he knew he had failings and frailties, as did his people, he saw beyond these weaknesses. He heard the voice of the Lord calling him to prophesy the word of the Lord. He was called to challenge the people when they were too comfortable, and comfort them when they were too challenged – to call them to just beliefs and behaviour. He responds, "Here am I; send me!" May it be so for us when we are so called!

In God we trust

At least, in God we are supposed to trust. In this passage, the prophet Jeremiah is expounding on what is a basic, deep, broad and wide theme of all the biblical prophets: human beings, made in the image of God, are to place our trust in God, always and completely. Prophets must proclaim this message because people seem to need constant reminding that our trust must be in God. In the time of Jeremiah and Isaiah, misplaced trust was often manifested in the making of political alliances with one country against another. When it seemed that political instability in the known world was rampant, leaders kept turning – against the strongly worded advice, counsel and prophecies of prophets – to political alliances with other countries. Those political alliances were thought to protect the people from other peoples who were aggressively and militarily on the move through the Ancient Near East.

This scenario should sound familiar. In our post-9/11 context, these words from the Book of the Prophet Jeremiah could hardly be more relevant. That is why I am committed to the use of the Old Testament in the church. It is relevant for all Christians in all times and places. Certain situations, such as famines, are all too real in Africa, for example. Other parallels speak to the church in North America, too.

In New Testament times, the nation of Israel, in which our Saviour and Messiah was born, brought up and lived out his ministry, was an occupied country. The political situation in much of the Old Testament times, therefore, was actually more like our own. The nation of Israel, both when it was united and when it was divided into the northern and southern kingdoms, had some political autonomy; it had diplomatic relationships with neighbouring countries; it had the potential and the power to make the political alliances of which the prophets often disapproved; it had economic and trade relations with other nations. Does all this sound familiar? Preach this passage drawing, in as much detail as you can, on the similarities between the time of the Prophet Jeremiah and our time.

All for the best

Joseph and his amazing technicolour dreamcoat are back, but this time Joseph is without the dreamcoat. In this part of the story, Joseph has all his brothers in tow, and there is a happy ending. The whole Joseph saga is a wondrous story of the relationship of God with the people, even though God is rarely mentioned throughout the 14 chapters. That was not a concern to the first readers and hearers of the saga. The early hearers of the stories, prophecies, instructions and wisdom believed that everything in life belonged to God and was under the sovereignty of God. That belief was the foundation for every part of their life as a people. Regardless of the fact that the saga directly mentions God so rarely, the Joseph narrative is one of the better known of the Old Testament stories. (In preaching, mention at least the bare bones of the story each time.)

The fact that the first two verses of the chapter are omitted by the lectionary does not damage the plot line, but it diminishes the portrayal of Joseph and of our humanity (though verse 15 relates some of the living colour). No matter where you start the reading, a key point to draw out is stated in verses 5 to 8. Although Joseph had been sold into slavery by his jealous brothers, he was able to say that the brothers were not to feel bad about what they did. It was part of God's plan to preserve life: when the famine came to the land of Israel, Joseph was in such a high position in Egypt that he could help his family. For them, his help meant the difference between life and death by starvation. The God of the promise of many descendants to Abraham has ensured, through the fourth generation, that the promise lives.

This point can lead into a discussion of providential theology. One does need to tread carefully there. Some people will say that losing their job was God's will because it prompted them to explore other visions and vistas, and ultimately there was a good outcome. But what about the death of a child, or the slaughter of 800,000 Rwandans? Can there be a good outcome from those tragedies? Can God be working through them for good? Well, no and yes. God does not will such things in order that some good might be accomplished. The biblical witness, when seen in its entirety, always emphasizes that God is the God of life. Sometimes terrible and tragic things happen that are no one's fault or will. Can good be inspired as a response to tragedy? Of course. Is that good inspired by God? Of course. Were those dire tragedies willed so that the good might result? Never. In a free and sometimes turbulent world, God is always the God of life. We are called to work with God to preserve life.

All things bright and beautiful

The Old Testament contains many references to nature and to the interconnections between nature and the people of faith. God is the creator of *all* things. Many references in the Old Testament make this point, but most of them are not included in the lectionary. Isaiah 55:10-13 is one example that is found there.

This passage was written during the exile of the people in Babylon, sometime in the approximately forty years after 586/7 BCE. It concludes that part of the book of the prophet Isaiah sometimes called Second Isaiah. This joyous piece of poetry celebrates the reality of God's word and power. Rain and snow come down and nourish the earth, and so does God's word accomplish God's will. As Walter Brueggemann says, "God's word produces real outcomes in public life."[89]

In dealing with this passage, note a number of particular details. In verse 12, the phrase "go out in joy" means to be released from exile. ("Go out" is technically used for release from exile.) The homecoming of Israel from exile in Babylon will be celebrated by nature. This is a poetic way of saying that human political realities are bound up with natural realities. In verse 13, the text most deliberately talks about "cypress" and "myrtle" as a sign of restoration, in comparison with the "brier" and "thorn," which are formulaic phrases in Isaiah for life diminished by God's judgment, by the repercussions of acting contrary to God's will. (The same point about the connection of human and natural realities is made in the New Testament stories of the crucifixion, when Scripture refers to the darkness that happens at noon as Jesus is hanging on the cross.)

In an age of environmental disruptions and looming ecological crises, we may understand this kind of biblical passage anew. You may wish to use this text to connect to our human actions and greed, and our decision to ignore what is deep justice for all God's people and all

---

89   Walter Brueggemann, *Isaiah 40–66*, 161.

God's Creation, with the destruction of nature. If we in the West are able to return from our exile in the empire of materialism and a life that not only consumes too much of the world's resources but also says that our value comes from our possessions, might not the mountains and the hills burst into song?

Let us pray

The last building block has been laid, the last golden lamp stand lined up, the last dish for incense perfectly positioned. The Ark of the Covenant has been installed in the Holy of Holies. The Temple of God in Jerusalem has been completed according to King Solomon's vision, mandate and plan. With all the details in place, now that all has been built and established there to the glory of God, it is time to pray. King Solomon begins with a speech, followed by a long prayer. It is parts of that prayer, which goes on for 31 verses, that form this Sunday's Old Testament reading.

Solomon stands before the altar of the Lord in the presence of all the people of Israel. Their presence witnesses to their full support and participation in the building of the Temple of God in Jerusalem. Solomon starts to pray using words of praise that declare that God keeps covenant and steadfast love. There are two things I want to note.

First, Solomon begins his prayer with praise. Prayers of intercession and petition are all very well, and are often necessary and central parts of our worship, but as the biblical witness reminds us here and in the Psalms, we are to praise our God, the Holy One. Our Jewish sisters and brothers have remembered this point. Even their mourner's prayer, the Kaddish, is a prayer of praise, in the very face of death.

Second, verse 23 makes it clear that in this time and place in the life of the people of Israel, monotheism is still not established. God is the supreme God, the God of the people of Israel, to be sure, but the existence of other lesser gods is acknowledged. In the faith of the people, relationship with God continued to develop and grow. As the Epistles of Paul tell us, the faith of the early Christian communities was also still developing. The words and actions of their faith continued to be revisited in the light of their belief in the reality and new life of the Risen Christ.

The second part of this reading could be entitled "Shameless Universalism." There is to be no exclusion of those whom some consider beyond the boundaries of the people of Israel. God's name, mighty hand and outstretched arm will be so famous, glorious and well known that people of other lands will hear of them. Solomon asks that God hear the prayers of "outsiders" and respond. His prayer is a kind of witness. God's response to the prayers of those who are not of the people of Israel will ensure that all peoples of the earth will hear of and respond to the presence of God in the same way that the people of Israel do.

To veil or not to veil, that is the question

What an encounter with the living God can do to you! Moses, prophet extraordinaire, mediator for God to the people and for the people to God, had given the people "the ten commandments." The Ten Words, as they are sometimes called, are the "rules of engagement" for how to live as God's people in God's created world. The people made a rather bad slip immediately afterwards. They lost faith. They got discouraged. They wanted a god they could see and touch, so they made a golden calf. God and Moses got angry. The tablets on which the Ten Words of instruction and ways of response to God's love from the starting point of grace were written had been broken. As soon as peace was restored among God, Moses and the people, it was back up the mountain for Moses. Back up the mountain for the covenant to be renewed, for the tablets to be redrawn, and for Moses to acquire the need for a veil.

One look at the story of the Transfiguration of Jesus in the Gospels will make it clear why this text was chosen for this Sunday. But the story in the book of Exodus can also stand alone, as it does for our Jewish sisters and brothers.

Moses was so transformed by his experience up on the mountain that when he came down with the second set of tablets, his face shone with the wonder and glory of the presence of God. He did not realize it at first, but those who saw him were awestruck. They knew why his face shone so brilliantly and they were afraid. Moses drew them all to him by stages, and communicated the covenant of relationship. The people seemed to be able to stand to see his shining face for a while. He did not put a cover on it until after he had talked with them and, presumably, given them the second set of tablets, but for daily life, he wore a veil. When relating directly to God, he removed it. But note that he regularly did not put the veil back over his face after being in the presence of God until he had communicated God's words and instructions to the people.

The experience of the reality and presence of God makes Moses' face shine in a way that is almost unbearable to see. The light of the reality and presence of God is not a gentle, glowing haze of candle-light; it is powerful, brilliant, transforming and almost too much to bear, at least long-term. Archbishop Desmond Tutu is humble, warm, friendly, gracious and lovely to work with. To be in his presence, though, is what I imagine it might have been like for the people of Israel to be in the presence of Moses after his encounters with God. Being with Archbishop Tutu is mesmerizing, powerful; the light that shines from him is almost too much to bear. Others in our world and in your experiences of God in the world might also fit this description: Jesus, first and foremost, but others, too. As you wrestle with this passage, name some for your congregation or invite them to name some for themselves.

We give thee but thine own

It is the very first of all the fruits and crops of the land that the people are to bring before God in thanksgiving. This gift is given in gratitude for the love and grace of God and the great blessing of a home and an inheritance. In a time and place in which agriculture was often at a subsistence level, when famine often lurked just around the corner, it was significant to give in this way. It would be significant now if many of us in North America gave like this. Some of our ancestors in the faith, not too many generations back – my grandparents' generation, in fact – gave like that: they gave to God through the church the first of what they had. Today, those of us who respond in praise and thanksgiving, tend to give to God – through the church or through other important routes in our society – not the first of all we have and make, but rather the last, the left over, the excess. As a nation, we are unwilling to give in foreign aid to the starving, dying peoples of the world – even 0.7% of our gross national product, something that our country originally proposed would be a way to heal God's hurting children of the world. It is a scandal.

I am not saying that the people of Israel always, or even often, measured up to this proclamation of the text from the book of Deuteronomy, but it was the proclamation and the imperative. It was seen to be the way to respond in love to God's great love. Note that what comes after the giving of the first fruits is a recital of the concrete ways in which God's love has been made manifest in the life of the people. The story of the Exodus is told, and often retold, throughout the biblical text as the most daring and grace-filled action of God on behalf of the people. It and its frequent recital showed the people who God is and who they were. The phrase "A wandering Aramean was my ancestor …" is considered by many biblical scholars to be one of the oldest parts of the biblical tradition. This liturgical phrase, which perhaps reflected the ritual and identity of the people, was recited at cultic gatherings as the people remembered who they were and whose they were. The Aramean mentioned is probably Jacob/Israel; he is probably so named because of living for a time in a part of the land that could be known as Aram.

This passage, with its proclamation of what is to be given to God in response to all the blessings received, has even more punch when we remember that of the five books of the Torah or Pentateuch, Deuteronomy is the one which is seen, within itself, to sum up the others. The people are poised to enter the land that God has promised them. Most of Deuteronomy is Moses' farewell speech. He is not able to go with them into the land, but he tells them everything he thinks they need to know and to keep close to them in the journey and life ahead. In our time and place, how do we articulate what we need to know and keep close to us for our journey and our life ahead?

Lord, I believe; help my unbelief

God has promised, God is promising, God will promise again. Over and over in the Book of Genesis, we hear that God has promised to Abram/Abraham and Sarai/Sarah descendants who will be as numerous as the stars in the heavens, descendants who will be a blessing to all the earth. Again and again we hear the promise. Abram/Abraham and Sarai/Sarah seem to have a hard time holding on to their belief in the promise, but God keeps making it. In terms of historical-critical scholarship, it is likely that this biblical text reflects the coming together of two or more sources or traditions about Abram/Abraham and Sarai/Sarah, which may partially explain what seems like a lot of repetition in this part of Genesis. It is a common biblical methodology to include multiple traditions or sources, even ones that disagree with each other. The text we have was ultimately put together intentionally, as an expression of faith. We read and strive to find meaning in it.

It is problematic that verses 13 to 16 are left out of this lectionary reading. Without them, verse 17, where the reading picks up again, does not make sense. Verses 1 to 18 really must be read right through. Another difficulty in dealing with this text is the temptation to dismiss verses 9 to 11 as primitive, pagan types of ritual. The ritual they describe has not been used for centuries to mark the power of our faith in God. However, it is important to try and discern what the meaning of such a ritual was in that time and place. What does it say as part of our canon of Scripture? We may not like it, not at all, but we cannot just dismiss it out of hand.

A helpful way to understand those verses comes from *The Abingdon Bible Commentary* of 1929. (Current biblical commentaries are not the only ones worth reading!)

> The covenant is ratified by means of a ceremony which is familiar to us also from other quarters: ... toward evening, as the sun is about to set, he falls into that peculiar state into which God throws men when

he wished to act directly through them. Though the sun is not yet below the horizon, the world grows suddenly and mysteriously dark to his senses, and in the midst of the gloom he sees Jehovah, in the form of fire, passing between the pieces of the victim. Doubtless previously he himself had walked between them, for the essence of this form of covenant ritual lay in the fact that both parties walked between the pieces of the victim. Thus they both entered into it, became part of it, formed one continuous living entity with it, and therefore with one another.[90]

Although this is not the way we would or should mark a covenant relationship, in that time and place it was a way of marking a signifi-cant relationship – in this case, a relationship between the Divine and the human. This is a good time to prayerfully reflect on the ways in which we mark and believe in the promises made to us by God.

90   *The Abingdon Bible Commentary*, Abingdon-Cokesbury Press, 1929, 230.

Loaves and fishes

The people are not to be deceived. Living life in the shadow of, in the confines of, in the boundaries prescribed by the Babylonian empire is costly in all the wrong ways. The people are buying into the "bread" of the empire, the way of life that the empire says is needed; it is costing them money and labour and yet it does not satisfy. The people are being called to turn instead to God: in God, as has always been the case, is the gift of life truly a gift. It is given freely from God's graciousness and it truly satisfies. It is the bread of life, indeed. It is wine and milk. These were the three elements needed for life.[91]

This is not the first time the people have heard about the gift and bread of life. God had made an everlasting covenant with David. God has not forgotten, even though the people seem to have been seduced by the powers and ideology of empire politics. It is a reminder that God's covenant is so awesome and so broad that the nations round about will see it and align themselves with Israel. (Babylon seemed to be an exception.)

So who are the wicked? Possibly the Babylonians, but more likely those who have been completely seduced by the ways of the empire. They are spending money and labour to be so accommodated to life in Babylon that they can barely hear the prophet's words, and will need much persuasion to return from the exile to their homeland.

Be careful where you go next with this passage. There is much talk in some Christian traditions these days about "empire," whether of the U.S. administration and the Canadian accommodation of it or of the deep, wide and broad materialism of our culture. I have heard, in church circles, many speeches, presentations and sermons on the evils of empire. Isaiah would agree, but only to a point. We must not

---

91   Wine may seem to be a kind of extra that points to beauty and joy in life, but in the times of Isaiah and Jesus, wine was an essential item. It often had to be added to unclean or unsafe drinking water in order to make that water drinkable and life-sustaining rather than life-destroying.

condemn empire without exploring the alternative: what God's vision and reality of the bread of life looks like and tastes like for all the people of the world. Isaiah specifically refers to the covenant with David. The people of that time would have known what the alternative to empire was. The opposite of empire is the reign of God, the justice and righteousness that are both individual and corporate. When encouraging people today to turn from the bread that does not satisfy to the rich food that is free gift, be specific about what that means for individuals, for the community, for the church and for the world. And how, specifically, are God's ways truly higher?

Now what?

Forty years of wandering in the wilderness after the Exodus are over. It is time for a new generation, a new leader, a homecoming into the land. Now what? These people have known only wandering. It was their parents' generation who knew both the slavery in Egypt and the grace of the Exodus, who did most of the grumbling in the wilderness and who experienced most of the leadership of Moses. The current generation was years younger when the ten commandments were received and the people made the golden calf. Moses, knowing all this, gathered this generation as well as their elders to hear him sum up the details and responsibilities of the people's relationship with their God, a summing up that is the book of Deuteronomy. Now the new generation is ready and has entered the land under the leadership of Joshua. This lectionary passage comes in the midst of a series of passages in the Book of Joshua that describe what these people do next.

The Jordan River has been crossed and the Ark of the Covenant is with the people. The males have just been circumcised; there having been no circumcision during the wandering in the wilderness. Somehow, in all those things, but particularly in the circumcision, God says that the disgrace of Egypt is rolled away from this new generation. The Bible abounds in interesting and intriguing and sometimes amusing uses of language. God has a sense of humour, and this is one of those places where it really shows. God has rolled away from the people the disgrace of Egypt, and so the place where God does so is named in a way that picks up the word "roll."

It is time to keep the Passover. The ritual that is so totally bound up with that great act of grace, the Exodus, is now to be kept in the new place by the new generation. They are to enact it, to bring together the words and actions of remembrance, hope and grace for themselves in what is the dawn of a new era. For the first time, the people eat the produce of the land. Then, since they no longer need it, the manna that sustained them in the wilderness ceases. The people are to live and grow in their new context. How frightening it all must have been at times! Completely new – and in some cases, painful – rituals and the awareness that their life was now integrated with the land, a land that neither they, nor their parents' generation, nor some generations before had ever seen.

It might seem less frightening if we continue reading verses 13 to 15. They use military imagery, to be sure, as was the norm for all people and places at that time, and is still, alas, the norm for many people and places in our time. But those verses also contain the assurance of the reality and presence of God. Joshua, like Moses, is told to take off his shoes for he is standing on holy ground.

To paraphrase the title of a book by theologian Paul Tillich, it takes "courage to be." The assurance that God is with us and can and does sanctify where we stand is bread for the journey indeed.

The point is ...

This lectionary passage illustrates very well the point and the passion that brought this book of mine into being. Although Old Testament commentaries (Walter Brueggemann's Isaiah commentary being one example) would designate verses 14 to 21 of chapter 43 of the Book of the Prophet Isaiah as a poetic unit, the lectionary chooses to begin the text at verse 16. By skipping verses 14 and 15, the specific context and people that were originally addressed by this text are, in a sense, removed. The text can then more easily serve a Christological purpose and focus on "the new thing" God is doing in verse 19 as the coming of God in Jesus Christ into the world. It is a Christian use of Scripture to interpret in that way. It is all right to do so as long as we do not disparage our Jewish sisters and brothers as a result. We can still make the same Christological point about Jesus Christ being the "new thing" for us, however, without removing from the text its historical grounding and context, as the lectionary does.

In verse 14, in the typical prophetic phrase "Thus says the Lord," God identifies himself as the Redeemer of Israel and then goes on to declare what that redemption will look like. The captivity in Babylon will be finished and the people of Israel set free.[92]

Verse 16, where the lectionary picks up the text, again starts with the prophetic declaration, with some very specific detail about the characteristics of God. Verse 19 declares that God is about to do a new thing, also with some very specific detail about the characteristics of that new thing. The "former things" or "things of old" are likely the Exodus or possibly the Creation. They might also be the earlier prophecies of the Book of the Prophet Isaiah, which spoke of the judgment

---

92   Many lectionary texts – often, though not always, those taken from the Books of the prophets Isaiah and Jeremiah – are grounded in the Babylonian exile in some way. This event had such an impact on the life, faith and being of the people, it was such a defining experience, that it shaped the identity and the relationship of the people to their God through the centuries.

to come. Whichever events the text is referring to, "The new thing is a massive miracle that transforms all of life."[93]

A final note about balance in the Old Testament. There are many places where the wondrous deeds and love of God in the Exodus and in Creation are recited. As Christians, we must remember this point and honour the history and faith of our Jewish sisters and brothers. The "new thing" that is being wrought must be seen in continuity with the past, for Christians and Jews, but also as a clear statement that biblical faith always points to the future, for Christians and Jews.

It would be very interesting, and faithful, to bring together a group of Christians and Jews to study these texts together. If the location of your congregation does not permit that, try a Bible study that uses both Jewish and Christian commentaries to look at the same Old Testament passages. See what is to be seen.

---

93 Walter Brueggemann, *Isaiah 40–66*, 59.

Lent 6/Palm/Passion Sunday – Isaiah 50:4-9a

See the entry for Palm/Passion Sunday, Year A.

Holy Thursday – Exodus 12:1-4 (5-10), 11-14

See the entry for Holy Thursday, Year A.

Good Friday – Isaiah 52:13–53:12a

See the entry for Good Friday, Year A.

"To boldly go ..."

God says, "I will rejoice in Jerusalem, and delight in my people." God will rejoice in the "city of peace." (In Hebrew, "Jerusalem" means "peace established.") The God of Creation is creating anew; that new Creation is both of the natural world and of human existence. Verse 17 flows from verse 16, with the "former things" (see Lent 5, Year C) forgotten. It is not that those "former things" should be completely forgotten; the faith of Jews and Christians is a deeply historical one that believes God acts decisively in linear history. But the former things should not impinge on the fact that the faith of Jews and Christians is one that points to and orients itself to the future. God can create, does create and is creating a new thing. God goes boldly into the future.

This new thing God is creating involves new life in a newly reconstituted city. Many biblical stories and much biblical theology revolve around cities. God's new Creation of a new Jerusalem, in relationship with a new heaven and a new earth, is very specific. The glorious new Creation will mean no more infant mortality. This reference in verse 20 is not a symbol or a metaphor. God's reign, the fulfillment of the reign of God begun in this time, will mean that babies no longer die. (Clearly, given the infant mortality rate in some countries in God's world, an infant mortality rate that our actions could also directly affect now if we so chose, the reign of God is not completed. God calls us as Christians, in the Resurrection light of Christ, to participate in the new creation of a time when babies do not die.)

Verses 21 to 22 tell us that the new Creation, the new city, will also be a place of economic stability. People will build houses and will get to live in what they have built. People will plant vineyards, work in the agricultural necessities of life, and eat of what they have planted and nurtured. They will not lose the rights to their homes and produce to others – political powers or economic corporations. All this will be in line with God's will for justice, expressed throughout Scripture, in Leviticus and Deuteronomy and the prophets. Jesus said that he came not to abolish the law but to fulfill it. When we use this passage from the Book of the Prophet Isaiah on Easter Sunday, that is exactly what we are proclaiming the Resurrection to mean.

Verse 23 then reiterates both the value of labour, which produces independence and the necessities of life, and the forward-looking vision of God for a new Creation in which the most vulnerable members of society, children, are not at risk. They will be blessed.

The city and nature will be in harmony. What is harmful, the serpent, will be deprived of its power. Things that seemed impossible, that seemed to be a permanent part of a violence inherent in the order of the world, will be newly and differently created. God is doing this work, but the biblical witness always states very clearly that we who are made in the divine image are called to be active participants in God's plan. In the words of the sermon that opened the German Kirchentag in 2007, "Do not be afraid. He is risen. You are witnesses." Go from this Easter Sunday service reverberating with the trumpets and the hallelujahs to be and act the new Creation.

The dignity of difference

Every biblical passage is a great passage to preach from, including every Old Testament passage. But in all three years of the lectionary, the
Old Testament passages chosen for Pentecost are particularly engaging. The New Testament passage from Acts 2 that is usually the focus
of this significant day in the life of the church is crucial to our life and
faith, but do not neglect the Old Testament lections for it. Let the
Old Testament lections inform it, just as the early church was always
informed by its previous texts, even and especially when it was in the
process of compiling the New Testament.

Here we have the very early peoples of the earth speaking the
same language and settling in the plain of Shinar, Babylonia. They
build a tower or ziggurat in the Babylonian model to reach up to God
and to stand as a sort of central rallying point for the peoples of the
earth. God is not amused. The people are, in a resonance with the
story of the Garden of Eden, trying to usurp the divine imperative.
God says, "Come, let us go down, and confuse their language there,
so that they will not understand one another's speech."[94] The people
are scattered and their language confused; the Hebrew word for this is
obviously related to "Babel" but also to "Babylonia."

This Tower of Babel passage is not the opposite of Acts 2, as is
sometimes claimed. The Acts passage does not involve restoring humanity to one language. Rather, because the Apostles are filled with
the Holy Spirit and speak various languages, each person hearing the
wondrous Gospel about God's deeds of power hears it in a recognizable and comprehensible way. The confusion of languages that occurs
in Genesis 11 is not so much a punishment, not so much something
that needs to be fixed by the coming of the Holy Spirit; rather, it is a

---

94   The fact that God says "us" is not a usage of the royal "we," however we might wish
     that it was. This style of speech carries over from a very early time in the faith and
     reflects belief in a kind of heavenly court. It might help to think of God's conversa-
     tions with the adversary in the Book of Job, or God's sending of messenger angels.

recognition by God of what is necessary, a recognition that being truly human means not striving incorrectly to become divine. It is also a proclamation of diversity. In Acts 2, that diversity continues.

In his book *The Dignity of Difference*, Rabbi Jonathan Sacks states his belief that difference is not a punishment of God, but a gift of God. It is a gift that enables us to be truly human as we are meant to be. We are not meant to strive to be divine: this would be a denial of our true humanity. But we are made in the divine image, and that is how and why we perceive diversity as a gift. As Scripture and Christian Trinitarian theology also so clearly articulate, God is truly diverse and in relationship in God's self. Although we are to worship no other gods before God, and that includes ourselves, we are to mirror God's own diversity. As Scripture in its entirety clearly witnesses, God is the God of all peoples and all places. We are to speak all those languages, to be scattered over the face of all the earth, and to proclaim the Dignity of Difference.

I was there

The Book of Proverbs is not an either/or but rather a both/and. Much of the book consists of short, pithy statements that express a truth about human behaviour – statements that are often very concrete and that focus on making people better at their relationships with family, colleagues and community. The book is ascribed to King Solomon as the epitome of wisdom, but the material in the book, the proverbs, comes from a variety of times in the life of the people of Israel, some of which are later than the time of Solomon.

A comparison of the Proverbs material with the literature of other peoples of the Ancient Near East shows that this part of our biblical tradition had the most in common with the traditions of other peoples. Some of the proverbs in the Book of Proverbs are the same as those found in similar texts of countries such as Egypt. This is not a bad thing. It shows that there was conversation and communication among countries and peoples, and that they shared some high points of their traditions, not just the lower points such as military alliances and battles.

The Hebrew word for proverb has, as Hebrew words always do, a multitude of meanings, encompassing "taunt," "oracle" and "allegory." All through the book, the reader is assured over and over again that "The fear of the Lord is the beginning of Wisdom." These taunts, oracles and allegories are completely grounded in the Lord of Creation and Life, who cares deeply in everlasting covenant for the details of our lives. Also throughout the book, Wisdom is personified as a female figure who is constantly calling out to people, trying to pull them into the correct way of being and doing. She is somehow part of the divine.

This is what we hear and read in the passage for this Trinity Sunday. A personified female Wisdom is calling and raising her voice. She is proclaiming to the people, to all who live, that they are to learn prudence and acquire intelligence. The lectionary passage then jumps forward to an explication of the relationship of Wisdom to divinity. That is no doubt why it was chosen for Trinity Sunday in the Christian tradition, but it is an explication that has much depth and resonance and meaning in the Jewish tradition as well. Wisdom is a Creation of God – God's very first Creation, in fact – and she is not just a passive creation. Wisdom was beside God, as God's first creation, throughout the whole process of creation, as the mountains were shaped, the heavens established, and the earth and fields and soil brought into being. The text calls her a "master worker" who was daily God's delight, rejoicing in the world and in the human race.

Given all this proclamation of the nature and role of Wisdom, as shown to us in the Book of Proverbs, it deserves much more attention in our preaching and in our lives.

And the winner is ...

In the world of real estate, the catchphrase is "Location, location, location." In dealing with biblical texts, the catchphrase is often "Context, context, context." When I use the word "context," I mean a number of things, depending on the nature of the text itself. I let the text guide which parts of the context need to be considered to deepen the meaning we are called to see and hear.

In this text from 1 Kings, the most important part of the context is the nature and depth of the drought and the famine. The broad text gives us this context, though not, alas, in the portion selected by the lectionary. The beginning of chapter 18 tells us that the drought had been going on for three years. The result was a famine – one of many famines we encounter in the biblical text. The famine was so severe that one of the Lord's faithful hid some prophets in a cave and provided them with bread and water, fearing for their lives at a time when Queen Jezebel took the lives of the Lord's prophets lightly. The famine was so severe that King Ahab sent that same man to scour the countryside to find enough grass to keep the livestock alive. We need to see this big picture to understand the power and magnitude of what will happen next.

We hear that King Ahab thinks that the dire situation is the prophet Elijah's fault, but Elijah points out that the fault lies with the king and his predecessors, who have forsaken the commandments of the Lord and followed the god/gods Baal.

Now we get to the contest. In God's corner is the prophet Elijah; in Baal's corner are the prophets of Baal. The contest is to see who will respond and bring the rain that is so desperately needed; whoever does this will be the God to follow. Read on through the details of how the contest is to be set up. (The limping that is mentioned in relation to the prophets of Baal is probably a kind of ritual dance.) When Baal does not respond to the call of his prophets, Elijah has a great line. "Cry aloud! Surely he is a god; either he is meditating, or he has wandered away, or he is on a journey, or perhaps he is asleep and must be awakened." Prophets are never meek and mild!

Listen to and look at what Elijah then does with the water, remembering that there was practically no water available. He not only makes the contest harder for God and for the parched people to watch, he uses the remaining precious water in full confidence that God will respond and bring rain. God responds with the fire appropriate to the contest, the people respond with the faith thus produced and then, in verse 41, God responds with rain and life is preserved.

This is not a text that encourages us to be profligate with scarce resources of creation – to think so is to have missed the point. The point is that it is God who is the Lord of Life and Creation, and is to be acknowledged as such. How do we do that acknowledging in our time and place?

Proper 5 – 1 Kings 17:8-16 (17-24)

Outside the box

Moving backwards through the biblical text we now encounter the story of the Widow of Zarephath.[95] The story reflects an earlier stage in the drought and famine context discussed in the previous entry. The Prophet Elijah, who is abruptly introduced for the first time in the text, declares that there will be a drought. It is important to be aware from the beginning, in working with this passage, that while Elijah is a prophet of Israel, the Widow of Zarephath is not an Israelite. (Zarephath was a Phoenician part of the land.) A careful reading of the text therefore nips in the bud the all-too-common stereotype that Israel was a rather closed nation and people, and that it was only with Jesus and especially the Apostle Paul that the message of God's love, faithfulness and challenge was made visible to people "outside the box." Although the people of Luke 4:25-26 seem to have forgotten, as we sometimes do, that God is truly the God of all peoples, Jesus reminds them of this story of the Widow of Zarephath. It is not a popular reminder. Even today, traditions that consider themselves very inclusive do not like to be told that they must also welcome traditions that they consider exclusive!

Elijah is to be given bread and water by the widow, in spite of the fact that she is gathering one last little bit of firewood so she can cook one last meal with the meagre amount of food she has before she and her son curl up and die of starvation. Elijah, using that common biblical phrase "Do not be afraid," tells her to cook for herself and her son, but first to feed him. She is assured that her supplies of food will never run out until the rain comes and the famine ends. How hard that must have been to believe! How many of us would have been able to be-

---

95 Remember that the lectionary matches Old Testament texts to New Testament ones, with the New Testament as the guide.

lieve these words and to put our lives and the lives of our family even further into peril?

It is a miraculous feeding by a prophet who moves in an atmosphere of miracle. (The text moves on from this story to relate the story of Elijah then resuscitating the son of the very same widow.) The miraculous feeding story, the miraculous resuscitation story combined with other stories about Elijah, such as his assumption into heaven at the end of his prophetic career, make it obvious why he, along with Moses, is considered a figure of faith who speaks to and about the wondrous nature of the Messiah.

How do we perceive God interacting in our time and place with people we do not see, cannot see, or struggle to see as part of our own community?

Signed, sealed, delivered

Here we have a classic biblical story about injustice. The powers that be want what they want, and when they are refused there is sulking, plotting, lying, deception and death. This is one of those passages that is easily related to our current context. God makes it clear through the words and actions of the Prophet Elijah that this injustice is unacceptable.

We must avoid reading this story in a self-righteous way, though. Not many of us write letters making false charges against someone who has something that we want, to the point that we are willing to have someone die so we can get it. But go deeper. Many of us who read this passage are indeed people of power in our societies. We have some wealth – never as much as we think we want, but some. We have health care, we have education, we have the ability to influence at least a couple of people in our world. And we are often willing to put our own wants ahead of justice for people who have barely enough to survive.

Through the Prophet Elijah, God makes it clear that there are consequences for acting unjustly. The lectionary concludes this passage at verse 21a, which does not serve to reinforce the biblical belief that consequences for injustice are corporate. But consequences are articulated, and if we read just a few verses further, the corporate nature of the consequences of injustice can be seen.

It is not faithful to the biblical text to use this passage as an opportunity to disparage Queen Jezebel and to make her into either some kind of a whore or a super villain, as has often been done. What she does is of course terrible. It is evil. (In another story in this biblical book, she kills prophets of the Lord. And her death in 2 Kings 9 is also terrible.) But compare the details of her deception, official lies and death-dealing actions with those of King David in the matter of Uriah the Hittite. The prophet Nathan's response to David's actions is similar to Elijah's response to King Ahab and Queen Jezebel. And yet, though there are consequences, David goes on ruling Israel. Jezebel, and such details as her applying makeup before her death in 2 Kings 9, has been used through many ages to condemn women. This is a misreading of the text for a misplaced agenda that has perpetrated a great deal of injustice. To avoid such an interpretation, hold this text in relationship with the story of King David and Uriah the Hittite. Power corrupts in an equal opportunity way.

Go, continue on your way

Moving backwards in the biblical text again, we read of Elijah killing prophets of Baal. Queen Jezebel is of the faith of Baal. She is married to King Ahab of the faith of the God of Israel in a kind of political marriage. Jezebel, not at all happy with Elijah, prophet of the God of Israel, who has killed the prophets of her faith, vows to kill him. Elijah is afraid; he flees. Not only is he afraid, he is discouraged, to the point of death. It was Elijah, after all, who proved in that great contest with the prophets of Baal that it is the Lord, the God of Israel, the God of Creation, the God of Life who has the power and might to bring rain and relieve drought and famine. In words and feelings that resonate closely with those of the prophet Jonah at the end of the book of his name, Elijah just wants to die. He has been zealous for God, he has said and done all the right things; there is no doubt of that, but still people seek his death.

After being ministered to by angels, a wondrous and miraculous part of the story that the lectionary lists as optional, Elijah gets himself to Sinai, the very same mountain where the ten commandments were given.

After some whining and complaining, he encounters the vital, dynamic, challenging presence of God. God did not manifest to the Prophet Elijah in the rock-breaking power of the wind, in the awesome shaking of the earthquake, or in the light and heat of the fire, though at other times God does manifest divinity in all those ways. Instead, God manifests the Divine Self to Elijah in silence and in a quiet voice, though even in that gentle manifestation, Elijah must shield his face from the power of God's glory. When Elijah makes his case about his tremendous and correct efforts on God's behalf, God's response is somewhat disturbing. God does not pat Elijah on the back or commend him or sympathize with him or empathize with him. God just tells him to get back at it. What follows this lectionary passage is a concrete and precise list of all the things that Elijah is to do.

On June 8, 2008, the sermon at Christ Church Deer Park in Toronto set out the fundamental message of the Bible as "Do not be afraid. Just believe. Now get up." Elijah would agree.

To cross on dry ground

In the Book of Joshua, chapter 4, the Ark of the Covenant crossed the River Jordan.[96] Now the prophets Elijah and Elisha are crossing this river on the way towards Elijah's ascension into heaven.

The books of 1 and 2 Kings are filled with narrative stories of the events of the kings and prophets of Israel over a period of about 500 years. These stories are built and told around the covenant of the people with their God. Whether the stories are historically accurate is irrelevant. Both the liberal and the literalist interpretations of history – both interpretations based on an understanding or not of events that observably happened exactly in the manner in which the text describes them – are constructions of the past few centuries. What matters is that these are stories of deep meaning. They detail the ways that, in the midst of the realities of politics, economics, relationships, power and lack of power, life is lived in covenant faithfulness to God or falls short of that covenant faithfulness.

The Prophet Elijah and his successor, Elisha, are on their way from Gilgal, a well-known ritual site, to Bethel, another well-known ritual site and the place of Jacob's dream. In an echo of the story of Ruth and Naomi, Elijah tells Elisha to leave him, but Elisha refuses. Keep reading through verses 3 to 5 for more of the flavour of the story.

It is his mantle, both the symbol of his calling by God and the physical manifestation of God's power in him – the very same mantle that Elisha will pick up and use to replicate his master's action – that Elijah uses to part the waters. Elisha wants a double portion of Elijah's spirit before Elijah goes from him; since Elisha is able to watch Elijah's ascension in the divine whirlwind, even though they are separated by a chariot and horses of fire, his wish is granted. Elisha is devastated by the loss of Elijah, and yet he then picks up the mantle of his mentor

---

96   This is not the time or place, but it would be interesting to look at all the biblical instances of the parting of waters and people crossing over on dry ground. What are we to understand from those stories?

and replicates Elijah's action, making the point that the authority of God, the role of God's prophet, now truly rests in him. Although it is not a call story exactly, this is a story about vocation. It is a story about a journey that ends in a way that Elisha does not want it to end. He knows, however, that the mantle of prophecy is now his to bear, just as it is our role and authority in our world to proclaim faithfulness to God's will for peace and justice, to bear the mantle of proclamation of covenant and its promises from God and its requirements of us. As always, in proclaiming God's will for peace and justice, be specific for your time and place. Is it a ministry of presence in the face of anti-Semitism or racism that your congregation is called to; a ministry on behalf of the homeless; starting a reading program in a local school for children who need extra care; holding the hand of the dying and suffering; reminding all and sundry that God is love, grace, mercy and forgiveness? Pick up the mantle.

'Tis a gift to be simple

Read the story and go lightly in terms of commentary on it. It is, like the previous entry, a story of the people of Israel told in the light of their covenant with their God. It gives us many details of life in that time and place, some of which resonate with us still. It is a story of the people of Israel and the prophet of Israel, Elisha, but it is also a story of people in a nation around Israel and God's relationship to them. God heals even if the person in question is a little resistant to the methodology of the healing and must be convinced by a piece of common sense that is in line with the Book of Proverbs. It is being made clear in the history and faith development of the people that God is not contained or containable.

The lectionary text ends with the healing of Naaman the Aramean, but the story goes on. It is a vivid story that ends with a moral. For some reason, we in the Christian tradition are very fond of morals. We like sermons and particularly children's stories to end with one. Yet most of our biblical stories do not have a moral. This one does, however, as we will find out if we read to the end of chapter 5. A suggestion for "preaching" this text is to have different members of the congregation be the voices in the story. Afterwards, reflect on what God is saying to the church today.

The herdsman of Tekoa

The Book of the Prophet Amos is one of the books of the twelve minor prophets. Unlike Isaiah and Jeremiah, who are part of the priestly upper class, Amos was a herdsman. He came from the village of Tekoa in Judah, the southern part of Israel. In spite of the fact that Amos was from the south, or perhaps because Amos was from the south, God called him to go to the north to prophesy. He prophesied during the reigns of two kings, Uzziah and Jeroboam, whose reigns were ones of relative peace and prosperity. Amos afflicted the comfortable at the call of God, because the economic prosperity was not being shared. In fact, the time of peace and prosperity was accompanied by a huge amount of social corruption, as the Introduction to the Book of the Prophet Amos in the New Revised Standard Version tells us.

Amos's prophetic ministry probably lasted only about 10 years, but during that time he was able to make himself very unpopular. It was unpopular to pronounce judgment on the northern kingdom and insist that true faith must and would lead to social justice. One could not be rich and prosperous and think that one was righteous and faithful in God's eyes while others suffered from poverty and injustice.

Prophets often spoke and dealt in images of great vibrancy. They also proclaimed their word from God through actions that were signs and symbols, as the Prophet Isaiah does in chapter 20 of his book. In this text, Amos uses the image of a plumb line. A vision from God had shown him, through this common method of ensuring that walls were built straight, that the people of the north were not, in effect, straight, as they were called to be. They were not measuring up and there were going to be repercussions from God.

This message did not sit well with the powers that be. Amaziah, the priest of Bethel, objected vigorously. At this point in the history and faith of the people of Israel there was controversy around the site of Bethel. When the nation of Israel had split into north and south after the reign of King Solomon, the south had maintained the worship of God in the Temple in Jerusalem. The kings of the north, however, had re-established two older northern shrines for worshipping God. Of course, the south did not accept the reinvigorated shrines of Bethel and Dan as legitimate. This background information illustrates how unwelcome in the north Amos, a prophet from the south, would have been. Amaziah, the priest at Bethel, accuses him of conspiracy against the king of the north and sends him packing. The trouble is, for the north, all that dire stuff that Amos said came to pass. Prophets always declare what will happen, but also always hold out the possibility of repentance. The north did not rectify its social injustice. The country of Assyria invaded.

Who are the prophets in our time and place to whom we do not want to listen?

Sandals and silver

John Sawyer's fascinating book *The Fifth Gospel* has deeply influenced my understanding of the use of Scripture in the church through the centuries. The premise of his book is that throughout our whole Christian history and faith we have used and emphasized different parts of Scripture, even different verses of the same book. In the time, place and context in which I write, the Book of the Prophet Amos, particularly the verses that make up this reading, are popular with those who see direct parallels between social injustice in Amos's time and in our time. These verses, therefore, may be more familiar to us than some of the other lectionary texts we encounter. We live in a time of rampant social injustice on a national and global scale. Have we responded to the prophetic call of Amos, though?

As preachers, we need to approach this text with fear and trembling and be very specific in our response to it. The Bible and the prophets continually comment on politics. So does Jesus. We trample on the vulnerable when we do not work for affordable housing. We buy the poor for silver and the needy for a pair of sandals when we cut back on health care. We bring to ruin the poor of the land when we buy from large corporations rather than supporting local producers and craftspeople. The United Nations' Millennium Development Goals could have a significant positive effect on the lives of the poor and oppressed globally.[97] Through this initiative, poverty, suffering and injustice, all themes of the Prophet Amos, can be reduced. Speak about these vital goals to your congregation. Speak about the United Nations. In spite of its flaws, it is the only global body that brings nations together to attempt common action on behalf of the widows, orphans and sojourners of God's world.

The image that begins this passage is a play on the Hebrew words for "summer fruit" and "end." This vivid image is connected through the sound of the language to the message of the prophet. Painful as it may be, explore the connection.

---

97 http://www.un.org/millenniumgoals/ (accessed June 18, 2008).

What's in a name?

Hosea is one of the twelve minor prophets, the one whose book stands first of the twelve.[98] Hosea's prophetic ministry, as a prophet of the north to the north, followed that of Amos. Hosea's message has basically the same content as Amos's, but the balance is a little different. Both prophets cry out for the social justice that is the will of God and the faithful expression of liturgy and ritual. Both prophets cry out that judgment is on the way because of the lack of that social justice. Both prophets know that God truly, deeply loves the people and hopes for their faithful response. Without that faithful response, repercussions are on the way at the hands of the invading nation Assyria.

God tells Hosea to act out the message, so he marries Gomer. Gomer may have been a prostitute in the way that we understand the term today, but likely was a temple prostitute, a ritual part of the worship of the non-Israelite peoples of the land. Such a possibility makes Hosea's point more clearly than our modern understanding of the term: the temple prostitutes were part of the fertility rituals, part of the local worship of the local gods, and therefore antithetical to the worship of the God of the people of Israel. It would be implied, therefore, that the people had slipped in their fulfillment of the command to have no other gods before God.

The names of the resulting children of the marriage of Hosea and Gomer are then signs and symbols of the message of the prophet. Names are always significant in the biblical text, and these are especially pertinent: Jezreel (God sows), Lo-ruhamah (Not pitied) and Lo-ammi (Not my people).

---

98 The reason for the ordering is now lost to us, except for the obvious conclusion with the Book of the Prophet Malachi. The Book of the Prophet Malachi, whose name means "my messenger," concludes the Old Testament and sets up the transition to the New Testament and the proclamation of the Messiah for Christians. The messenger, in Christian theology, comes to prepare the way.

The "and yet" begins in verse 10. The behaviour and unfaithfulness of the people have been dire. The symbol of Hosea and Gomer's marriage relationship gets more dire in a subsequent passage. Yet it is crucial for the prophet to also proclaim that God still stands by the covenant. The language used here immediately brings to mind the language of covenant with Abraham in the Book of Genesis. The future will still proclaim that the people are the children of the living God. No matter how dire the circumstances, no matter how unrepentant the people, with God there is always faithful covenant and hope in love.

How often has our behaviour made us seem to the world as if we are not the people of God? God shakes the holy head but then calls us back anyway.

Bands of love

This passage from the Book of the Prophet Hosea contains lovely, warm, intimate language portraying God as a doting parent who loves Israel in spite of itself and who is intimately involved in Israel's life and development, even when the people keep trying to turn away. The ever real repercussions are spelled out, but the ever real bands of love are passionately portrayed. It is easy to like this passage, but it must have been hard for the Prophet Hosea to utter it and hard for whoever eventually wrote it down. Hosea lived and prophesied in the last days of the existence of the northern kingdom of the nation of Israel. The conquering nation, Assyria, was visibly on the move and northern Israel had six kings in 25 years. In those times of insecurity, bleakness and dread, Hosea comforted the afflicted.

As is often the case in Old Testament texts, the primary image used for the wondrous love of God is that of the Exodus. God's great act of grace in freeing the people from slavery is remembered and held up. Yet in spite of that great act of grace, the people turn to the worship of foreign gods that may not even be real. Apparently, we hear, such worship involved sacrifice and the offering of incense. Could the "idols" bear any relation to the golden calf that the people of the Exodus make, or statues used at the two shrines of Dan and Bethel to rival the Temple in Jerusalem? The worship of calves or bulls is a long-standing tradition in many cultures, perhaps because of the association of these animals with power and potency.

The repercussion for the unfaithful behaviour is going to be a return to the kind of conditions people had to endure when they were in Egypt, but this time Assyria will be the overlord. Violence and destruction are inevitable – both of the cities and of the systems that turn the people away from God. And yet, you can hear the ache in God's voice, the agonized resistance to giving up Israel, even in the name of God's own justice and call for righteousness. No matter how deep or groundless Israel's rejection, God's compassion grows warm and tender. God's justice demands justice, but even in the face of the righteous call for the just repercussions, God's love overwhelms. Always, eventually, the children return. They return to the sound of God's voice, like the dove in the time of Noah, with peace and security and freedom.

The people were worshipping idols that represented power and potency, something very familiar to us in our time and place. The names of the idols have changed in 2,500 years, but what they represent has not changed. Today we call them nuclear weapons, jam-packed schedules for ourselves and our children, wealth disguised as the value of personhood and personal convenience over environmental health.

Let us argue it out

The first verse of the first chapter of the Book of the Prophet Isaiah, that book of Old Testament prophecy that has so much meaning for Christians that John Sawyer calls it "the fifth gospel," begins by situating the time and place in which the prophet spoke. Although there are always deep recurring themes, biblical prophecy is not an abstract concept whose words and meanings can always simply fit any time and place. The biblical prophets were keen observers of their peoples and nations, keen observers of what was happening on the political and religious fronts. Although they are not fortune-tellers, their prophecies can apply to our time. That is the case because human beings tend to wallow in particular sins, not because the biblical prophecies are "one size fits all." Biblical prophets name names and name places, as we see in this opening verse of the Book of the Prophet Isaiah. The prophet has a vision, a common feature of the prophetic persona. In that vision he sees something concerning the south of the nation, Judah, and its capital, Jerusalem.

The Book of the Prophet Isaiah marks a new beginning in biblical writing. It was written down (at least some of it) fairly soon after it was spoken. The prophecies of Isaiah were uttered and written during the dark time in which the nation of Israel was in decline and the might of the superpower Assyria was expanding. Isaiah (or his school of disciples) afflicts the comfortable with the news of the coming disaster, which he believes is a result of the people's unfaithfulness to God and their lack of understanding of God's call for social justice. He, or his disciples, then comfort the afflicted during the exile in Babylon and point to a return to the land. Both streams of prophecy are interwoven throughout the book, which cannot be divided into First, Second and Third Isaiah as easily as was thought in recent years.

In verses 10 to 20 of this first chapter, the bulk of the lectionary reading for this Sunday, the prophetic writing certainly does not mince words. A few further pieces of context will be helpful in preaching the Gospel through these verses. The cities of Sodom and Gomorrah, which appear in Genesis 18, are reviled there for their lack of hospitality and their lack of righteous inhabitants. Also, Isaiah may have been a priest in the Temple. Although we can and have read these kinds of prophetic verses as a push for a complete abolition of the sacrificial system, we do well to remember that Isaiah never denounces the Temple and it sacrifice system. The message of verse 17 is the lynchpin. Empty ritual worship, of which we, too, may be guilty, is not pleasing to God. We, too, are to learn to do good, to seek justice, rescue the oppressed, defend the orphan, plead for the widow. Then our sins, too, will be washed clean.

If listening to a glorious organ postlude by Purcell is not held together with ensuring that all children, near and far, have the resources they need to learn to read, Isaiah will be afflicting us.

The vineyard of the coming of the Lord

God is at the holy wit's end. The case is clearly, articulately and poetically stated that God has done everything possible to enable the people of Israel to be and do all they can. God had the right to expect a harvest of righteousness and faithfulness. God expected justice, but saw bloodshed; righteousness, but heard a cry! And so there will be repercussions. The conquering invader Babylonia is coming.

Speaking theologically about the nature of repercussions requires careful reflection and prayer. In ages past, the church sometimes said that a disaster, such as the plague, could be sent by God as a direct punishment for bad behaviour. This kind of theology leads to conclusions that are untenable from a biblical point of view. The biblical witness, often best seen in the Psalms, tells us that the rain falls on the just and the unjust; in the Book of Job and elsewhere, it explores the question of innocent suffering. We resist believing that, for instance, newborn babies suffer because of anything they or their parents have done. Likewise, God does not use genocide or famine to punish a nation or people. Then how do we understand these words of God in this text in Isaiah? (Here we are speaking of God's actions, not natural disasters or human acts.)

In biblical thought, everything is a part of God. If God is truly all-powerful, then anything and everything must come from God. At the same time, God is a God of justice, which means there will be repercussions for injustice. Keep reflecting as a community on this deep question and keep praying about it.

It is a difficult question, and so it should be. Difficult questions are real, and we must face them.

Proper 16 – *Jeremiah 1:4-10*

See the entry for Epiphany 4, Year C.

Get your priorities straight

"Hear the word of the Lord" – this classic prophetic formula authenticates the one who utters it and the word itself. So this passage from the Book of the Prophet Jeremiah begins before moving on to a rhetorical question: What did the ancestors of the people find to be wrong in God that caused them to move away from God and go after worthless things? It is easy for each of us to list all the things we think God would consider worthless in our society – such as our obsession with electronic devices, the quest for wealth and power, and so on. Yet our faith tradition calls us to gather regularly *in community* to pray and reflect together on the deep question of what it means to be faithful to God, as well as on what is worthless in our world.

Reading further in the passage, part of the definition of "worthless" is somehow connected to the fact that the people have simply forgotten or are ignoring all that God has done and is doing for them. The people are not connecting God with that wondrous act of grace that was the Exodus. The rulers have transgressed, and sectors of society are pursuing things that do not profit, a theme that we saw in Isaiah 55 (Lent 3, Year C). Verse 9 raises the same kind of difficult question we struggled with in the previous entry. After the people are to see if any other nation has behaved as badly as they have, there is a call for the heavens, for the natural world, to be appalled. Note this connection between people's actions and the natural world that is so foundational to the biblical way of thinking.

In dealing with this passage homiletically, include a recital of all God's great acts of grace in our history and lives of faith, as many Christian traditions do in the Great Thanksgiving prayer during the Eucharist. Or in the Prayers of the People, include lots of prayers of thanksgiving instead of just making petitions.

Pottery class

Chapters 18 and 19 of the Book of the Prophet Jeremiah contain powerful narratives about the contemporary relationship God has with the people. These chapters use the image of pottery, a common household object at the time. The story and the image are vivid. A creative way to delve into this passage in a liturgy that has allowance for some informality would be to invite a potter to join you. Working with a potter's wheel as the Scripture passage is being read, he or she can model what Jeremiah sees. Pottery making was an everyday activity; suddenly the congregation views it, and perhaps some of the everyday activities of our lives, in a new way.

This passage raises questions we explored in the entry for Proper 15, Year C. It also highlights several other key theological points, all through that powerful visual image of pottery. It reminds us of the freedom of God. God is never at our beck and call, though sometimes, especially in our prayers, we may slide into that way of thinking. What's more, God can and does change the divine mind. If a particular people or nation corrects its behaviour, God changes in response. In many of the stories in the books of Genesis and Exodus, the personal and passionate intervention by a figure such as Moses dramatically causes God to reconsider a planned action or response to the people's behaviour. There is clearly a vital and dynamic relationship between God and humanity. God is both totally other from us and totally involved with us. What does not change is the reality that God's response to us as human vessels is always based on the absolute truth that God is God of justice and faithfulness. Passages such as this one call us to reflect deeply on where in our world God may be acting in ways that we personally find disconcerting, but that are ways of deep justice.

The windy city

In no way.can this passage be classified as a text filled with sweetness and light. In fact, upon hearing this passage, some people may wonder why they came to church this Sunday. They gave up going to the cottage or camping to hear this?

In the Middle East, a hot wind is not a good thing. It can, in fact, bring death; the text tells us that this wind is too strong even to be a winnowing or cleansing wind. It is a wind connected with God's judgment on the people – God's foolish people who are skilled in doing evil and do not know how to do good. God is angry. Various parts of the land and the cities are quaking and in ruins as a result. What the people have done to merit such anger is typical in the prophetic literature – they have put their faith in alliances and idols and things that are worthless, rather than in God the Creator and Lord of Life. They have lived in ways that promoted injustice rather than justice for God's poor and vulnerable ones, which is divine will.

The verses at the end of this passage are even more difficult than the early ones. (See also the previous entry.) In verse 28, we hear that God has spoken. God has a purpose; God has not relented and will not turn back. The congregation is definitely wondering now why it got out of bed this morning. But in the last line of verse 27, God says, "I will not make a full end."

The calling, both biblically and for us, is one of justice and deep relationship with our God. God is a God of justice. When justice is not being served, God must speak out. In this passage, Jeremiah is working in the "afflict the comfortable" mode, but he also prophesies in the "comfort the afflicted" mode. He provides what the people need to hear to maintain their belief in that divine balance between justice and mercy, righteousness and being cherished by God.

No balm in Gilead

"Summertime and the living is ..." well, not entirely easy, if your life is anything like mine. But it is sometimes possible to squeeze out a few nanoseconds for reading. One book I read recently was Karen Armstrong's *The Great Transformation*. Among the many interesting, challenging and startling things she says there, Armstrong reminds us that in many cultures and traditions in the ancient world, the gods that were worshipped were often conceived and perceived to be arbitrary and uncaring towards humanity. The myths of the Greek gods certainly fall into this category. This is never the case with the God of Israel. The God of Israel gets exasperated with the people, to be sure, and gets angry with their unfaithfulness and injustice. The God of Israel is even known to rant about the people's whining, stating clearly the repercussions of such bad behaviour. But the God of Israel is in eternal covenant with the people; loving them truly, madly, deeply; always eager, encouraging and enthusiastic; wanting the people to straighten up and fly right in terms of faithful worship, which is intertwined with just behaviour. The God of Israel cares about the people. That is the message we hear flowing through the Prophet Jeremiah in this Sunday's passage.

The repercussions for the people's bad behaviour this time is that the Babylonians are coming. God does not want it or will it, but they are coming. This raises a profound theological point, as biblical texts always do. Asking how history might be different if the people had worshipped God in faithfulness and truth and truly cared for the widows, orphans and sojourners in the land is to ask the wrong question. The people have not been all they were created in the image of God to be. The world has not been all that God meant when God declared it to be good. The Bible believes that these things are connected. It is best not to push too hard from the rational methodology of the Enlightenment period at that connection.

The grief of God, through the prophet, for what is to befall the people is real and visceral. God hurts and mourns and weeps. God's heart is sick. God longs for healing for the people. In the poetic form of a hymn, God longs for the balm of which Gilead was famous (Genesis 37:25). In the context of the whole witness of the biblical faith, the response is that, yes, "There is a balm in Gilead."

Just when you think it cannot get any worse ...

When the Prophet Jeremiah receives this particular word from the Lord, the army of the king of Babylon is besieging Jerusalem. Whether, like St. Augustine on his deathbed when the army of the barbarians was besieging Hippo, Jeremiah could actually hear the battering at the gates, we do not know. But even though Jeremiah had seen this coming and had been prophesying it loud and long, it would still have been terrifying. To make matters worse, Jeremiah's prophesying of the coming disaster had made him so unpopular that he was under lock and key, confined in the court of the guard in the palace of King Zedekiah of the southern part of the nation, Judah. The verses omitted by the lectionary contain the content of the prophecy; these verses give a deeper understanding of both the nature of what is to occur and why it would make Jeremiah so unpopular.

In those dire and depressing circumstances, the word of the Lord comes to Jeremiah and tells him what to do. What he is to do is unusual – we may even think it crazy – but it is in line with the prophetic, biblical message and hope. Jeremiah is to buy a field. In the bulk of the verses of this lectionary reading, we get more details of land transactions in the sixth century BCE than we probably thought possible or wanted to know. According to the land transaction system of that time and place, and in a manner not unlike the marriage system as described in the latter half of the Book of Ruth (Year B, Proper 27), it seems that Jeremiah has first dibs on the land his cousin was offering for sale. Verses 6 to 8 of this passage illustrate a major feature of biblical prophecy: the way to know that a prophecy is indeed the word of the Lord is if what is prophesied actually happens. Clearly, in verses 6 to 8, this is the case. Jeremiah hears that his cousin is going to offer him the field for purchase, and it is so. Then Jeremiah knew that it was the word of the Lord, pulled out his cash, got deeds signed, rounded up witnesses and made sure the deeds were properly recorded and stored.

(The process does not sound much different from our current process for such transactions.)

The point of the land transaction business is found in verse 15, the last verse of the reading. What Jeremiah is to do falls into the category of prophetic sign/actions. The situation, although dire, is not hopeless. The army of the king of Babylon may be besieging the city. They will take the city and will force many of the people into exile. But, "thus says the Lord of hosts, the God of Israel: Houses and fields and vineyards shall again be bought in this land." The land has a future. Life will return to what is normal, more or less, and people will live more or less normal lives in the land. This powerful message of hope is given just as it seemed that things could not get much worse, for Jeremiah or for the people as a whole. Hope it is. Life it is. This is the will and word of the Lord.

To lament is human

To lament is both human and biblical, but it is something we resist today. Laments are depressing, and many people want sermons that are filled with hope and light.

Yet lamentation is very much a part of our biblical tradition, not only in this book but throughout the biblical text, especially the Book of Psalms. This short book of Lamentations is grim, dire and depressing, and so it should be. It was written in response to the fall of Jerusalem to the Babylonians and the complete destruction of the Temple, the physical, earthly centre of the people's faith. This was a crushing and heartbreaking series of events. To make a modern comparison, it is what we might feel if Rome, Canterbury, Istanbul and Riverside Church in New York were simultaneously destroyed. The author of Lamentations is anonymous, but the book has been traditionally ascribed to the Prophet Jeremiah. It comes from his time period, he witnessed the events it describes, and he obviously had some relationship with the writing and preserving of texts.

The book as a whole recognizes that the destruction of Jerusalem and the Temple, if seen as a judgment, is righteous and just. This book begins in deep lament and ends with repentance. Although the book indeed is one of lament, it also appeals for mercy in the deep belief that "the steadfast love of the Lord never ceases, his mercies never come to an end; they are new every morning; great is your faithfulness. 'The Lord is my portion,' says my soul, therefore I will hope in him."

Walter Brueggemann has written widely on the nature of biblical lament and the crucial role it plays for human beings.[99] Frederick Buechner has written much on the nature of being honest about pain and reality, and how human beings must admit to and accept the fact that there is darkness in our lives, both as individuals and corpo-

---

99 Walter Brueggemann's *Ichabod Toward Home: The Journey of God's Glory* (Grand Rapids, MI: William B. Eerdmans, 2002) is but one example.

rately.[100] The biblical author of Lamentations knows this truth: only by admitting the existence of and walking through the valley of the shadow of death can we truly feel and accept the truth of God's mercy, and live in and with a hope that is not sweetness and light but sustaining bread for the journey. Only then can we proclaim with the poets and prophets of our faith, "Surely goodness and mercy shall follow me all the days of my life, and I shall dwell in the house of the Lord my whole life long."

100 Frederick Buechner, "The Two Stories," in *Secrets in the Dark: A Life in Sermons* (New York: HarperOne, 2007), 82.

Settle down!

The word of the Lord is embedded in a letter that the Prophet Jeremiah sent from Jerusalem to those who had been exiled in Babylon. Through this letter, the God of Israel directly addressed the people, declaring that it was he, their God, who had sent them into exile. The point of the letter, though, is to tell the elders, priests, prophets and all the people taken into exile how they were to spend their time there. They are to settle down. They are to build houses for themselves, feed themselves through their own gardens, intermarry with the Babylonians and have children with them. But there is more – much more. The people in exile are to "seek the welfare of the city" and to pray for it.

The lectionary passage ends there, but reading on a few verses lets us know that some prophets and diviners are spreading a different message. The text implies that these prophets and diviners are saying that the exile will be over soon. Yet they are not sent by God and are not to be listened to. God is clear, however, that the exile is going to last 70 years. (Whether 70 years is historically accurate does not matter; numbers are often used in symbolic ways in the Bible. The point of the text is to proclaim how the people should live while in exile.)

Karen Armstrong, in her book *The Great Transformation*, discusses this passage from the Book of the Prophet Jeremiah in some depth. She sees it as a development in the faith tradition, saying,

> If [the exiles] could come through this time of trial, they would develop a more interior spirituality. [God] would make a new covenant with them … Having lost everything, some of the people of Israel were turning within. Each individual must take responsibility for him- or herself; they were starting to discover the more interior and direct knowledge of the Axial Age.[101]

---

101 Karen Armstrong, *The Great Transformation: The Beginning of our Religious Traditions* (Toronto: Alfred A. Knopf, 2006), 170.

Historically, we know that the exiles were well treated in Babylon, but it was major dislocation nonetheless. For Armstrong, as the above quote indicates, the Book of the Prophet Jeremiah, in this passage and in its broader context, reveals a developing awareness that relationship with God, while often greatly deepened and aided by ritual and location, might not be dependent on those realities. Life as the people of the God of Israel is to be lived without resentment and with the conquering powers. Most important, it is to be lived as the people of God. The people will end up back in the land, though reading ahead in the Books of Ezra and Nehemiah shows that this life will not be entirely smooth. They can and must be the people of God wherever they are.

Sour grapes – not!

One of the wondrous and challenging realities in preaching the Gospel through the Old Testament texts is that some passages, which on the surface seem to be challenging, turn out to be less difficult after we delve into them. Others, which on the surface seem easier to preach on, turn out to be more difficult than we first thought. This lectionary passage, in my opinion, falls into the latter category. We risk preaching this passage in a way that can lead to anti-Semitism or anti-Judaism. If we say that God is creating a new covenant to replace the old covenant that God made with the people of Israel, and that the people of Israel broke, we denigrate the covenant with Israel and our Jewish sisters and brothers. If we say that those earlier ways of understanding covenant and ritual are no longer the way to understand relationship with God, and that it is now all about our personal relationship with God, we assert the superiority of Christianity over Judaism and the replacement of Judaism with Christianity. For too long, this approach has been used to speak of the Christian church as a new kind of Israel in the mind and heart of God.

Verse 30 is frequently mentioned in any preaching on this passage because it puts forth the concept of individual responsibility. The text itself contrasts this concept of individual responsibility with the concept of corporate responsibility, which is set out in the parable quote of verse 29.[102] Verse 34 then goes on to tell us that God is remaking the covenant with the people of Israel: "I will put my law within them, and I will write it on their hearts; and I will be their God, and they shall be my people." This is not a replacement of the covenant with Israel; God, who is already in covenant with the people of Israel, is remaking, re-forming the nature of that covenant, but God always remains faithful. In this lectionary reading we see God ensuring that all

---

102 Thomas Cahill, in his book *The Gifts of the Jews*, discusses this notion of individual responsibility as one of the great contributions of Judaism to the Western world.

the people of Israel will know the Holy One. God is forgiving iniquity and remembering sin no more, re-expressing the relationship that is always there.[103]

This is a passage of Holy Scripture written by a Jew for Jews, and known by our Messiah, Jesus Christ, who was himself a Jew. The God of Israel has always had a very personal and vital relationship with the people of Israel. (See the entry for Proper 22, Year C, about deep hope.) Although the people broke the covenant, God never did. The law as guide and instruction and gift of grace stands. The faith now understands the law to be deep within the people. God is forgiving, again. The day of judgment has passed, as Jeremiah said it would. The hope is real, as Jeremiah said it was. Thanks be to God!

---

103 For further comment on covenant and the reality that God is in covenant with both Jews and Christians according to the biblical text, take a dance through "The Two Covenants" section in the Introduction.

Dream keeper

My children used to be drawn, in a kind of horrified fascination, to Judith Viorst's illustrated book entitled *Alexander and the Terrible, Horrible, No Good, Very Bad Day*.

Much of the ministry of the Prophet Joel must have felt like a terrible, horrible, no good, very bad day much of the time. Joel, whose name means "The Lord is God," was a prophet in Israel during a severe plague of locusts. It is difficult to date the time of his prophetic ministry – it may have been before the fall of the northern part of the kingdom to Assyria and the fall of the southern part of the kingdom to Babylonia, but plagues of locusts were a devastating and all too frequent occurrence in the Ancient Near East. In this subsistence agricultural economy, such a plague could and often did mean starvation. The Prophet Joel saw one particular plague of locusts, along with a severe drought, as an indicator of what he called the coming "great and terrible day of the Lord." He saw this coming day, in no uncertain terms and in some pretty brutal language in the first few chapters of the book, as a punishment on both Israel and its neighbours for the usual list of suspect behaviours – injustice and unfaithfulness.

Verses 30 and 31 remind us of a key biblical point – God's relationship with humanity is interconnected with the natural world, which God also created. This understanding is much more than a jumping-off point for a worthy sermon on climate change. God is the God of all Creation: and what happens in the relationship between God and humanity is never separate from Creation. But there is always the opportunity for repentance and the assuring call to "Return to the Lord, your God, for he is gracious and merciful, slow to anger, and abounding in steadfast love …" (2:13). This lectionary passage proclaims, after the warning of the dire coming of the judgment of the Lord and the call to repentance, God's gracious response. The drought will be over. The damage caused by the locusts will be repaired. God's relationship with the people (and, it is intimated, with all people) will be permanently restored.

In preaching the Gospel (and I do mean *the* Gospel, not one of the four gospels), it is important to emphasize that the spirit is poured out on *all* people. The Spirit of God is not contained by any of us, as this text makes clear. The sons and daughters and those enslaved by the forces of power in our world can and will prophesy and dream dreams and see visions. A question for discernment in any sermon and in congregational/parish life is what those dreams and visions and prophecies look like. The next question is how we work together with God for their fulfillment.

The right question?

Each year, as part of my Lenten discipline, I read through Sir John Polkinghorne's wonderful little book *Searching for Truth: Lenten Meditations on Science and Faith*. One entry, entitled "The Right Question," follows an entry entitled "The Wrong Question." One way Polkinghorne defines the "right" question – the kind of question that we as people of faith should be asking of ourselves and our world – is whether it is a question that gets to the heart of things, a question whose answer will illuminate what is going on in a situation, in the world. The Prophet Habakkuk, in the short book by his name, asks just that sort of right question. It is a bit of a mystery to me why this book of prophecy is so little used or remembered in the church: the question Habakkuk asks is profound.

The question he asks is also often asked by the Psalmists. In a way, it is the flip side of the question that reverberates through the Book of Job. Job asks why the innocent suffer; Habakkuk asks why the wicked prosper. There is trouble, violence and injustice, and it seems that God is not listening to the people's cries for help. The wicked seem to be surrounding the righteous. It is hard to imagine anyone who has ever read Habakkuk trying to claim that the Bible is irrelevant! Many of us wonder on an almost daily basis why the wicked prosper.

Having asked the question, Habakkuk then stands by for the answer. God is not a "tame" God, to use the term C.S. Lewis rejects for the messianic Aslan the Lion in his Narnia saga. God's answers and responses to our questions and cries, as Job discovered, too, are not always the rational, tidy, immanent answers that we think we want. God answers Habakkuk that there will be vindication in the end. In other words, God's purpose is for justice, and ultimately, there will be justice. Some patience may be required in the interim, but the righteous live by faith. Much as we might like instant solutions to the problems and injustices we see, we are sustained by faith and by being in the community of faith for the long haul. This is a key point to make in our current context. One reason, I believe, that our response to various world crises, from global warming to HIV/AIDS, has been so little, so late, is that the problems and injustices seem so large and overwhelming. In the West, we are a quick-fix culture. This text from Habakkuk is a wondrous reminder that we are to protest injustice, to work alongside of God for God's ultimate justice, and to be sustained by faith. Habakkuk 3:18 proclaims, "I will rejoice in the Lord; I will exult in the God of my salvation."

Lieutenant-General Roméo Dallaire, who witnessed the Rwandan genocide, says that it will take 60 years of our patient but active participation to bring peace to the Great Lakes district of Africa. Blessed are the peacemakers.

Fear not, for behold ...

Although the prophecies of the Prophet Habakkuk cannot be dated with any certainty by scholars, those of the Prophet Haggai can be dated precisely to the year 520 BCE. Cyrus of Persia, who had become the leader of the new superpower in the Ancient Near East, had allowed and encouraged the Israelite exiles in Babylon to return home. It would be naive of us to believe that Cyrus's motives were particularly noble. Persia simply had a different foreign policy and way of dealing with captured peoples than did Babylonia. (It is interesting, though, to read what the Prophet Isaiah [e.g. 45:1] says about Cyrus, describing him as the servant and instrument of the Lord and using the Hebrew word for "messiah" for him.)

Once the people were back in the land, the rebuilding of the Temple had lagged behind the rebuilding of homes. The first part of the Book of the Prophet Haggai commands the people to get going on the Temple. By the second part of the book, that rebuilding had been fulfilled, even though we know from the books of Ezra and Nehemiah that it had not been easy. Some had vigorously opposed rebuilding the Temple, and the project had stopped and started. When it was finally finished, some who remembered the previous Temple in all its glory found it a disappointment.

This lectionary passage begins with the word of the Lord commanding Haggai to speak to the governor and the high priest and to the remnant of the people back in the ravaged land. Haggai is to tell them that things are going to get better. Haggai is to proclaim to them that God is with them according to the faithful promises of previous generations. They are not to be afraid or discouraged. The way this is all going to be made visible is through the restoration of the Temple to a house of splendour of silver and gold. Verse 8 says the silver and gold will be "shaken" out of all nations. This sentiment comes from a longing for the kind of political authority on a global scale that was seldom the reality for the people of Israel, and from a desire to show all the nations that the glory of God, shown through the glorious Temple, is a glory above all else.

God's spirit abides among the people. Appearances of their new, post-exilic life in a ravaged land to the contrary, they are not to fear. Living in a country and context so much more stable than that of the people Haggai is addressing, we need to pay attention and be less fearful. That is the faithful response.

The possible dream

A rabbi colleague of mine has often commented that it must be very difficult for Christian preachers to preach at Christmas, because the people in the pew come to Christmas services certain that they know the meaning of the stories they are about to hear. The stories and the images are so familiar to everyone that people think they have their meaning all wrapped up.

This passage from the Book of the Prophet Isaiah is a bit like that. It is so familiar, it may be difficult for people to truly hear what it has to say.

These words of God, in the glorious poetry of the Book of the Prophet Isaiah, are probably addressed to a particular context of the people of Israel. The text speaks of their challenging return from exile in Babylon. The theme of restoration and new creation, however, is one that travels all through the Book of the Prophet Isaiah. Even when Isaiah is proclaiming judgment to come, which he does a great deal, he also always proclaims God's comfort, tenderness, compassion and mercy. Here, God is creating new heavens and a new earth in which the former things – either the time of exile and tribulation, or the prophecies of judgment, or both – will be forgotten. God is going to rejoice and delight in Jerusalem and in the people. This passage is a good reminder of the high profile that cities receive in the biblical text. Obviously, much of the land and context of the people of ancient Israel was pastoral, rural or small villages. Yet the city of Jerusalem plays a prominent role all through the text: as a political centre and as the site of the Temple, where the connection between God and the people is so strongly felt. But it is also more than that. In texts like this one and Revelation 21, the city of Jerusalem models and becomes the fulfillment of God's reign of peace and justice on earth.

In verse 19 of this lectionary text, the prophecy gets very specific. It is God's will for the fulfillment of the holy reign of peace and justice that there will be no more suffering. No more newborn babies will die. (This was a radical announcement in a time and place where the infant mortality rate might be as high as half of all babies born.) Every person will live a long life. People will build and live in their own homes, and plant and eat their own crops. This prophecy does away with landlords and large agricultural conglomerates and transnational corporations. It speaks to dignity and self-sufficiency in the midst of community. The natural world, too, will manifest this divine will for peace and justice, making possible what was thought to be impossible. With God, nothing is impossible.

King of kings, Lord of lords and Shepherd of shepherds

The liturgical purpose of the Sunday that we call "Reign of Christ" is to close the church year before we begin the season of Advent next Sunday. It does that closing by proclaiming who Jesus Christ is for us as Christians. Although we proclaim this belief each and every Sunday, we do so in a special way this Sunday. We read this passage to understand the image of the shepherd. There is plenty of information in the passage about what a bad shepherd does – scattering the flock, driving them away and not taking care of them – and there are repercussions for the bad shepherd for not doing his job. God, as the good shepherd, on the other hand, will bring the flock back to their home and safety, and they will live with all the benefits of security and stability. There will be no more fear, nor will any be missing.

Much can be done homiletically with this image of the good shepherd ensuring that none of the flock will go missing. Jesus' parable of the Good Shepherd leaps to mind for Christians. Sheep going missing was a real problem in biblical times. There was much danger from rough terrain and predators, and much risk to the shepherd, probably alone and in the dark, trying to find the missing sheep. One helpful place to go with this passage is to set it beside the parables of Jesus and show some of the ways in which he was in line with his Jewish tradition.

This lectionary passage then goes on to declare that God will raise up a king, a righteous king in the line of David. As we have seen before, the role of that righteous king will be to execute justice in the land. The biblical tradition always equates justice and righteousness. It is incomprehensible to me to hear that Christians should not be involved in issues of politics and social justice. The Bible says otherwise. The prophets and other parts of the Old Testament are crystal clear: we are all called to be bearers of justice to all God's world. As Karen

Armstrong says, the Deuteronomist stream in the Old Testament insists upon the importance of justice, equity and compassion.[104]

Justice, righteousness, salvation and safety are all part of the same package: all are part of the fulfillment of the reign of God in Christ.

---

104 Armstrong, *The Great Transformation*, 163.

Thanksgiving – *Deuteronomy 26:1-11*

See the entry for Lent 1, Year C.

Appendix
Roman Catholic Readings[105]

---

105 where they differ from the Revised Common Lectionary

Year A

Third Sunday in Ordinary Time/Epiphany 3 –
Isaiah 8:23b-9:3

See the entry for Year A, Epiphany 3 in the Revised Common Lectionary section. Although the numbering of the verses is slightly different, this is basically the same passage.

Fourth Sunday in Ordinary Time/Epiphany 4 –
Zephaniah 2:3, 3:12-13

Humble is as humble does

The prophet Jeremiah had warned the people. The prophet Nahum had warned the people. The people had not listened. Now it was the prophet Zephaniah's turn. King Hezekiah had launched a significant religious reform. And then, years later, King Josiah had launched a significant religious reform. These reforms had not fallen on completely deaf ears at the time, but the years went by, the everyday concerns of everyday life multiplied and the temptations to self-centred living increased. The people were again concerned with themselves rather than God and others. The purpose of the religious reforms of the two kings, and of the warnings of the prophets, were to call the people to repentance, to right relationship with their God and their neighbour, but the reforms, warnings and call were not being heard or addressed.

As is so often the case with biblical names, the name of the prophet carries great meaning. "Zephaniah" means "the Lord hides or protects." The text contains many references to the people seeking the Lord and the Lord hiding the people on the day of the coming wrath. It also contains many references both to the coming wrath, which is a direct result of the people's failure to follow the paths of right relationship, and to the people who heed the warning and return to faithfulness, seeking refuge in the name of the Lord.

The purpose and message of the book as a whole is to announce to the people of the southern part of the kingdom of Israel that since God is a God of justice, the consequences of not being in right relationship with the divine and the neighbour are about to come. And they will be dire consequences. Chapter 1, verses 2-6, gives an idea of how dire. While it is not always helpful to our understanding of the biblical text, when the lectionary picks up such short sections and, as in this case, puts together verses that do not come together in the text itself, there is a point being made that resonates with the message of the prophet Zephaniah. The dire consequences of injustice and unfaithfulness may indeed come, yet God's ultimate will is always one of mercy, compassion and love for the people. There is always the opportunity to turn towards God, to turn in the right direction; this is what we see proclaimed in verse 3 of chapter 2 and verses 12 and 13 of chapter 3. Seek the Lord, we are told; be humble, we are told; take refuge in the Lord, we are told.

We read the prophet Zephaniah in the context of the prophets Isaiah, Jeremiah, Amos, Jonah and others, and we read the prophet Zephaniah in the context of the first five books of the Torah. All these parts of the biblical faith tradition are clear in the ultimate message they proclaim. God is the source of life and love; we are called to respond to that life and love *with* life and love. One might "translate" Zephaniah into the context of our time by wondering what he would think of the fact that we let homelessness continue, that malnourished children die by the thousands in our world every day, that we seldom raise questions about dehumanizing aspects of science and technology, that we rarely protest our country's participation in the manufacture and selling of the small arms that result in countless deaths of our sisters and brothers in conflict-torn countries. What would it look like if we were truly the humble of the land (chapter 2, verse 3) and truly did God's commands?

Sixth Sunday in Ordinary Time/Epiphany 6 –
Sirach 15:16-21

The choice is yours

The book from which the text for this Sunday comes gets the prize for the most versions of its title of any of the biblical books from which lectionary texts are drawn. "Ecclesiasticus, or The Wisdom of Jesus the Son of Sirach" is also known as "The Church Book" and is not to be confused with Ecclesiastes. The Roman Catholic and Orthodox traditions of the church regard Sirach as sacred and canonical. At the same time, parts of the Protestant tradition regard Sirach and such other books of Wisdom as Tobit and Judith as worthy of being read but not quite of the same status as other books of the Old Testament because they were never part of the Jewish Scriptures. (For those who are keen on the colourful history of these books, which Protestants refer to as the Apocrypha, look up the Council of Trent, April 8, 1546.)

For a basic description of the Book of Sirach, I can do no better than to quote the introduction to it in the Revised Standard Version: "Sirach is a significant link in the history of the development of ancient Jewish thought. It is the last great example of the type of wisdom literature represented in the Old Testament book of Proverbs, and the first specimen of that form of Judaism which subsequently developed into the rabbinical schools of the Pharisees and the Sadducees." The Prologue to the book sets its context; I always mention it in any sermon on Sirach as a way of encouraging the congregation to connect with the living reality of the text and its dynamism for its early readers. It has so much to say about translation – the relationship of various parts of Scripture to each other and the nature of both the transmission of tradition and community.

The specific text for this sixth Sunday in Ordinary Time reminds the community of its choice in acting faithfully. God knows us, sees us and does not want us to sin, but also gives us the freedom to choose between life and death in words that call to mind Deuteronomy 30:19. To emphasize how this text speaks to us in the first part of the 21st century is the mandate for preaching. God is mighty in power and sees everything, but having given us the gift of freedom in our creation (God being God, not a puppet master), desires us to choose life for ourselves, others and all Creation. God does not compel our choice. How do we as Christians, living in community – local, national and global – thus choose life? Note the connection that the Prologue to the book makes with the reading of the law and the prophets, both of which contain the strong and strongly interwoven themes of faithfulness to God and social justice. What does all of this look like in your particular parish? An "out of the cold" program, substantial support of Development and Peace, working with neighbouring congregations of different Christian traditions to alleviate child poverty? God knows all of our deeds, thanks be to God!

Year A

Tenth Sunday in Ordinary Time/ Epiphany Last/ Transfiguration – *Hosea 6:3-6*

It was the worst of times

It was the worst of times and the worst of times. Hosea was a prophet to the northern part of Israel in a period of dire circumstances. The superpower, Assyria, was on the move: it seemed inevitable, at least to the prophets, that the darkest of dark days were coming. And come they did. It was only a few years after the ministry of Hosea that the northern capital, Samaria, was captured and the people sent into exile, wiping out the northern kingdom of Israel (722–721 BCE).

The thing about prophets is that they paid attention. They were not, were never, fortune tellers. Rather, they read the "signs of the times," made connections among events and behaviours near and far, and then told it like it was. In telling it like it was they used signs, symbols, images and poetry and they made two basic points. The people's behaviour was unfaithful to God, in worship practices and/or in unjust social practices. No matter how unfaithful they were, however, God would always take them back.

These two basic points are clearly made in this lectionary passage. The context of the broader passage, within which the lectionary passage sits, is a call to repentance. The specific verses of the text for this Sunday revel in the assurance of the appearing of the Lord. The presence of God is linked with Creation. The transitory nature of the love of the people for God is also connected with Creation. Because of the permanence and assurance of God's love, and because of the transitory and fickle love of the people, the Lord has sent the prophets to pay attention, to read and proclaim the "signs of the times." Judgment is sure, but love is over and above judgment. Love and knowledge are to be our response to the covenant – not merely actions performed with scant attention to their meaning.

I have said before and I will say again, it is an unfaithful interpretation of this phrase, unfaithful in terms of the whole canon of biblical witness, to use this passage to denigrate any peoples past or present. The most common misstep with this kind of prophetic passage is to use it to denigrate the worship/sacrificial system of the Israelites of history or the Jews of our time and place. The passage was addressed to the people of the covenant; if we truly believe that we, too, are in covenant with the Lord of Life, then the passage has an original context and is also addressed to us.

To what do we pay scant attention in worship or in our daily lives? It might be the actions, motions and listening in worship. It might also be the ease with which we avoid taking part in global initiatives for justice, dismissing the ability of an individual to make a difference. It might also be the ease with which we avoid participation in and discussion of the pros and cons of proposed electoral reform, dismissing the ability of any societal system to make a difference. From this day forth, emulate the prophets and pay attention! Then emulate them some more and speak God's love to the world.

Year A

Lent 1 – *Genesis 2:7-9, 3:1-7*

Good and not so good

The same and yet different. The second half of this passage is also the second half of the lectionary reading for the first Sunday in Lent in the Revised Common Lectionary, so consult the entry for Year A, Lent 1, of the RCL section.

Both sections of text declare that God is continually with us. In the first passage, we are midstream in what has been called the second Creation story. God has created the earth and the heavens, but there were as yet no plants, no herbs, no rain, nor anyone to till the ground. There was a stream, however, which watered the ground. And then, "lo and behold, God created a being from the dust of the ground, breathed into its nostrils the breath of life and the being became a living being." Hebrew is a very "punny" language; it uses plays on words often and well. This is one example. The Hebrew word for the being God created is *adam*, because it is taken from the ground, *adamah*.[106] Other Hebrew words refer to gender-differentiated man and woman, but they are not used until later in the passage, when there are two beings.

God plants a garden; in goes the created being as well as "every tree that is pleasant to the sight and good for food," including the tree of life and the tree of the knowledge of good and evil. We who know how this story is going to move may well start holding our breath or sighing at this point. And indeed, the story continues in its depiction of disobedience and the prideful desire to be like the Creator rather than the created. The first Sunday in Lent is a time for remembering

---

106 One can use the name "Adam" for this creature, but to do so misses the sense of the Hebrew. The biblical scholar Phyllis Trible suggests "earth-creature." This is awkward in English, but it expresses the biblical relationship between the creature and the ground from which it was made, as well as the fact that at this point in the story there is no gender differentiation.

who we are and whose we are. It has also been a time in the church for focusing on temptation as a part of the human creaturely reality and sacrifice as a part of the struggle against that temptation. The second part of this lectionary passage is a focal point for our understanding of temptation, which is about the knowledge of good and evil, about seeing ourselves as God. Lent, therefore, begins with a passage that calls us to look deeply at who we really are, not who we and the world think we are; that, of course, is the point of the penitence, fasting, sacrifice, almsgiving, prayer and all the actions that are a part of this season of the church year.

Who are we in God's eyes?

Eleventh Sunday in Ordinary Time – _Exodus 19:2-6a_

God is in the details

Many parishes sing the popular hymn "On Eagles' Wings," based on Psalm 91. The phrase "And I will raise you up on eagles' wings" is one of those phrases that resonates throughout our Holy Scriptures. Here we find it, slightly varied, in this passage from Exodus.

The Israelites have been liberated from slavery in Egypt, they have crossed the Red/reed Sea, they have complained – a frequent theme in their wandering in the wilderness – and God has responded – also a frequent theme in their wandering. Now, in this passage, they have reached Mount Sinai. There is much wandering ahead of them, but for now they are camped in front of Mount Sinai. They are poised on the brink of being given the great gift of grace which is the ten commandments. They are poised on the brink of serious rejection of their gracious God in the golden calf incident. They are poised on the brink of the second reception of the ten commandments, of God never giving up on the people.

The message of that day, the message we thus hear this day, is that God has actively intervened in an act of freedom from oppression. God has carried the people into the holy presence; the people are to respond to this great grace by holding firm and fast the covenant relationship between them and God. If they do so, they will be God's treasured possession, a priestly kingdom and a holy nation. But what does this mean? It is a difficult biblical idea. (Who said that the Bible contained easy ideas?) It is a difficult idea for us to live out. (Who said that Christian living was easy?) In the context of the whole biblical witness, it meant for the people of Israel, and is interpreted by Jews of our time and place, to mean being a particular and strong witness to the love and justice of God. The people of Israel believed, and 21st-century Jews believe, that being a treasured possession, a priestly kingdom and a holy nation means being focused on God in a way that is obvious to the world, in a way that manifests to the world both faithful relationship with the Lord of Creation and a response to that relationship that deeply and actively cares for the "widow, the orphan and the sojourner," the poor and vulnerable. One might say that such biblical witnesses as the holiness theme of the Book of Leviticus are about proclaiming that the details by which we live our lives matter. In the details of life, we bear witness to who we are and whose we are, to the truth that we have, in effect, been borne on eagles' wings to God.

The priests were those in Israel who facilitated the relationship between the people and their God. Being a priestly kingdom, therefore, in our time and place, would mean that we, in spite of, or perhaps because of, our frail humanity, facilitate the relationship between our world and our God. We are instruments, channels of relationship, treasures of God who, for that purpose, are borne up by God's strong and sustaining presence. Thanks be to God!

Twelfth Sunday in Ordinary Time – *Jeremiah 20:10-13*

What would you do?

The prophet Jeremiah was in the stocks in the upper Benjamin Gate of the house of the Lord. He was there because the priest Pashhur, chief officer in the house of the Lord, had heard what Jeremiah was saying publicly. Prophets do not say popular things. Or at least, true prophets do not. The biblical text often makes it clear that if people like what prophets are saying, if it makes them feel comfortable, the prophets are probably false ones. Jeremiah's message could not have been any harder to hear. He proclaims in no uncertain terms that the nation of Judah, the southern part of the kingdom of Israel, the only part still more or less standing at this point in the history of the nation, is about to fall to the superpower Babylon. In the verses before this reading, Jeremiah details exactly what is going to happen: it is beyond dire. And he has a personal message of doom for Pashhur the priest. Although this particular version of Jeremiah's prophetic message comes after he has been released from the stocks, it is the same kind of message that he has already been proclaiming, the same kind of message that got him put in the stocks in the first place.

We need to tread very carefully when we read biblical texts and place our lives and context, either consciously or unconsciously, into them. It is easy for us to side with Jeremiah. But what would we do if an unpleasant, loud, persistent voice was continually raised against us, continually condemned us for what we thought we were doing right? What if we were constantly being threatened, or so it seemed, with a coming dire destruction that was said to be completely our fault?

In this lectionary passage, Jeremiah makes it very clear what those surrounding him in his time and place did. Jeremiah is whispered against and denounced. His very friends plot revenge and are his persecutors. What could be worse? But Jeremiah, newly released from the stocks, actively persecuted by those he held dear, hangs on to and proclaims his faith. It must have been difficult, but Jeremiah proclaims that the Lord is with him, that his persecutors will not prevail and that he has committed himself to God. "Sing to the Lord; praise the Lord! For he has delivered the life of the needy from the hands of evildoers."

Heaven help us not to be like the priest Pashhur and refuse to hear the Word of the Lord because it brings dire news. Heaven help us to be those who act and speak in the face of persecution and who proclaim and praise the Lord.

Thirteenth Sunday in Ordinary Time – *2 Kings 4:8-11, 14-16a*

"Lord, I believe; help my unbelief"

This is a miracle story, portraying, as the telling of miracle stories often does, divine power and significance, in this case mediated through the prophet Elisha. Tell the story. There is no need to leave out verses 12 and 13; tell the story in all its vibrancy and detail. It is so often by hearing the details of the stories of our ancestors in the faith, by reflecting on the humanity so portrayed, that we experience our own humanity in its relationship to the divine.

Elisha is one of the early prophets of the people of Israel, a prophet who does many colourful things, which we read about in the books of first and second Kings.[107] Elisha seems to have something of a regular route that causes him to pass by Shunem from time to time. The text does not give us the reasons that the wealthy woman supports the prophet, but it is important in the story that Shunem is not one of the towns and places that we are used to hearing about in the biblical text. The woman is off the beaten track, not linked to the places that play a larger role in the narrative of the faith tradition. What does that mean to us to whom the text is also addressed? Here is someone living perhaps on the margins, someone who recognizes the nature and power of the prophet. God help us indeed if we fail to listen to these kinds of texts and start to believe that we are the mainstream and therefore corner the market on truth. To do that is to be unfaithful to our biblical tradition. Who on the fringes of our community right here and now may be giving shelter to one of God's messengers? Who on the fringes of our community right here and now may be experiencing the benefits of holy presence?

When asked specifically what reward she would like for her care of Elisha, the Shunnamite declines any reward. The favours that might be had from the powers that be, the king or the commander of the

---

107 These books are called the "Former Prophets" in the Hebrew tradition.

army or both, have no meaning or worth for her. Not only does she not ask for anything in the first place, she even declines an advantage when it is offered to her. On the suggestion of his servant, Elisha determines to give the woman something that is impossible: a son. Hear the vibrant presence of the God of life in story and detail, in the unexpected and the unlikely. For God so loved the world.

Fourteenth Sunday in Ordinary Time – *Zechariah 9:9-10*

The Lord remembers indeed

The prophet Zechariah's name means "the Lord remembers"; the book of Zechariah is one that proclaims both memory and vision.[108]

Historically, the ministry of the prophet Zechariah took place in the post-exilic period in the southern part of the land of Israel. The people were returning from the exile in Babylon to their homeland and dealing with all the issues that such a return and resettlement into a devastated land entailed. One of those issues was the rebuilding of the Temple. Zechariah also, however, focused on the spiritual renewal of the people. He was constantly warning them, hence the emphasis on "remembering," that they should listen to all the things that God had said to them through the other prophets. Solidarity in prophecy.

This book of prophecy also contains many Messianic passages: the passage for this fourteenth Sunday in Ordinary Time is one of them. It will sound familiar to many Christians, immediately evoking images of Palm Sunday. In its original context, this messianic passage proclaims the coming of the Messiah-king. It is a coming in meekness, gentleness and peace. The Messiah-king to come is at one and the same time both victorious and humble; he obviously has power, able not only to banish weapons and unite the northern and southern parts of the land (symbolized by the names "Ephraim" and "Jerusalem" in the text), but also to proclaim and bring about peace for the whole world. It is obvious why Christians see this passage resonating with our proclamation of Jesus Christ as Messiah. It is unnecessary to debate homiletically

---

108 The prophet Zechariah is one of what are called "The Twelve Minor Prophets," so named for the length of their books, not as a theological assessment. At least, that was the original thinking. The fact that down through the ages there has been theological assessment made is clearly shown in the very structure of the lectionary. In the Revised Common Lectionary, fully one third of the Old Testament passages are taken from the Book of the Prophet Isaiah. A theological judgment to be sure about the role of the prophet Isaiah in Christianity.

whether this passage is an actual "prediction" of Jesus, which is something that prophets do not usually make, or whether the Gospel writers wrote their stories of Palm Sunday in such a way as to mirror this passage. The point is that these words of the prophet Zechariah had meaning for the people of his time and place, and have meaning still for Jews now, anticipating the Messiah. At the same time, they have meaning for Christians, albeit a somewhat different meaning. We believe that the Messiah has come and that all the world is encompassed in a transformation and redemption that will someday be fulfilled, and that we are called to actively participate in that world. How do we hold together that truth with the humility we see in this passage?[109]

---

109 It is only one animal that is being referred to here. The parallelism that is a key feature of Hebrew poetry makes it sound to Greek and English readers like two animals.

Year A

Fifteenth Sunday in Ordinary Time – Isaiah 55:10-11

See also Year C, Epiphany 8, in the Revised Common Lectionary section.

Word and deed

This is such a joyous passage of Scripture, even more so when seen in its slightly broader context. It comes towards the end of the Book of the Prophet Isaiah, the part of the book that speaks to the homecoming of the people from exile in Babylon. The passage directly before it speaks about a God who is rich in forgiving; the passage directly after it speaks about leaving in joy and being led away in safety as the mountains and hills and trees put on a vibrant concert. It would be easy to proclaim this passage in that context, to proclaim the joy of being, as Christians, in such relationship with God and either leave it at that or turn quickly to the New Testament, which for Christian preachers often *seems* more straightforward to preach from. But at the same time that this passage proclaims such joy, it also raises questions – questions that I think faithful Christian pastors and congregations must wrestle with in our time and place.

To begin with, the passage captures the movement that is always part of the biblical proclamation of the "word." In the movement of creation, we hear God's "word" that it is good. In the beginning of the Gospel of John, we hear that the Word was with God and indeed was God, active in Creation and time. So here, the "word" goes out from God's mouth and carries out God's will, succeeding in what it was sent to do. It would be helpful to explore with a congregation what that might mean specifically in terms of God and in terms of our *response* to God as Christians in our time and place. To put it in a basic way, how does the "word" go out from God and not return to God empty?

To Christians, that word is Jesus, who carried out God's will and succeeded in what he was sent to do in redeeming the world. In the context of this passage in the Book of the Prophet Isaiah, the question is also very much what the "word" is for the people of Israel and for our contemporary Jewish sisters and brothers, and how that resonates for us. Is it the word of God's forgiveness, which is mentioned in the verses above? Is it the word of God's forgiveness combined with the continual prophetic call to repentance, which is a common combination in prophetic literature? A problem arises since we all know that the prophets continually call for repentance in the name of God, and we all know that often they are ignored. How do we describe God's will and God's word succeeding in what it was sent to do? And then there is that cliché that when things go awry or there is great pain, it is "God's will." How could we possibly proclaim these words to a Rwandan woman who, like hundreds of thousands of her sisters, was brutally raped and forced to watch her husband hacked to death with a machete? Part of the answer – only part – is that we are to hear the way that God's word carries God's will, and we are to succeed in being bearers of it.

Sixteenth Sunday in Ordinary Time – *Wisdom 12:13, 16-19*[110]

Our judge and our hope

"For there is no god, other than you, who cares for anything." What a proclamation of the unparalleled sovereignty of God! God cares for everything, we are told, and there is no other god.[111] This passage proclaims that God does not have to "prove" it, that God has never judged unjustly.

The lectionary then skips verses 14 and 15; read these verses before going on to verses 16 to 19, which proclaim that God's justice has its source in strength, and God's lenience has its source in God's all-encompassing sovereignty. Verse 19 describes the effect of this cause. God's actions, as they have just been detailed, have been a lesson to the people. As God has acted, we are to act to all people.

What if we were truly to live this way? C.S. Lewis talks about living in real forgiveness for others. He points out that it is often much harder to forgive those with whom we live in great proximity than it is to forgive, in a sort of abstract way, those who live far away from the daily realities of our lives.[112] But can our calling be to anything less?

---

110 Like Tobit, Judith and Eccesiasticus, Wisdom has a kind of varying status in the Christian tradition. These books were not part of the canon of Scripture for the people of Israel. Books such as Wisdom were written in Greek; they were known to the writers of the New Testament, who make use of them. While they are still not accepted as Scripture in Judaism, they are in Roman Catholicism. Some Protestant bibles contain them and some do not. Like the Book of Ecclesiastes, this book of Wisdom is attributed, internally in the case of this book, to King Solomon, but its style reveals it to come from a time many centuries later than Solomon, written by a Jew in well-educated Greek.

111 A proclamation of monotheism is not as common in the Old Testament as we sometimes think. Much of the Old Testament is based on the belief in monolatry, which is the belief that God is the only God for the particular people to worship and relate to, but it does not deny the existence of other gods for other people.

112 C.S. Lewis, "On Forgiveness," in *Fern-Seed and Elephants and Other Essays on Christianity*, Walter Hooper, ed. London: Fount Paperbacks, 1975.

Year A

Seventeenth Sunday in Ordinary Time – *1 Kings 3:5, 7-12*

See the entry for Year B, Proper 15, in the Revised Common Lectionary section.

Year A

Eighteenth Sunday in Ordinary Time – *Isaiah 55:1-3*

See the entry for Year C, Lent 3, in the Revised Common Lectionary section.

Nineteenth Sunday in Ordinary Time – *1 Kings 19:9a, 11-13a*

Neither earthquake nor fire

Elijah was on the run, fearing for his life. He had won the dramatic and all-consuming contest with the prophets of Baal, which had not gone over well with the regal powers who were supporting those prophets. (I mention this context because the lectionary skips a number of verses. I suspect that this selection is an attempt to make the passage more universal somehow, but the whole point of the biblical text is particularity. We see the actions and grace of God in the details of particular people in particular contexts, which allows us to see the actions and grace of God in the particular contexts of our lives.)

So Elijah was on the run. He felt he had successfully and dramatically done everything that God wanted of him and had, just before this passage, lain down in despair and wanted to die. God would have none of that behaviour, however, and had supplied him with food and drink and an angel to nag him. In this next passage, while Elijah hid out in a cave, God challenged his despair. Elijah laid out the sorry tale of having done all he has done and still having been deserted by the people. For good measure, he declares that the people have deserted God, too. In a way that we will hear again in the Book of Job, God does not answer Elijah's protest directly. Rather, God reveals the Holy self as it is to be truly experienced. Not in the mighty wind or earthquake or fire, but in a gentle breeze. Although the passage chosen for this Sunday does not take us on any further than that point, it is striking that Elijah, just as in the passage that preceded this one, is instructed to get on with the job.

We, too, are to hear and experience the reality of the presence of God – not necessarily in big, dramatic events, though God is revealed in the Bible in them too, but in the gentle breezes of our lives. Experience God in the comforting hug of a good friend when you have been having a bad day. Experience God in the soft purple of a sunset. Experience God in the satisfaction of a job well done and in the passing of the peace in a regular Sunday service. Be strengthened by those experiences, because gentle and comforting as an experience of God can be, there is no option of wallowing in despair for any reason. The calling is always to get on with the job. The discernment is to determine the specifics of our particular job or role but then, with the gentle breeze sustaining us, we go.

Year A

Twentieth Sunday in Ordinary Time – Isaiah 56:1, 6-7

No membership form required

One of the reasons that the Book of the Prophet Isaiah is such a feature of the Christian lectionary is its "universal" passages such as this one, in which the broadness of what is being said can easily be incorporated into the faith tradition of Christianity. The passage can be seen as coming from the third part of the Book of the Prophet Isaiah, a third part that deals to some extent with the complex and often discouraging details of resettlement in the land after the return from the exile in Babylon. Much of the focus of chapters 55 to 66 of Isaiah is on that time of figuring out how to live in the land again in a changed time and with changed demographics.

The chapter and this passage begin with a statement declaring God's reality and purposes. "Have a care for justice, act with integrity, for soon my salvation will come and my integrity be manifest." Then follows a detailed description of God's inclusiveness, which is not in the lectionary, perhaps because of what seems like obscure and graphic detail to the modern reader. Those verses, however, help to spell out the depth and breadth of that inclusiveness. If those verses make us feel a little uncomfortable in their somewhat graphic nature, that is a good thing. We should be continually challenged by our biblical texts, and challenged to be as inclusive as this passage says that God is.

Verses 6 to 7 reinforce the inclusiveness of God further by outlining the minimal requirements God asks for from those traditionally perceived to be outside the covenant. God's house will be called a house of prayer for all the peoples. It seems obvious when we read it in a text like this, but how can we translate this concept into our lives?

We must all step outside the box of our own tradition and truly live, regardless of the cost, the depth and breadth of God's vision as it is set out in this Sunday's message. If another faith tradition does the same with us, from the depths of its tradition, how will we respond, exactly?

Twenty-First Sunday in Ordinary Time – Isaiah 22:19-23

Take me to your leader

"Bad Steward, Good Steward." That is what Walter Brueggemann entitles the section of his Isaiah commentary that deals with this passage. Brueggemann says,

> This portion of the text purports to give a glimpse into the internal workings and internal tensions in the royal household. It contrasts two officials who functioned as "chancellor," that is, second in command to the king. The narrative contrasts *Shebna,* who is condemned and rejected for unacceptable actions and *Eliakim,* who is commended and endorsed as a faithful and effective official. The juxtaposition appears to be informed by the historical notes of 2 Kings 18:18; Isaiah 36:3 and 37:2, in which Eliakim is the senior officer and Shebna ranks next in authority. On the face of it, the text concerns the wise and the irresponsible use of public power.[113]

Brueggemann then goes on to detail the fact that there is scholarly debate about whether both these figures, around which this passage revolves, are historical. Whether they are historical or not, the point of the passage is that the figure of "Shebna" is portrayed as having messed up – probably by abusing the trust placed in him, probably by being an unfaithful leader who has tried to advance himself at the expense of the household and the realm. He is being replaced by the figure of "Eliakim," who is portrayed as a good steward or leader, who does what he does for the faithful care of the household. Eliakim is held up as a model, an ideal, a major participant in a pure, perfect and secure regime.[114]

It is certainly possible that this text had an influence on the way that Matthew 16:19 was expressed, which can be seen in the setting of the two texts into the same week in the lectionary. And in the Roman

---

113 Brueggemann, *Isaiah 1–39,* 178-79.
114 Brueggemann, *Isaiah 1–39,* 180.

Catholic tradition, this text obviously plays a very important role in the articulation of the Petrine theory of church authority.

It is in the juxtaposition of the two figures around which this text revolves that we are called to do some discerning about what leadership should and should not look like as the church considers its role in working towards God's future. The Petrine theory of church authority has given substantive thought and articulation to the role of the pontiff. But what about the faithful stewardship role, the faithful leadership role that individual Christians are called to play in the world? This passage calls us to consider ways in which we have advanced ourselves at the expense of God's will for peace and justice for all peoples. The Book of the Prophet Isaiah makes clear to us that God's will is for faithful stewardship from us, from the church. Both are very much a part of the movement towards the fulfillment of God's reign.

Verse 11 of this chapter, a verse not included in the lectionary reading, says, "But you had no thought for the Maker, no eyes for him who shaped everything long ago." How will we encourage all parts of the church to go further in care and faithful stewardship?

Twenty-Second Sunday in Ordinary Time – *Jeremiah 20:7-9*

To whine is human

A cliché about prophets says that their role is to comfort the afflicted and to afflict the comfortable. This passage from the Book of the Prophet Jeremiah seems to be just about afflicting. Jeremiah, prophet of the southern part of the land of Israel, Judah, for the years leading up to and including its destruction by Babylon, is not a popular figure. Mind you, most prophets are not. Jeremiah keeps warning the people about judgment to come because they have forsaken God; they have forgotten that they are accountable to God. Although he points out, as prophets do, that repentance is always possible, it is his message of "affliction" to which, naturally, the people take the most exception. And for that, he is himself afflicted. At times he is imprisoned down a well for his uncomfortable message. In the verses right before this passage, he was in and out of the stocks. So here we read a detailed, heart-rending account of how and why he feels afflicted.

If you read the verses right before this text, verses 4-6, it is graphically clear why people feel afflicted by Jeremiah's message. But Jeremiah, in this text itself, rails against God for seducing him, for overpowering him so that he is not only afflicted by what feels like everyone else in the world but is also a laughing stock. His message of judgment, pulled from him by a God stronger than he is, means constant insult and derision for him. He tried not to be a bearer of God's word. It was not only God's strength that prevented him from rejecting his call, but the fact that the call burned within him.

This is not a cheery passage, but then again the Bible has never claimed to be cheery. It reveals God to us, God's will, God's purpose for all people and all Creation. It is not a cheery message to us, this Sunday, that we are called to "speak truth to power." It is not a question of banding together with those of like mind (though that can certainly be helpful), and, in the comfort and reinforcement of such a like-minded group, challenging the death-dealing powers that be. Jeremiah is unpopular and afflicted by everyone. It is hard for us even to imagine what message we might proclaim that would be both so faithful and so unpopular that everyone in our context would reject it and us for it. Reflect on that, though.

What is also powerful about this passage is how real it feels in its graphic language and in the power of its imagery. Jeremiah can say whatever he is feeling to God and about God, and he does. God can take it. The call does not lessen, the affliction by others does not lessen, but Jeremiah is in a real, vibrant, honest relationship with his God. The Bible is challenging to us in all kinds of ways: obscure sometimes, uncomfortable sometimes, but always a portrayal of real, vibrant, honest relationship between God and God's people.

Read it that way, hear it that way, live it that way.

Twenty-Third Sunday in Ordinary Time – *Ezekiel 33:7-9*

Take me to your leader – Part 2

These passages from the prophets, that we hear week after week, are a great deal less than cheery!

Ezekiel's name means "may God strengthen," an important message to his time and place when the people of Israel were in exile in Babylon. They knew that their entire country, the city of Jerusalem and the Temple, where they believed God dwelled, were in ruins. Ezekiel was both a prophet and a priest, as were other figures in the history of the people of Israel; and his message carried much detail about the Temple and its importance, design and ritual. At the same time, Ezekiel was very clear that God was not limited to any temple or city, responding to his people in all times and places. This general theme of the prophet Ezekiel offers great sermon potential about the wondrous combination of God's freedom to be God in, of, through and around the world, and the necessity for sacred spaces and places in which we can particularly focus ourselves on God's revelation to us. The Rev. Dr. James Christie, President of The Canadian Council of Churches, may have had this passage from the Book of the Prophet Ezekiel in mind when he said,

> While God may be encountered everywhere and anywhere, God is not a part of creation. No matter how much we love the world and admire what we refer to as God's handiwork, we meet God when and how God chooses. That is the phenomenon that Christians call "revelation" … And so we have "sacred spaces" dedicated to providing believers with an atmosphere of security and some sanctity to consciously develop their intimate personal relationship with God who loves them.

We also encounter in the specifics of this Ezekiel passage the fact that the prophet is being presented as a kind of sentry. Prophetic leadership consists of being a watcher. When the prophet hears a word from the mouth of God, the prophet is to warn the people. Note the assumption in this passage that the word is always going to be one of warning or judgment or both. It is crucial to keep in mind the reality and truth that the prophets give the warning and convey the judgment they are called to convey, sure that repentance is always possible and that God's ultimate will is always one of forgiveness and grace. Ezekiel knows that, but in this passage the warning predominates. The prophet is to warn the people, for that is what a sentry does – warn the people of what is approaching. If there are to be consequences for wickedness on the part of an individual, the prophet is to declare that. Should the prophet hold back from such warning, he becomes responsible for what befalls the individual. But if the prophet so warns and repentance does not follow, the prophet will escape the repercussions which will surely come to the people.

So who would want to be a prophet? As we saw above, in the entry before this one, the call to prophecy can be unwanted, and prophecy as a career can be unpleasant, but the call is irresistible. Here we have another depiction of what being a prophet means. What about for us? The call is irresistible, too. We must watch the signs of our times; we must engage in our society; we must be ready, willing and able to speak. We may or we may not be listened to, but that makes no difference to the reality of the call.

So are we really acting as sentries for the word of the Lord of Creation? Pope Benedict XVI has taken up the call to environmental stewardship in the name of God. What are we sentries poised on the ramparts saying to industry and to individuals to safeguard this planet for those who follow us?

Twenty-Fourth Sunday in Ordinary Time – *Sirach 27:30–28:7*

No road rage

As I write this entry it is the very end of November. Christmas plans are afoot. My second daughter mused that a number of her university colleagues did not want to go home for Christmas. There is anger in their families, and so there is little appeal in going home for the holidays/holy days. I myself have several close colleagues in whose families there is such anger between parents and children that communication has ceased, even on birthdays. As we all know, anger is a powerful thing. Road rage, too, is on the rise. It is all too easy to erupt in anger when we are stressed – whether at home or in the car.

Now, there is anger and there is anger. The anger of the prophets against injustice is part of their role. The anger of God against behaviour that diminishes anyone's humanity is divine. The anger that we should all feel about the unending suffering and neglect of the poor and vulnerable, despite international, national and regional promises made years ago to address these issues, is part of our calling as Christians. This kind of anger motivates and inspires us to action.

In this text, it is the road rage kind of anger that is being spoken about. Vengeance is ruled out – thou shalt not cut off the driver who just cut you off. Keeping track of slights against you is not allowed; remembering the number of meetings at which the same person kept overruling your very good ideas for the parish finance campaign is not permissible. If we are angry, one against the other, if we keep track of what we consider to be the sins of others, how can we then expect compassion and forgiveness from God? It is our human failing to cherish resentment. Goodness knows, God knows, we all do it, but it is not part of God's plan. We are, this passage from Sirach tells us very clearly, to get over it. We are to remember the commandments of life and live by them, including how we live with our families and those who share the roads of our community with us.

This book of Scripture, also known as Ecclesiasticus, its Latin name, is in the Roman Catholic tradition of Scripture, but not so firmly in the Protestant tradition because it is not a part of the TaNaKh (Torah, Nevi'im, Kethubim – Torah, Prophets, Writings) of the Jewish tradition. Although originally written in Hebrew, it was translated into Greek in 132 BCE. As the introduction to it in the Jerusalem Bible says, this book "consists of maxims and aphorisms of worldly wisdom and social prudence ...." Wisdom books in the Bible, such as Sirach, may sometimes sound to us a bit "secular," but this book, as with all Scripture, is set in the overarching care and concern of God. All of life is God's purview.

Year A

Twenty-Fifth Sunday in Ordinary Time – *Isaiah 55:6-9*

See the entry for Year C, Lent 3, in the section on the Revised Common Lectionary.

Twenty-Sixth Sunday in Ordinary Time – *Ezekiel 18:25-28*

The big picture

With the biblical prophets, it is never a question of choosing between collective responsibility and individual responsibility. Although there is ebb and flow in biblical theology around this issue, the big picture always contains both corporate and individual responsibility for sin and falling away from God, and for repentance and turning back to God.

In this passage from the Book of the Prophet Ezekiel, the emphasis is on individual responsibility. It sounds as if there was some sort of groundswell accusation that God is unjust. (Remember that much of Ezekiel's prophecy occurs in the context of a people who are in exile, having lost their land, city and Temple.)

Ezekiel is taking no nonsense, though. He fires back that it is what people do that is unjust. He does not, in this passage, go into specifics, though prophets often do. The sins of the people always seem to fall into two categories: the turning away from God as the sole source of life and the one and only to worship and rely upon, and sins of social injustice towards the poor and needy. Ezekiel does not go into specifics in terms of sin, but he makes it clear that it is a personal decision when integrity is rejected in order to commit some sort of sin. The repercussions that descend on the person who sins are therefore repercussions of his or her own making. And the reverse is true as well. When the choice is made to renounce previous sins, there are repercussions of life for the person making that choice. The next verses of the book continue in the same vein, though they are not included in the lectionary selection.

This is a good time to do some serious reflection on the nature of God's justice. Reading and hearing this passage and others in the biblical text, we could find ourselves quite disturbed, and rightly so, about the reference to death as a consequence of sin. We may ask how our loving, compassionate, forgiving God could allow or even seem to will such a reality. Three things are important to keep in mind in any reflection of this nature:

- God is not to be put in any kind of box, even a box whose look and feel we really like. As an Anglican prayer declares, God can do infinitely more than we can ask or imagine. God *is* infinitely more than we can ask or imagine. We are made in the image of God, and not the other way around.

- God is a God of justice, even though passages like this one deeply trouble us in the way they portray the ramifications of that justice. We have no choice about that, but even if we did, if we were to think through specific situations in our world and our lives, I believe we would find ourselves passionately wanting God to be a God of justice. We want to believe that God cares for those who are hungry and ill and living in fear and despair.

- There are ramifications for injustice. In the subsistence culture in which the biblical texts were written, injustice often resulted in death. Life was precarious. It still is precarious for countless people in our world today, although many in North America may feel removed from such incertitude. And even if actual physical death does not occur because of injustice, we know that it has ramifications for us and for our society.

Year A

Twenty-Seventh Sunday in Ordinary Time – Isaiah 5:1-7

See Year C, Proper 15, in the section on the Revised Common
Lectionary.

Year A

He's got the whole world in his hands

Chapter 24 of the Book of the Prophet Isaiah is one of the "afflict the comfortable" parts of prophecy. Chapter 25, however, is one of the "comfort the afflicted" parts. As we read Chapter 25, or the selected verses that are the lectionary reading for this Sunday, we must remember that God has standards and ideals of right relationship with the divine and with others, that God is the God of the whole of Creation, and that our behaviour affects that Creation.

Chapter 25 as a whole is a chapter of affirmation and confidence, to use the words of Walter Brueggemann in his Isaiah commentary, though a careful reading may challenge us around the exact nature of those "wonderful" things that God has done.[115] A city has been destroyed – perhaps Babylon, perhaps not, but a city, like all cities, that may stray into an emphasis on commerce and power and exploitation. The emphasis in verse 4, in contrast, on the people of Israel having been a refuge to the poor and for the needy in distress is not to be taken lightly. Verses 6-10a must be read in remembrance of them.

Verse 6 begins with an emphasis only on God and God's wonderful work. We get a vision of the details of the coming of God, the reign of God. God is in charge. Of course, there is a mountain, because there is always a mountain at momentous points in the biblical text – such as Mount Sinai and the site of the Transfiguration. People are thought to be closer to God, or God is thought to be closer to people, when a mountain is the setting. There is a fabulous feast in a time and place where such abundance was much more rare than it is in our time and place. As Christians, we partake in the Eucharist as, in all its deep reality and meaning, a prefiguring of the heavenly feast to come. Verse 7 then shows us the Lord of Life overcoming death. The power of death, all that diminishes God's will for shalom (health, whole-

---

115 Brueggemann, *Isaiah 1–39*, 197.

ness, peace, prosperity) for all people, will actively be overcome by the Lord of Life. Death is swallowed up; it is completely encompassed and rendered powerless by life. This is not "pie in the sky when you die" imagery, nor is it something that is somehow limited (though that is not possible, biblically) to the spiritual. The vision Isaiah proclaims, the vision of God, is a complete transformation of everything.

As I write these words, the west coast of Canada is preparing for the 2010 winter Olympics. Many cities have used the coming of the Olympics as an opportunity to "gentrify" their downtowns, an action that has resulted in the removal of the poor, who have lived there for years. They are considered unsightly when the world is watching. An interfaith campaign in Vancouver was created to ensure that after the Olympics are over, the city will be a better place for all its people than it was before – especially for its poor and vulnerable. Part of the plan includes building a solid network of interfaith leadership that is ready, willing and able to speak out on future issues that threaten some of God's children.

Reread Verse 4 of this 25th chapter of the Book of the Prophet Isaiah.

Twenty-Ninth Sunday in Ordinary Time – *Isaiah 45:1, 4-6*

Cyrus the messiah?

This is a good biblical reading to remind us that we are never to think that God is limited by our perceptions and beliefs, for any conversation about interfaith dialogue, and for making the point that God uses whom God chooses.

The time period is that of the exile in Babylon. Gloom and doom abound among the people, but thankfully it is time for the prophet to comfort the afflicted. That comforting takes an unexpected tack. God is going to free the people from exile, and is going to use a rather unusual tool to do so – at least, unusual to our way of thinking. God has always and does always use whom God chooses to use, often to our surprise or shock. In this case, it is Cyrus, King of Persia, who will be the instrument God uses to send the people back to the land. Historically, Babylon lost its position as the supreme empire; Persia stepped into the power vacuum. Babylon had a policy of deporting the peoples of the lands it conquered and either taking them to its own land or planting them in some other country all together – a sort of "divide and destabilize" policy. Persia, on the other hand, believed that people are better subjects if they are home in their own lands. The Persians were not being altruistic; this was a pragmatic governance policy.

In this Sunday's passage from the Book of the Prophet Isaiah, God speaks directly to Cyrus, in effect calling him by name, even though he does not know who God is. Cyrus is reminded in no uncertain terms that God is the one and only God preparing him to be the instrument of the divine purposes, which will both free the people and at the same time glorify God. Cyrus has been chosen for the sake of the people of Israel. Isaiah 45:1 in the NRSV Bible uses the term "anointed" for Cyrus. In the Hebrew of the original text, that is the same word we translate as "messiah." It is the same word that Christians use to proclaim the reality of God in Jesus Christ, and that Jews use to talk about the ways in which God's will is going to be fulfilled in the future.

I have often talked about this biblical text in public gatherings, bible studies, and workshops, and the result is always disconcerting. At times, people are uneasy about considering that the word we hold so sacred in describing God's action in Christ for our sakes could have been used earlier about another person, someone not of the people, someone who, according to the text, does not even know that God exists. But that is the call when we read and hear the Bible: to try and discern what it *is* saying, not just what we want it to say. The text could not be more clear. God uses Cyrus, and although the holy purposes will be fulfilled through him and God will be glorified by what is to happen, there is no demand or even request that Cyrus should recognize and worship the God of Israel.

What would it be like to use this text for an interfaith discussion? What would it be like to read this text in the presence of Jews, Muslims, Sikhs, Hindus? What would it be like if we specifically articulated, for our time and place, this proclamation that God can fulfill the divine purposes by using whomever God chooses? Who might God be using right now who might seem an unlikely "messiah"?

Thirtieth Sunday in Ordinary Time – Exodus 22:20-26

The widow, the orphan, the sojourner

The people of Israel have been freed from slavery in Egypt by God's great act of grace. In the course of their subsequent wandering, God meets them at Mount Sinai and gives them the gift of the ten commandments, the guidelines by which they are to live in right relationship with God and with each other. The text for this Sunday is part of an exposition of the ten commandments.

The people of Israel are reminded time and time again throughout the biblical text that they are to care for the poor and vulnerable because it is the right thing to do – a command from God, in effect. They are reminded time and time again, as here, that they were once poor and vulnerable. There is an extra imperative to care for others who are in the same predicament that they were once in.

God's response to any injustice on the part of the people sounds harsh to us – somewhat incomprehensible, even. There is no easy explanation I can give that will take away any discomfort or even rejection of this response. The Bible was written in a time in which life often hung by a thread more than it does for many of us; death was a closer companion. This is still true for much of the world, and still true for some in North America, but less so for most of us than in centuries past. The Old Testament thus often resonates very strongly for our sisters and brothers in more precarious living situations than ours around the globe.[116] In a time and place like that of the Bible, in which life often hung by a thread, and God was seen as the God of justice and indeed the God of everything, and there were seen to be consequences to human behaviour, this passage encapsulated that faith.

---

116 A significant book on this topic is *The Next Christendom: The Coming of Global Christianity* by Philip Jenkins (New York: Oxford University Press, 2007). Jenkins clearly and helpfully points out, with many statistics to back him up, that the weight of Christianity, in numbers, is shifting to the southern hemisphere. This situation will affect the way our biblical texts are read and the contextual nature of our faith, which can still seem very European.

Year A

Thirty-First Sunday in Ordinary Time – *Malachi 1:14b-2:2b, 8-10*

In a minor key

"My messenger" is his name, and bearing the message of the Lord is his "game" (or calling). Both prophets and priests were called messengers of the Lord; it is not clear whether "Malachi" is a title or a proper name. But no matter. What is important is what the book of the minor prophet Malachi has to say to his generation and then down through the ages to our generation.[117]

The book of the Prophet Malachi, which does not come up often in the Sunday lectionary, is a turning point in Christian scripture from the Old to the New Testament. This specific passage is directed towards the priests or leaders of the community. It is an exhortation to them to "shape up," to glorify God's name lest their priestly revenues (the meaning of the term "blessing") be taken from them. Reading the verses in between 2b and 8 and then reading on after verse 8 indicates more specifically what the priests have done that they ought not to have done, and what they have not done that they ought to have done. God had a covenant with the priestly line, and it stood for life

---

117 "Minor" prophets are minor simply because of the length of their books. "Major" prophets like Isaiah, Jeremiah and Ezekiel each take up a whole scroll, but "minor" prophets can share a scroll. It is not their message that is minor but their length. Malachi is the last book in that part of the Bible that Christians call the Old Testament. It is not, however, the last book in the Bible of our Jewish sisters and brothers, the TaNaKh. The texts of our Jewish sisters and brothers have been intentionally placed in a different order in the Christian Old Testament. The Jewish TaNaKh ends with the books of Chronicles, deliberately setting up an ideal of the ongoing kingdom of David as a vision of what the people are to be. The Christian Old Testament ends with the book of the Prophet Malachi, deliberately setting up an ideal of the Messiah, God's messenger to come, leading smoothly into the New Testament proclamation of Jesus as the Messiah. An interesting bible study idea would be to have people read Malachi straight into the first chapters of the Gospel of Matthew and then reflect on what they hear when reading in that way.

and peace. The priests were to walk with God in integrity and virtue, and to convert people from sin. They were to be guardians for knowledge and instruction. But instead, they have caused many to stumble. The covenant with the ancestors has been profaned and the faith has been broken. Allegiance has been given to "an alien god."

It would be a mistake for any Christian community or tradition to think that this passage is not directed at them. Yet this text must not be used to take pot shots at those in leadership. Rather, it is an opportunity for leaders to re-examine their way of enacting leadership, and an opportunity for all Christians to re-examine our way of enacting leadership in the world. How have we given allegiance to "an alien god," such as materialism? It used to be traditional for people to tithe, that is, to give one-tenth of their income to God through the church. This was in times when many people had more limited financial resources than they do now. One reason why fewer people tithe these days is that we tend to believe that we have what we have because of our own efforts and hard work, overlooking the many blessings that God has given us.

Thirty-Second Sunday in Ordinary Time – Wisdom 6:12-16

Wisdom is ...

Time for something completely different. For a sermon on the nature, meaning and specifics of Wisdom in our time and place, Wisdom that is bright indeed and does not grow dim, try making this a kind of interactive sermon. Different traditions offer different kinds of possibilities for doing this. One way would be to announce to the congregation two weeks beforehand that the sermon two weeks hence will be on the Gospel, as all sermons aim to be, but on the Gospel as proclaimed through this text. The text, Wisdom 6:12-16, could be printed in the bulletin or on some kind of a handout for people to take home. Ask the congregation to reflect prayerfully on how they would define Wisdom that is bright and does not grow dim, and to write a response with a particular emphasis on specific examples of such Wisdom as they see it around them. These reflections would then be returned to the priest the next week and used in the crafting of the sermon for the Thirty-Second Sunday in Ordinary Time. Such a methodology would be to live out the very words of the passage that "even to think about [Wisdom] is understanding fully grown." "Be on the alert for her …."

Thirty-Third Sunday in Ordinary Time – *Proverbs 31:10-13, 19-20, 30-31*

See Year B, Proper 20, in the section on the Revised Common Lectionary.

Year A

Feast of Christ the King – *Ezekiel 34:11-12, 15-17*

See Year A, Reign of Christ, in the section on the Revised Common Lectionary. Although the verses are not exactly the same for these two readings, they are similar. Since this is one of the passages that is helped by reading straight through it and not skipping verses, the commentary in Year A of the RCL section will apply to this version of the passage also.

Year B

First Sunday of Advent – *Isaiah 63:16b-17, 19b; 64:2-7*

See Year B, Advent 1, in the section on the Revised Common Lectionary. The selections from the lectionary are almost identical, so the same commentary applies to both.

Year B

Fourth Sunday of Advent – *2 Samuel 7:1-5, 8b-12, 14a-16*

See Year A, Proper 11, in the section on the Revised Common Lectionary.

Year B

Second Sunday of Lent – *Genesis 22:1-2, 9a, 10-13, 15-18*

See Year A, Proper 8, in the section on the Revised Common Lectionary. The verses of selections from the lectionary are almost identical, so the same commentary applies to both.

Fourth Sunday of Lent – *2 Chronicles 36:14-16, 19-23*

"Revisionist" history – not!

The Books of 1 and 2 Chronicles both have much in common with the Books of Kings, which relate some of the story of the people of Israel, and differ greatly from those biblical books. 1 and 2 Chronicles may have been written by the same person or same editorial school as Ezra and Nehemiah, but what is important to note in preaching on the texts generally, and this lectionary text specifically, is that whoever put these texts together had a particular point to make: this later audience in the history of Israel is still God's chosen people, despite the fact that there is no longer a Davidic king, and the return from exile is still both subjugated to the rule of Persia and taken up with all the complexities and problems of resettling and rebuilding in the land. The life and times of the people could not have felt any worse, but by focusing on the momentum to David as the ideal King and Solomon as his ideal son who builds the ideal Temple, the people are reassured of their place in God's care. God's promises to David still do have meaning for a changed people in a changed land in a changed time. There could be no better news. That point is reinforced by the emphasis the text places on the many and various religious orders and rituals that come from the time of the text, but that are projected back into the time of King David. If the contemporary practices can be shown to have their roots in the previous ideal age, the promises and contemporary care of God are confirmed that way, too.

These two books do not appear often in the lectionary (though they are found more frequently in the Roman Catholic lectionary than in the Protestant one, probably because of their emphasis on ritual and liturgical practices). This particular reading is fairly bleak. It tells of the shameful practices of the priests and people in the last years of the existence of the southern part of the kingdom, practices that resulted in the defiling of the Temple and the ignoring of all the messengers God sent to them to encourage them to change their be-haviour. After they ridiculed, despised and laughed at God's messen-gers, God was active in bringing about the end of the kingdom and the destruction of the city and the Temple. The destruction is vividly detailed and the prophet Jeremiah invoked; the whole picture looks bleak indeed. But then come the last two verses of this reading and of the two books of Chronicles as a whole. (Remember that beginnings and endings are always very important in biblical texts!)

The prophet Jeremiah is invoked again to show that it was also very much God's purpose that the bleakness should be not minimized – never minimized – but overturned, that it is God who uses Cyrus, King of Persia, to free the people from captivity in Babylon. (See Year A, Twenty-Ninth Sunday in Ordinary Time, in the Roman Catholic section of this book for more on God's use of Cyrus, but note that the Chronicles version of the relationship between Cyrus and God is quite different from the Isaiah version of that relationship.) The great and glorious good news for the people of the Chronicler's time and of our time is given in those very last lines of this reading. The faithful worship of God will be re-established; God is with them; they are freed again. There is no revision of the truth. The promises of God endure, forever and ever, Amen.

Year B

The Baptism of the Lord – *Isaiah 55:1-11*

See Year C, Lent 3, in the section on the Revised Common Lectionary.

Fifth Sunday in Ordinary Time – Job 7:1-4, 6-7

Curse God and die

"Curse God and die" is what Job's wife says to him in the second chapter of this book of Wisdom literature. We can probably understand why. Job, as this book adapts the story of a famous figure from ancient history, is a good and upright man who the text itself says "feared God and shunned evil." Job had all the material and familial comforts and strengths that we would all want to have. When God and the satan (the adversary) get to talking about Job, God proudly points out how upstanding this man is. The satan is less impressed. He thinks Job holds God in such high esteem only because he has so much good stuff. God then agrees to put Job to the test, which may disturb the way we view God. If Job's family and possessions are taken from him, will he still hold God in such high esteem? God does take them away, and Job does still revere God, but this is not enough for the adversary, who then challenges God to afflict Job's very physical being. The results are dire, but still Job does not do as his wife suggests and curse God, though he does end up cursing his own existence.

Then the "friends" show up. Their basic points, given in long, long speeches, are that all misfortune either comes from bad behaviour or is sent to try us. Job, throughout the many chapters of this book, maintains that this is not so. He maintains his innocence and is ultimately vindicated when God shows up in answer to his constant pleading. God does not specifically answer Job's questions and protestations, but clearly says that the friends were wrong and that Job was indeed innocent. The book ends with a restoration for Job – new possessions and a new family, except he seems to have kept the same somewhat colourful wife. It is a troubling ending, though, as we ponder the loss of Job's previous children and their families on a kind of a whim of God's.

This lectionary passage is a reply of Job's to his friend Eliphaz of Teman, who utters the first speech of the first friend. Job is maintaining his innocence, the truth that he does not "deserve" all the misfortune that has happened to him (6:24). He demonstrates his point by waxing bleakly about the human condition. Life generally is no better than hired drudgery, he says, in which both night and day seem endless. And yet, at the same time, life passes very swiftly, leaving no hope behind. However bleak life may be, and the text certainly paints a picture of it in that light, it is not so because of some sort of deserved punishment by God. Life is just bleak. The difficulties of life do not confront us because God wills that there be such difficulties. Remember that although God may seem problematic in the beginning of this book of Job, in the end, God appears in a whirlwind and says that Job is right to believe that he did not deserve what happened to him. A difficult text in a difficult book, but much past and current commentary help us in working with it. Some current thinking by those working in the convergence point of science and theology, such as the quantum physicist and Anglican priest Sir John Polkinghorne, offer some useful guidance. Polkinghorne, for example, says in his book *Searching for Truth: Lenten Meditations on Science and Faith* that as humans were created with the potential for freedom, so must the natural world have freedom, or the potential for random acts. Therefore, random stuff happens. Disturbing as the opening of this Book of Job is, really, misfortune is not the result of a vindictive God; it is random. Job knew that.

Sixth Sunday in Ordinary Time – *Leviticus 13:1-2, 44-46*

To life!

It would be easy to dismiss the Book of Leviticus, as many people to-day do. It would be easy to dismiss this particular text from the Book of Leviticus. But the lectionary challenges us to delve deeply into the Scripture as it is revelation to us, regardless of how difficult or removed from our lives it may seem. And that means all Scripture, including Leviticus, which is the physically central book of the Torah for our Jewish sisters and brothers. We interpret it as Christians, we understand the weight of its guidelines for life as Christians, and we take it seriously.

Leviticus is a book about the living of life. In its myriad details, it proclaims to us that God is the Lord of Life, caring deeply about the physical realities of our lives. The Book of Leviticus comes from a time in the history and life of the people of Israel in which life was much more precarious than it is now for many of us in the western and northern parts of our globe. Although understandings of some of the physical realities of life were therefore different than they are now, the deep meaning was and is the same: God cares about life in all its detail. God wills life.

In a book that can seem particularly obscure in the canon of scripture, this passage can seem particularly obscure in the book. Rabbi Gunther Plaut reminds us that while the word "leprosy" is used with a bit of reckless abandon in some English translations of the book, Leviticus deals broadly with a wide range of skin conditions.[118] This lectionary text deals with leprosy as we know it, but many other Levitical texts in which the word "leprosy" appears in English actually concern other skin ailments. None of the texts makes any statements against what we now experience as modern medicine; the texts often consider it possible that ailments may clear up.

---

118 Plaut, *The Torah*, 328.

In texts such as this one, there is a difference between what is described to be done for it compared to what is described for other skin ailments. Leprosy was sometimes thought to be a sign of divine displeasure; the person manifesting it was to be barred not only from the sanctuary, as was the case with other skin conditions, but from all human society. Some biblical stories that depict people with leprosy seem to indicate that divine displeasure may have arisen from lack of faithfulness towards God and God's purposes, though other stories do not. Very unfortunately, readings of biblical texts that deal with leprosy influenced some thinking in the early stages of the HIV/AIDS pandemic, resulting in un-godlike behaviour on the part of some people towards those with the disease. The point of this passage, and, indeed, all of Leviticus, however, is the connection between the Holy One and the realities of life. There is no abstract, theological-only realm in which God exists far away from the realities of human life. The relationship we have with God is intimately connected with our physical lives and surroundings. The people of Israel knew that, just as our global sisters and brothers in the developing world know it. If we listen to Benedict XVI, and countless others speak out on our current environment crisis, that truth will again become clear and real. God cares about Creation in all its details.

Tenth Sunday in Ordinary Time – *Genesis 3:9-15*

Where, who, how, when and WHY?

So few words, so much meaning. Pages and pages and volumes and volumes of biblical commentary have been written on this text. St. Paul the Apostle, the Church Fathers, saints, popes, reformers and even the comic Bill Cosby have reflected on and written on this text. To comment on it in just a few words here feels rather overwhelming. One place to start, though, is to say that this is one of the Old Testament texts in which there is a substantive difference of opinion between the Jewish and Christian traditions.

Jewish scholar and rabbi Gunther Plaut writes:

> Christianity, building on certain, largely sectarian Jewish teachings, taught that after Adam's transgression all men were inherently evil. In this interpretation the event has come to be known as "the fall of man," an expression absent from the Bible itself and from Jewish literature. "By one man, sin entered the world," says Paul in the Christian Scripture and again: "by the offense of one, judgment came upon all men to condemnation." This was man's original sin, a fatal flaw, from which he could be redeemed only after Jesus came into the world as the Christ. Without faith in him as the redemptive saviour men would live and die in their original sin. In the course of centuries the doctrine of man's inherent sinfulness led to a thoroughly pessimistic view of man and a heavy emphasis on the right kind of faith. The mainstream of Judaism refused to make the tale of Eden an important part of its world view and maintained that the only road to salvation was through godly deeds (mitzvoth), rather than through belief in a saviour, and that, while man tended to corruption (Gen. 6:5; 8:21), he was not basically a corrupt creature.[119]

So says a Jewish scholar about the Christian interpretation of a text that was and is still a part of the Jewish faith as well. And of course, as mentioned above, there are countless volumes of Christian

---

119 Plaut, *The Torah*, 38.

interpretation written about this text and even within Christianity, there are differences of opinion about the meaning of it.

Some scholars maintain that it is an etiological text – that is, a text that explains things. It explains why snakes slither and women often have so much more pain in childbearing than any other mammal. Feminist scholars maintain that this text has been much misused to justify the subjugation of women, interpreted to say that the first woman brought sin into the world, and it has certainly been used to castigate women as a whole for centuries. It has also carried the weight of the interpretations, often in combination, that it depicts the beginning of sexual knowledge, that it depicts humanity's rebellion against God and humanity's loss of innocence in the acquired awareness, like God has, of good and evil.

It is a deep and complicated story. Right after it, the man and the woman are expelled from the Garden of Eden into a very different, very challenging life out in the wild world. It certainly portrays a vital and vivid relationship between God and those beings created in God's image who have taken the freedom to make decisions – decisions that, in this case, profoundly affect their lives. There are consequences, to be sure. In the very next chapter, we see death by violence come into the world. God remains a God of faithfulness and relationship, in spite of or because of what we may choose to do.

Year B

Eleventh Sunday in Ordinary Time – *Ezekiel 17:22-24*

Alliance peril

Wondrous and slightly obscure visions, bizarre prophetic acts (eating a scroll!) and a plethora of historical detail – all of these are contained in the Book of the Prophet Ezekiel. This particular chapter, chapter 17, contains a combination of historical story and poetic point. Ezekiel is a prophet of the exile. He prophesied in Babylon when the rulers and upper classes were exiled there by the Babylonians after their destruction of Jerusalem and the Temple. Then as now, the people who worked the land and lived in poverty were not thought to have much value: it was those with power and money who were worth bothering about. The story in this chapter is about the puppet prince installed in the land after the Babylonians deported the people. But although he was to be "modest and without ambition and so maintain his treaty faithfully" (v. 14), he rebelled and turned to Egypt to make an alliance there. The king of Babylon would not be amused, and neither was God. Dire consequences were predicted for the puppet prince at the hand of the king of Babylon, but because the prince had ignored God's oath and treaty, there would be consequences at the hand of God as well. The current state of political affairs, the supremacy of Babylon, was considered by the biblical text to be at the hand of God. At this time in the history of the people of Israel – not later and not always, but at this time – to rebel against the structures that God had called for as a consequence of the people's unfaithfulness to God was to rebel against God.

What follows, forming the verses of the lectionary reading for this Sunday, is a poetic piece detailing God's initiative and control over all Creation, which is one of Ezekiel's major themes. An interesting and engaging way to illustrate the text and its theme of God's initiative and control over Creation would be with a number of pieces of music that revolve around the same theme. There are endless examples. The specifics would depend on the musical characteristics of individual congregations. The words could be printed and the congregation encouraged to reflect on the theme as the music reverberates around them. John Rutter's *For the Beauty of the Earth* is one example; or use the hymn by that name, which is well known in many Christian denominations. The music could be sung by the congregation or by a choir or both. The point is that God is the Lord of Creation.

Year B

Twelfth Sunday in Ordinary Time – *Job 38:1, 8-11*

See Year B, Proper 24, in the section on the Revised Common Lectionary. Even though the verses of that reading are not the same as this one, the theology and context and the role of the texts in the Book of Job are shared.

Thirteenth Sunday in Ordinary Time – *Wisdom 1:13-15, 2:23-24*

To be or not to be ...

Five-year-olds are fascinated by the topics of sex and death. The fascination with both occurs at the same stage of development probably because it is at approximately five years of age that children become aware that there are beginnings and endings to life.

We proclaim all the time, as I do throughout this book, that God is the Lord of Life, but what is the relationship between God and death? Our Christian hope is grounded in the Resurrection of Jesus Christ from death. We ask in words of Scripture, "O, death where is thy victory?" But at the same time we acknowledge the dire and dreadful reality of death. We know that Jesus suffered terribly on the cross on the way to his death; we know that he was in pain and, because of the nature of crucifixion, died of suffocation. We know that bodies rot after death, though often we try to forget that fact. But how and why does death exist? I am not seeking scientific answers here, though such answers are important. I am asking about death from a theological point of view, which is the point of view of this lectionary text.

The first part of the reading from the Book of Wisdom for this Sunday makes it clear that death is not God's doing. The Lord of Creation has created all life. The second part of the reading affirms that God made humans imperishable – indeed, in the divine image itself – but that another force, which the writer of Wisdom calls "the devil," brought death into the world. This explanation does not necessarily make it any easier to understand death. It more than implies that this other force has a lot of power, power that even God, the Lord of Life, cannot overcome.

Christian theology has often looked to the story of the Garden of Eden to explain death. By the human choice to sin, to defy God,

Creation was altered and death came into life. Genesis 3:19 speaks to this understanding.

Sir John Polkinghorne writes,

> This [Holy Week] is all about a death. The agony of Gethsemane and the darkness of Calvary make it clear that death was a reality for Jesus, as it will be for us. There is no pretence in the Bible that death is somehow not a real end. But it is not the ultimate end. Only God is ultimate and Easter shows us that reality is not terminated by death.[120]

In any discussion about death, based in this lectionary passage or any other, the final word can be understood through this statement of Polkinghorne's: God is ultimate, not death. The Resurrection of Jesus Christ declares that the power of death is overcome. Easter declares that God is the ultimate end. Thanks be to God!

---

120 Polkinghorne, *Searching for Truth*, 143.

Fourteenth Sunday in Ordinary Time – *Ezekiel 2:2-5*

The prophet next door

This text relates the call of the Prophet Ezekiel – a call that shows us a God who is irresistible. Many of us who have experienced a call to ministry know this to the core of our being. Over and over again in the biblical texts, prophets or messengers of God are called, and despite the somewhat dramatic objections of some of them, they cannot resist that call. Ezekiel falls into line with the call, obeying God's instructions. And, in the case of Ezekiel, the call to eat a scroll, not to mention other bizarre manifestations of his prophetic ministry, seems to be irresistible.

Although this passage from the Book of the Prophet Ezekiel does not mention specific proclamations he is to make, there is a lot of talk about him being sent to a rebellious people – a defiant and obstinate people, even – and the reality that they will know that there is a prophet in their midst. Generally, prophets are called to comfort the afflicted or afflict the comfortable; generally, people are urged to reject alliances with secular powers and other gods that they have made in defiance of God, and to act in justice towards the poor and oppressed. Ezekiel, prophet during the Babylonian exile, both challenges and comforts. His message focuses on faithfulness to God, the mysteriousness of God's working and the new heart and new spirit that God is giving the people. It is always important to note that Ezekiel was both a prophet and a priest. There is no dichotomy between the two. He concentrates on the Temple and its being as a key way of working out the relationship between God and humanity; at the same time, he is clear that God's sovereignty is not limited to any place in particular. God is the God of all Creation.[121]

---

121 For more on this theme, see Year A, Twenty-Third Sunday in Ordinary Time, in the Appendix: Roman Catholic Readings.

To take this passage into the lives of its hearers and your congregation, tell some stories of prophets in our time and place. Remember that prophets both comfort and challenge, calling from the margins of society or from deep within society and systems and structures. They do unusual, colourful things to model their messages, and they are often unpopular. Watch the newspapers in the week leading up to this Sunday for stories of those who are carriers of God's message in your own context. Fear not the stories of those who might be unpopular in our society or in our churches. Watch for the prophets who, in effect, eat a scroll, being satisfied in their lives with the nourishment of the Word of God. Watch for the prophets who are so much a part of your context, they live next door.

Fifteenth Sunday in Ordinary Time – *Amos 7:12-15*

Not the prophet next door

Prophets can live right in our midst and context like Ezekiel, from whose book we read last week. They can also speak from outside the context to which they are prophesying, as is the case of the prophet Amos. The readings for these two Sundays in a row are even more interesting when juxtaposed. Amos, one of the shepherds of Tekoa in the south of the land of Israel, is called by God to prophesy in the north of the land of Israel. Amos has a particularly forceful message about social justice, using very sharp terms like "cows of Bashan" for the many whom he considers are "trampling" the poor. He states clearly that there will be dire, graphic consequences for the many who have "sold the poor for a pair of sandals." This message does not go over well in the north, into which he parachutes himself.

In that time before the fall of the northern part of the kingdom to Assyria or the southern part of the kingdom to Babylon, Jerusalem was the holy sanctuary of the south. Since the political split of the kingdom after the time of King Solomon, there were also, however, two sanctuaries in the north, which the people of the north thought to be holy as well. One of these was Bethel, which had a long history as a sanctuary in the land. It was Amaziah, the priest of Bethel, who took great exception to the "outsider" Amos charging around condemning the northern society left, right and centre. Amaziah got the king on his side by reporting a more minor part of Amos's message: that there would be unpleasant consequences for the king, as well as for the people. Amaziah tells Amos, in no uncertain terms, to get out, to go back to his own part of the country. We learn from his words that there seemed to be some kinds of "guilds" of prophets who actually earned their living by prophesying. Amaziah thinks that Amos is one of those, come to earn a living in the north. Amos corrects him, however, saying that he had been a shepherd and a tender of trees until God's irresistible call. As unpopular as Amos is, he gets his message across.

Here we have, in a sense, the opposite of Ezekiel's text last week. Amos is not the prophet next door; he is from outside the context. Yet God's call is just as irresistible. We ask a similar question, then, to the one we asked last week. Who are the prophets from outside our context who speak God's message to us? Having just returned from my third visit to Africa, I cannot help but think of the vibrant people of faith I encountered there, people with so much less materially than many of us have here but people whose faith resonated from them in word and spirit, in joy and enthusiasm. In Canada, the question for those of us who are not Aboriginal could be to identify those Aboriginal prophets who speak to us about justice. As Amos says so very often, "Listen to the word of the Lord."

Sixteenth Sunday in Ordinary Time – *Jeremiah 23:1-6*

And there were in that same country ...

Think of everything we know from the biblical text about shepherds. "The Lord is my shepherd," the shepherd leaving the 99 to go out and search for the single one who is lost, the shepherds coming to the manger as the ones representing the poor and common people of the world, and so on. Those of us who live in a rural context will know even more about the meaning of a shepherd. In this text from the Book of the Prophet Jeremiah, the image of the shepherd is used to speak about leadership. Since Jeremiah was a prophet and was from a priestly family, if not a priest himself, and since throughout his book he was critical of both the political and religious leadership of his land as it moved towards its destruction by Babylon, it may be both kinds of leaders who are being addressed here. The distinctions between church and state that are a part of our time and place are a more recent development in the history of the world. The line between them in Jeremiah's time was much more porous.

Doom is being proclaimed for the shepherds/leaders of God's people because they have not cared for the people. They have let the flock/people be scattered and destroyed. There will be consequences for them, to be sure, but God the divine self will gather all the people back from a diaspora to a fruitful and nurturing context in which they have what they need, and they will prosper there. By God's will, new leadership will arise who will truly care for the people as God wants them to be cared for. There is the proclamation of the messianic king to come – wise, honest and with integrity. Both parts of the land – and therefore all the land – will dwell in salvation and confidence. The political and what we might call the religious are totally intertwined.

This passage is, for Christians, one of great messianic import. We believe that it speaks to the coming of Jesus Christ our Shepherd and Saviour, who came to us through the line of David, and we rejoice in both the amount of shepherd imagery in the New Testament and the number of times that Jesus is declared to be in the line of David. Yet it had another meaning for the people of Jeremiah's time and place, as it does for our Jewish sisters and brothers now. It is not a faithful reading of the text to use it to consider Jewish leadership as the shepherds who are to be doomed, and Christian leadership as the new shepherds. Rather, as Christians, we use this text to proclaim Jesus Christ as our true and wise king and, in the light of that proclamation and in the depth of meaning that the shepherd metaphor contains, to consider our own leadership. In what ways have we scattered and destroyed people? How can we be the leaders that God wills and provide true pasture and nurture for people? How can we truly follow the one whose name is for us "God-our-integrity"? How can we lead in that holy name?

Seventeenth Sunday in Ordinary Time – *2 Kings 4:42-44*

Barley, barley everywhere ... and much to eat

Jesus knew his Scripture. A Jewish boy in the Galilee of his time would have been well educated in the texts and traditions of the faith. Even small, poor villages such as Nazareth would have placed a priority on the education of boys.[122] Jesus would have known this story of the prophet Elisha, given to us in what is now the second book of Kings. Was it a coincidence that his actions, which we hear recounted in the Gospel reading for this Sunday, are so resonant with this Old Testament story? Probably not. As Christians, we believe and proclaim that in the Incarnation, God has truly come into the world in the person of Jesus Christ, who was and is truly God. In his words and deeds and very person, Jesus proclaimed God. The people hearing and seeing him in the story told in the Gospel of John said, "This really is the prophet who is to come into the world." This makes a clear connection with the prophet Elisha, who in the 2 Kings story declares that it is God's will for the people to eat and have some left over. Jesus is the Incarnate God: the connection is obvious between his real presence in a certain time and place and in the midst of a particular people, and the way that God has been manifest through the eons of time before coming into the world as the Son.

But in the beginning, in the history and faith of the people of Israel, a history and faith that Jesus knew to the core of his being, there was a tradition of prophecy. The early prophets such as Elijah and Elisha did not leave us texts of their prophecies, but Scripture contains the stories of all the ways in which they proclaimed the presence and justice of God to and in the world.

So in this story we hear that bread from the first-fruits was brought to Elisha. In the biblical tradition, as we learn in that abundance of

---

122 The education of girls has been a more recent reflection of the will of God for justice and the development of the whole person.

guidelines in the Book of Leviticus, the first-fruits are to be offered to God. They are a thanksgiving for all God has given us. Today, we tend to give to God what we think we can spare, after all other wants and needs are taken care of, rather than giving the first parts of all that we have. Elisha directs that those first-fruits, given to him as a representative of God, be given to the people, but his servant protests that it is not nearly enough. But God had declared that it was to be given to the people: that they could eat and there would be food left over. And it was so. With God, things that seem impossible are indeed possible. We know well the biblical tradition of justice and taking care of the poor, who do not have enough to sustain them. What if we, in the name of God, were really to share the abundance God has given the world?

Year B

Eighteenth Sunday in Ordinary Time – Exodus 16:2-4

See Year A, Proper 20, in the section on the Revised Common Lectionary.

Year B

Nineteenth Sunday in Ordinary Time – *1 Kings 19:4-8*

See Year C, Proper 7, in the section on the Revised Common Lectionary.

Twentieth Sunday in Ordinary Time – _Proverbs 9:1-6_

"You are invited"

Hospitality was very important in the ancient Near East – not only because it was the gracious thing to do, but because it could mean the difference between life and death. That land was then, and is still often now, challenging in its geography and climate. It contains mountains and desert, it can be very hot or very cold, and there is often a scarcity of water.

The Old Testament passage for this Sunday is about the hospitality of Wisdom herself. Much of the Book of Proverbs, which is ascribed to the wise King Solomon, consists of "short, compact statements that express a truth about human behaviour," as the introduction to that book in the New Revised Standard Version says. It adds, "Although Proverbs is a practical book dealing with the art of living, it bases wisdom solidly on the fear of the Lord."[123] The book both talks about the acquiring of wisdom and presents "Wisdom" as a female person who has always been present with God. This passage presents the hospitality of the personified "Wisdom," who has built a grand house and prepared a grand feast and then sent out the word that all those who are "ignorant," that is, without wisdom, are to come and partake of the feast. Being a guest at such a feast will enable them to leave their folly and "walk in the ways of perception."

So what does it mean, specifically, to leave one's folly and walk in the ways of perception? What does it mean to be wise? We can read specifics starting in the very next chapter, chapter 10, and read right through to at least chapter 25 without any break in the list of specific ways to manifest wisdom. Proverb after proverb after proverb speaks to that topic. In a homily, I would list some of those specifics for the congregation, balancing the selection between well-known proverbs and little-known proverbs that may seem obscure or even weird to us.

---

123 NRSV, Introduction to the Book of Proverbs.

But the most important thing, the paradigm overarching it all, is the oft-repeated phrase "The fear of the Lord is the beginning of wisdom." All of those practical two-line proverbs that seem like common sense for anyone and everyone, that sound like what we might call "secular" advice, are set and grounded in the reality of God. The beginning of wisdom is to live in awe of God, to live fully conscious of the sovereignty of God, to live in conscious fulfillment of the will of God. So "Wisdom" calls to us to come to her banquet, to ground ourselves in her feast of proverbs, and to do all that we do, even, or particularly, in those parts of our lives that we might call "secular," in awesome acknowledgment of God.

Year B

Twenty-First Sunday in Ordinary Time – *Joshua 24:1-2a, 15-17, 18b*

See Year A, Proper 27, in the section on the Revised Common Lectionary.

Twenty-Second Sunday in Ordinary Time – Deuteronomy 4:1-2, 6-8

Repeat after me ...

The word "Deuteronomy" means "second law," which is exactly what that book is. The Creation, the adventures of the early patriarchs and matriarchs, the visionary faith of Abraham, the Exodus from slavery in Egypt and the long wandering in the wilderness have all happened. The people are about to re-enter the land – at least, the younger generation is. Moses, who will not be able to enter with them, delivers what is a book-length final address. In Deuteronomy, much of what has been said in the previous four books of the Torah is restated for a different time, a different generation. In this restatement, attributed to Moses, the people are reminded of God's goodness to them throughout their long journey. God's gift of the laws is summarized, including a restatement of the ten commandments that is slightly different from the versions in Exodus 20 and 34. The love of God for the people is a constant theme, as is the loving response of the people for God.

This particular passage is a kind of exhortation in which the people are to take notice of the laws and customs of which the speaker, Moses, is reminding them. For it is by doing so that they may have life and may enter and take possession of the land. God's commandments, God's gift of guidelines by which to live in relationship to God and to others are not to be added to, and neither is anything to be taken away from them. It is stated that the keeping of those guidelines, which were a gift to the people, will manifest to others the wisdom and understanding of the people of Israel. The people's wisdom and prudence will be seen by all. It is also strongly stated that there is no other nation that has its gods so near as God is to the people of Israel.[124]

This passage and the entire book of Deuteronomy raise the difficult but crucial issue of scriptural interpretation. We must balance the need, expressed by the Bible itself, to interpret the will and ways of God in each new circumstance with the certainty of the eternal will of God for peace, justice and faithful worship and relationship. It is not an easy task, and there is no neat and tidy answer, but part of the way forward in faithful discerning is to gather in community, to hear together the words of Scripture, to pray through and around them in music and spoken prayer, and to constantly reflect together on the events of our time and place. I believe, to the very core of my being, that we are called to do such reflecting ecumenically, gathering as sisters and brothers in Christ from various Christian traditions. The proclamation of unity in diversity that is the Canadian Council of Churches endeavours to hold fast to Christ in any and all circumstances. At the same time, we are to discern in our work in the areas of Faith and Witness, and Justice and Peace, and Biotechnology a way of interpreting the will of God for justice, peace and faithful relationship in the particular context of our lives. The Book of Deuteronomy resonates for the ministry and work of the denominations of Christ together.

---

124 This kind of belief is what is called "monolatry." It reflects an early stage in the life of the people of Israel. It is not "monotheism," which is the belief in the one God to which the people come in a later era of their history and faith. Rather, it is the belief that a particular God is the god of a particular people. The particular people are to be completely faithful to their particular god.

Year B

Twenty-Third Sunday in Ordinary Time – *Isaiah 35:4-7a*

See Year A, Advent 3, in the section on the Revised Common Lectionary.

Year B

Twenty-Fourth Sunday in Ordinary Time – *Isaiah 50:4-9a*

See Year A, Palm/Passion Sunday, in the section on the Revised
Common Lectionary

Twenty-Fifth Sunday in Ordinary Time – *Wisdom 2:12, 17-20*

The Screwtape Letters

When I reread this Wisdom passage for the purposes of this book, I wondered if this is where C.S. Lewis got the inspiration for *The Screwtape Letters*. His satirical book muses, in an entertaining and pointed fashion, on the nature of God and Christianity and the possibilities of corrupting Christians. This Wisdom passage is not written for the same purpose of "corrupting," but is rather a reflection of "Life as the godless see it," as The Jerusalem Bible titles the beginning of the section. The tone of it, however, could have influenced Lewis.

Although written in the last century BCE in the very fine Greek of a well-educated, Hellenized Jew, as the introduction in The Jerusalem Bible tells us, the Book of Wisdom is attributed to King Solomon. Attribution was a common literary practice in the Ancient Near East; rather than seeing it as an underhanded technique, we are to see it as giving a good piece of work the status that it deserved.

Starting with verse 12, this passage has a rather humourous tone as it portrays what the "godless" plan to do: lie in wait for the virtuous but annoying person who reproaches them for their transgressions of that great gift of God's grace, the law. Then the tone of the lectionary passage begins to echo the book of Job, which can also be classified as Wisdom literature. If the righteous one is really, as he claims to be, a child of God, then God will take his part. While the satan or adversary tests Job to see if he really loves God as much as he says he does, the godless plan to test the righteous one's endurance. If he is really the son of the Lord, he can even be condemned to a shameful death but will be looked after. Here, of course, we can see a Christological interpretation of the passage and why Christian readers would particularly resonate with it.

One of the homiletic challenges with a passage like this is the identification of the "godless." We need to proceed carefully and thoughtfully. We all, in the dark places of our hearts, know who we might identify as "godless." But we also know, as many of the texts of the lectionary reveal to us, that God's perspective can be very different from ours. Someone else reading this passage might put us in the place of the "godless"! What are the challenges to virtuous behaviour in our time and place? What challenges our attempts to be children of God? Are there ways in which we test the ability of others to be children of God? Remember the overarching theme of all Wisdom literature that "the fear of the Lord is the beginning of Wisdom."

Year B

Twenty-Sixth Sunday in Ordinary Time – Numbers 11:25-29

See Year A, Pentecost, in the section on the Revised Common Lectionary.

Twenty-Seventh Sunday in Ordinary Time – *Genesis 2:18-24*

You are not alone

When I was studying for my Master of Divinity degree at Emmanuel College in Toronto, I took a course on Trinitarian theology at St. Michael's Roman Catholic College down the street. One of the major texts for the course was *The God of Jesus Christ: Meditations on the Triune God* by the Roman Catholic scholar Joseph Ratzinger, later Pope Benedict XVI.[125] The book delves deeply into its proclamation that we need to understand the Trinity as God being in relationship. At one point it used the analogy of a family as a way of wrapping our minds around the reality of the Trinity. In Ratzinger's analogy, God the Father was the father, Jesus stood in the place of the mother and the Holy Spirit was the child. The book helped develop my understanding of the Trinity.

If God must be in relationship within the Godhead, then when God creates, there must be potential for relationship in that action, too. God creates a human person with whom God can be in relationship. But then God realizes that the human creature needs not only relationship with God but also relationship with another creature very much like it. God's first try to accomplish that relationship involves all the wild beasts and all the birds of heaven. The human creature gives them all names but none of them could be a part of the deep relationship that was needed. God then takes part of the human creature and from it builds another human creature, similar but also different. Complementary.

This is one of those biblical passages that has been interpreted and reinterpreted down through the centuries of the Christian tradition. The church carries with it all that interpretation, both good and bad.

---

125 Joseph Ratzinger, *The God of Jesus Christ: Meditations on the Triune God*, Fort Collins, CO: Ignatius Press, 2008.

This passage has been used in a variety of times and places to oppress women. Scholars such as Phyllis Trible, working with the original Hebrew of the text, remind us that the words used for "man" in the English do not correspond to what is there in the Hebrew. In fact, some significant changes in language in the Hebrew are not caught by the English. The earlier use of "man" in this passage is, in Hebrew, a word related to the word for "ground." Awkward as it is in English, "Earth creature" is probably a better rendering of the Hebrew. It is only when the second creature has been created by God that the Hebrew distinguishes between the sexes, using distinct terms for "man" and "woman."

Several other key linguistic details are found in the passage. The Hebrew word that The Jerusalem Bible translates as "helpmate" does not in any way imply a secondary status; that same word is used of God in the Psalms (e.g, Psalm 10:14, 30:10). In the NRSV, the word is translated as "helper." There has also been linguistic work done to show that the Hebrew word translated in English as "rib" is sometimes used in descriptions of the Temple to refer to a whole side of the Temple.

What is most important to proclaim about this passage is that it is about relationship. God's relationship in the Godhead is a guide for the relationship we have as human beings with God and with each other. As human beings, we are to stand side by side in deep relationship, and in that relationship to mirror God. What will that look like in our time and place? In your homily, be specific.

C.S. Lewis says, "Next to the Blessed Sacrament itself, your neighbour is the holiest object presented to your senses."[126] Act that out.

---

126 C.S. Lewis, in *The Weight of Glory*, as quoted in *The Business of Heaven*, Walter Hooper, ed. (New York: Harcourt Brace and Company, London, 1984), 148.

Twenty-Eighth Sunday in Ordinary Time – Wisdom 7:7-11

Door number three

Scripture comments on Scripture. This passage from the Book of Wisdom, one of the later books in the canon of what Christians call the Old Testament, is commenting on another passage of Scripture. In 1 Kings 3, verses 4-15, a much earlier part of the canon, we hear the story of King Solomon's dream. Solomon had just recently become the king of what was still the united kingdom of Israel. As there was no Temple in Jerusalem, he went to worship and offer sacrifice at one of the ancient high places, a place where people had experienced God for many generations. While at Gibeon, God appeared to Solomon in a dream and asked what he would like to be given. Solomon responded that, for the sake of the people he had been entrusted to govern, he would like "a heart to understand how to discern between good and evil, for who could govern this people of yours that is so great?" God was so pleased that Solomon had asked for wisdom rather than for a long life or riches for himself, God granted him not only wisdom but riches and a long life as well.

In the 1 Kings text, the story sets up the nature of Solomon's kingship. Interesting reflection can occur around the fact that Solomon is considered wise, as the above story and the Wisdom text that is the lectionary passage for this Sunday make crystal clear. Yet it is Solomon's no doubt unwisely oppressive theories of governance that result in the nation of Israel separating into two parts when the north rebels over the enforced labour and taxation he imposes. Nonetheless, the biblical text always considers Solomon the epitome of wisdom, attributing much of its Wisdom literature to him.

Wisdom 7:7-11 speaks in the first person. Solomon alludes to his prayer and dream and the way in which God granted it. In wonderfully extravagant language, King Solomon speaks of his love of wisdom and of her unparalleled place in life (in the Bible, Wisdom is always perceived as female). She is precious, she is radiant. In the 1 Kings story, being grounded in wisdom leads one to all other good things as well.

This is all well and good, but it begs the question of what exactly wisdom is. In the Old Testament understanding, it can be briefly summarized as the kind of practical maxims for the living of life that we find in the Book of Proverbs. And over and around that it is also, as we see in such stories as that of Joseph in Genesis and in such books as Wisdom, the complete and total grounding of all of life in God. That kind of grounding of the practical, everyday details of our own lives is the call of Wisdom to us. It is not frivolously unbiblical to look at dilemmas and solutions in our everyday lives and ask, "What would the writer of the Book of Proverbs do?"

Twenty-Ninth Sunday in Ordinary Time – Isaiah 53:10-11

See Year A, Good Friday, in the section on the Revised Common Lectionary.

Year B

Thirtieth Sunday in Ordinary Time – *Jeremiah 31:7-9*

See Year A, Christmas 2, in the section on the Revised Common Lectionary.

Thirty-First Sunday in Ordinary Time – *Deuteronomy 6:2-6*

Hear, O Israel

If you live your whole life, meaning both the quantity of the days and the quality of the days, totally centred on the Lord your God, and if you follow in the guidelines for relationship between yourselves and God and yourselves and others that have been God's gift of grace to you, you will live long and prosper.[127] This is the promise of God, given to the ancestors in the past and now being repeated by Moses to the next and new generation as they prepare to re-enter the land of Israel. Moses is not going to be crossing over into the land. The generation that was freed from slavery in Egypt by God's great act of grace and then given the ten commandments as a way of responding to that grace is not going to be crossing over into the land. It is the next and new generation that will be making that journey. The Book of Deuteronomy is both Moses' farewell speech and his restatement of the faith to be lived out in the land.

The central core of the faith of the people of Israel is contained in verse 4 of this passage. It is called the "Shema" in Hebrew, which means "Hear," and it is recited in every Jewish worship service. It is also considered an essential statement of monotheistic faith. The people of Israel are directed to love God completely, with all of their being, with heart and soul and strength. Jesus, of course, knew this central tenet of the faith. What does it mean to us to love God completely with all of our heart, soul and strength? What are the implications of grounding ourselves in the understanding of the biblical wisdom tradition that we read just three Sundays ago, the understanding that all of life in all of its concrete, everyday details is to be lived in awe of God?

A detail of this passage that may seem disturbing for Christian theology is the clear assurance that loving God with heart, soul and

---

127 If this phrase sounds familiar, it is no coincidence. This was a deliberate choice for the character of *Star Trek*'s Mr. Spock. *Star Trek* went biblical!

strength will lead to long life and prosperity. We all know that this is not always the case. We all know very saintly people who truly, deeply loved God but also suffered hardship or died too young. In our time and in many places around the globe, the "prosperity gospel" – the belief that personal faith in Jesus will lead directly to such things as wealth – is alive and well. What we proclaim is that God loves us and desires us to be in loving relationship with God, and that it is the divine will that all people live lives of health, wholeness, peace and have the resources they need for dignity and self-reliance. What is crucial is to use a biblical definition of prosperity: the divine will that all people have hearth and home, their own vine and fig tree, what they need to earn a decent living, community and security.

"Give us this day our *daily* bread." Not excess – enough.

Year B

Thirty-Second Sunday in Ordinary Time – *1 Kings 17:10-16*

See Year C, Proper 5, in the section on the Revised Common Lectionary.

Year B

Thirty-Third Sunday in Ordinary Time – Daniel 12:1-3

Daniel in the lion's den or an alternate location

For an introduction to the history and purpose of the Book of the Prophet Daniel I can do no better than quote *The Jerusalem Bible*:

> The book of Daniel was written between 167 and 164 B.C.[E.] during the persecution under Antiochus Epiphanes and before the Maccabean revolt ... The aim of the book was to sustain faith and hope among the Jews in their persecutions by showing them the triumph of Daniel over his own severe ordeals and temptations of the same kind; and to hold before them the vision of a time to come when the wrath of God would be satisfied; and the kingdom of the saints would begin under a "Son of Man" whose reign would endure for ever ... the meaning of the book for its first readers was to be found in its insight into the present and the future in the purposes of God. It is the last expression of messianic prophecy in the Old Testament.[128]

The Book of Daniel can be said to resemble the story format of such other biblical books as the Book of Jonah. It was never intended to record empirical history but, rather, as the introduction above says, to sustain faith and hope for people in the midst of difficult circumstances. The Book of Daniel is considered to be of the biblical genre known as "apocalyptic" literature – a kind of literature that uses symbolic language as it tries to disclose matters inaccessible to normal knowledge.

By chapter 12, verses 1 to 3, the book has already related the story of Daniel and his three companions in and out of the lion's den, portrayed in a historical period that predates the period in which the book was actually written, and has moved into a section of visions. Hope is being proclaimed in a time that will be the end of time. There will be kings and invasions and attacks and a quest for booty, and it will be a time worse than anything since time began. But the people

---

128 *The Jerusalem Bible*, reader's edition (Garden City, NY: Doubleday, 1966), 1230.

to whom this book was written as encouragement will be spared. And there will be some kind of final judgment. Although there have been many times since the writing of the Book of Daniel that felt to those living through them like the end of time, and there are many in our world in recent times who feel that way, for those of us living fairly comfortable lives in the west and north of the world now it does not feel like a time of terrible persecution. The environmental crisis is very real, but it is not the kind of death and destruction that the writer of Daniel is talking about. A homiletic question might be how we as followers of God in our Lord and Saviour Jesus Christ manifest in real time and real place the hope of God to those who are in the midst of peril and persecution. Since the reading of this passage falls very close to Remembrance Day, one could also continue to remember the stories of those who in their faith in God despite desperate circumstances manifest hope for us today. For ourselves and for others we are to live God's hope.

Feast of Christ the King – *Daniel 7:13-14*

One like a son of man

There are two ways, at least, that one could go in a homily about this passage. One would be to retell the history and format of the Book of Daniel, as given in the entry above, to remind people why this book of Scripture is such an important witness in our faith. Such a presentation of the passage would include such details as the meaning of the term "son of man," which appears in the Book of Daniel in the Old Testament and then is picked up in the New Testament. William Neil's *One Volume Bible Commentary* (London: Hodder and Stoughton, 1962) offers a short definition of the term, "son of man," which speaks to both its original meaning in its concrete, historical context and its meaning in subsequent Christian theology:

> In the mind of the author of Daniel, this human figure is clearly representative of the faithful Israelites who will inherit the eternal Kingdom, appointed by God to supersede the kingdoms of this world. Man, as made in the image of God, and having the possibility of living in right relationship of obedience, is contrasted with hideous beasts, who typify the greed, hatred and cruelty that govern the policies of godless oppressors. The son of man comes on the clouds of heaven because the Kingdom of the saints is from God, and not from the primeval watery chaos from which the powers of this world emerged. It is thus prophecy of the same order as First Isaiah's doctrine of the remnant (Isa. 1:9), but its obvious messianic character led to later apocalyptic writers identifying the one "like a son of man" as the Messiah who would come from heaven to inaugurate the Kingdom of God.[129]

A second way to go about a homily on this passage would be to simply read from or, depending on the musical facilities of the congregation, have sung a wide variety of hymns that point to the na-

---

129 William Neil, *One Volume Bible Commentary* (London: Hodder and Stoughton, 1962), 278.

ture of Jesus Christ as King and Messiah. Explore with the congregation through music the height and breadth and depth of the ways in which the church through the ages has experienced that eternal sovereignty.

Second Sunday in Advent – *Baruch 5:1-9*

Arise, Jerusalem

Although written centuries apart, the Book of Baruch sounds a great deal like books of the Old Testament prophets, particularly Isaiah, another book whose passages are often proclaimed in this season of Advent. Baruch is a short book under the name of the secretary of the prophet Jeremiah. It follows both the Book of Lamentations, attributed to Jeremiah, and the actual Book of the Prophet Jeremiah. Baruch was probably written in the first century CE, in response to the destruction of the Temple and the city of Jerusalem by the Romans in 587 BCE, but it is set in Babylon, where an early wave of exiles hears about these terrible events.

The major theme of the book is a confession of the sins that have led to this disaster and a plea for God's forgiveness.[130] The people have not walked in the ways of relationship with their God and with each other which God has set out for them; destruction is the result. Yet there is also comfort to come for the people. The city of Jerusalem is personified as both a widow who comforts her children, and as one who is to be comforted. The lectionary passage for this week is the very last section of that comforting in the book before we move into reading a piece of the correspondence of the Prophet Jeremiah.

This lovely passage of comfort and hope tells Jerusalem to put on the beauty of the glory of God forever. This statement reminds the city and the people that the name God gave it forever is "Peace through integrity, and honor through devotedness." God has decreed that the people "walk in safety under the glory of God." This is a lovely passage indeed for the Advent season, in which Christians proclaim that the hope and glory of God, the incarnate forgiveness of God, have come in the person of Jesus Christ.

---

130 Neil, *One Volume Bible Commentary*, 325.

A lovely passage indeed for the Advent season, a season when our congregants sometimes come to worship wanting to hear particularly lovely passages and might sometimes be a little resistant to the challenge that is part of the message, too. Note the use of the word "integrity" in verse 4 of the passage. It is a word that is used in other places in the Book of Baruch (e.g., 1:15, 2:6), and also crops up frequently in our contemporary culture and literature – in the latter case, surprisingly, frequently without definition. The homily for this week could focus on a Christian definition of "integrity." What an Advent gift!

Year C

The Baptism of the Lord – *Isaiah 40:1-5, 9-11*

See Year B, Advent 2, in the section on the Revised Common Lectionary.

Seventh Sunday in Ordinary Time – *1 Samuel 26:2, 7-9, 12-13, 22-23*

The Lord's anointed

It would be an understatement to say that things are tense between the current King of Israel, Saul, and the up and coming King of Israel, David. Saul was appointed as the first king of Israel, at the request of the people, against the better judgment of the prophet Samuel and with the somewhat resigned agreement of God. Saul has not worked out well as a king, and God has called the prophet Samuel to appoint and anoint David in Saul's stead. The transition is not smooth; battles are fought and loyalties are divided. By this point in the story, Saul's kingship is winding down and David's is on the rise, although this passage reveals David hiding in the wilderness of Ziph. In what happens next, David is able to portray Saul as vulnerable, but will not go so far as to have him killed. David declares that a hand cannot be lifted against the Lord's anointed, for Saul was indeed the anointed king of Israel. Although he would not allow Saul to be killed, David is certainly not above taunting him. Standing on a mountainside across from Saul's camp, David waves around Saul's captured spear and makes it clear that he is the "good guy" who would not raise his hand against the Lord's anointed.

An interesting story with lots of interesting bits in between the verses that form the lectionary passage for this Sunday. In the verses chosen for this passage, the concept of "the Lord's anointed" is reinforced. The broad context of the biblical text makes clear the fact that Saul has many flaws as a king. It is also clear that David, in spite of having a number of flaws himself, ultimately becomes the ideal king of Israel, the model held up for ever and ever, in both Jewish and Christian theology. The act of anointing a king was a sacred act in biblical times that is still practised in monarchies today. Holy oil is used to mark parts of the king's (or queen's) body, and an anointing can never be cancelled. Anointing is also an important part of the consecration of priests to God's holy service, and, in some Christian traditions, in baptism and in the anointing of the sick and others desiring healing. In Hebrew, the very word for "messiah" means "anointed."

To anoint someone is to mark them in a way that symbolizes a calling or a role. This action is a way of enacting what is believed to be the presence and purposes of God in the world. Of course, there is plenty of room for that calling or role to be abused or misunderstood but anointing is a way of showing and marking the significance of the holy in and around and through human life. From the beginning of its usage among the people of Israel, anointing was believed in some way to transfer qualities associated with the Divine to the person being anointed. Later in the history of the people, the use of the term "anointed" could indicate that a person was acting in accordance with the Divine qualities or purposes. This ancient practice resonates down the ages to our time and place, in which sign and symbol, ritual and meaning matter still.

Eighth Sunday in Ordinary Time – *Sirach 27:5-8*

Think before you speak

Although it is more common to hear the phrase "The devil is in the details" than "God is in the details," one does hear both. Both statements can be made, depending upon the point you want to make. This passage from the Book of Sirach for this eighth Sunday in Ordinary Time chooses the latter. More precisely, it witnesses to the fact that what we say – the words that come out of our mouths – reflects the depth, or lack thereof, of our faith in God.

Sirach, named after the writer to whom it is attributed in a very personal introduction by his grandson, who translated the work from Hebrew into Greek in 132 BCE is also called The Book of Ecclesiasticus (from the Latin, meaning the "Church's book"). It is worth reading the introduction, also called the "translator's foreword," for its intimate quality and for the way it lays out the process by which this book came into being. It provides an insight into some of the ways in which Scripture came to be the canon that we have. The book is not a part of the Jewish canon and therefore not part of the Protestant canon, but it was considered sacred text by the early church and then on into the Roman Catholic tradition. Sirach is a part of the Wisdom literature tradition; it consists of pithy sayings for living life in all its details. Some sections may sound "secular" to our ears today, but this would not have been the case for its original hearers because of their absolute deep belief that all of life was to be lived in a sense of awe for the sovereignty of God. Wisdom texts do not feel the need to mention God in every second sentence; they see God weaving the divine presence through every aspect of life.

This passage reminds us that a person's words betray what they feel, since speech is the test of one's character. To paraphrase an old cliché, great minds talk about ideas, ordinary minds talk about events, and small minds talk about people. That maxim could have sprung from this lectionary passage from Sirach. What does this mean for us in our Christian witness in our everyday, concrete lives? Like the biblical exhortations against gossip, slander and bearing false witness, this passage tells us to watch our words. But more than that, what are we called to say in the face of a suffering world? How do we use words to speak on behalf of others? Our speech is indeed a test of our faith.

Tenth Sunday in Ordinary Time – *1 Kings 17:17-24*

See also Year C, Proper 5, in the section on the Revised Common Lectionary.

The power of prayer

Elijah's encounter with the widow of Zarephath continues. When her son died, the widow blamed Elijah. He then performed some specific, concrete actions, something not unusual for prophets, and prayed in specific, concrete ways that could be said to challenge God. God heard Elijah's prayer and the son of the widow of Zarephath was resuscitated. The widow declared that she knew that Elijah, whose name means "the Lord is my God," was a man of God, and that God's word in his mouth was truth itself.

This event is a resuscitation, not anything that resembles the resurrection. Here, and in the story of the raising of Lazarus in the Gospel of John, someone who has died is brought to life again in the same form as they were before. In the resurrection, on the other hand, Jesus is transformed. He is both recognizable and not recognizable. He both eats fish for breakfast as he did before death, and also seems to be able to enter locked and closed rooms. He is new life in a new way.[131]

This lectionary passage also encourages us to reflect deeply on the meaning and power of prayer. Elijah clearly has a very dynamic relationship with God. The widow blames Elijah for the death of her son, but Elijah blames God. Elijah believes that God has killed the widow's son, but also that God can restore life to the son. The dynamism of the relationship between God and Elijah is powerfully portrayed as Elijah, in effect, takes God to task. Although we hear only Elijah's side

---

131 The writings of C. S. Lewis, particularly *The Great Divorce, The Last Battle* and *The Voyage of the Dawn Treader*, point to what this new life in a new way may mean for us. See also N.T. Wright, *Surprised by Hope: Rethinking Heaven, the Resurrection, and the Mission of the Church* (New York: Harper One, 2008).

of the relationship, we know that God did answer his prayer. There is much that we do not know about prayer. The biblical witness is clear that whether or not what we pray for is granted, a dynamic, engaged relationship with God in prayer is our calling.

Sir John Polkinghorne describes prayer in this way:

> ... in prayer we offer ourselves to become fellow workers with God. We have been given some power to bring things about. God has also retained some providential power to bring things about. Prayer is seeking the alignment of our possibilities for action with God's possibilities for action ... Prayer is a spur to action and not a substitute for it ... it is good to have many people praying for the same thing ... there are then more wills available to cooperate with the divine will. In petitionary prayer we are offered the privilege of becoming fellow workers with God ... when we pray ... We are saying what it is we really want, what is our heart's desire. We are called upon to assign value, to commit ourselves to what comes first in our lives.[132]

Let us pray!

---

132 Polkinghorne, *Searching for Truth*, 101–104.

Eleventh Sunday in Ordinary Time – 2 Samuel 12:7-10, 13

You are the man!

David – the great king of Israel, David the model of an ideal king, David from whose line will emerge the Messiah – has done a terrible thing. The chapter before the one from which this lectionary text is taken relates the well-known story of David and Bathsheba. David forces Bathsheba into relationship – a woman in that time and place having little choice when summoned by the king – and Bathsheba gets pregnant. After trying various other bits of subterfuge, which fail, David arranges to have her husband, Uriah, killed. Needless to say, God is not pleased. God sends the prophet Nathan, who tells David the parable that accuses him. Why, after all that God had done for him, would David act this way? There are consequences. When confronted by the fact that he is the villain of the parable, David immediately recognizes his sin.

If we read through this passage without skipping verses as the lectionary does, we find that it holds together two facts: that there are indeed consequences for sinful behaviour, and that in God there is forgiveness. The consequences, as laid out in verses 11 and 12, are dire. But the forgiveness is real. What is also important is that David knows he has sinned against God. Obviously, he has sinned against Bathsheba and Uriah, but the sin of failing to live in right relationship with others is also a sin against God. The same is true for us. When we fail to live in right relationship with others, when we carry a grudge, when we think petty thoughts about others, when we do not look out for the ailing neighbour next door, when we do not give more than we can spare to the crises at home or abroad, when we refuse to take climate change seriously, or when we break faith with the vulnerable people of the world, we are not only failing to live in right relationship with others, we are also failing to live in right relationship with God.

I began this entry by stating that David is considered the ideal king and that the Messiah is of David's line. But how can this be when David has done such horrific things? Challenging as it is, this is one of the ways that the Bible proclaims and manifests God's grace. In the Old Testament we see flawed human beings, who sometimes do such terrible things, and yet are instruments of God. There are serious consequences, to be sure, and there is always the vibrant and passionate challenge and calling to live in right relationship with God and all other people, but forgiveness is always available and we receive the assurance that we can move on from our flaws and sins and be instruments of God. Thanks be to God indeed!

Twelfth Sunday in Ordinary Time – *Zechariah 12:10-11, 13:1*

Zechariah's Messiah

Zechariah's name means "the Lord remembers." Although, because of the length of the Book of the Prophet Zechariah, he is considered one of the twelve "minor" prophets, Zechariah's message is not minor. Zechariah was both a prophet and a priest. His ministry took place after the return from exile in Babylon, sometime around 480 BCE. He was concerned about rebuilding the Temple and encouraging the people to listen to the messages of previous prophets, because he saw these as ways of preparing for the coming or the recognition of the Messiah. This passage is one of the many in the book that are messianic, that speak about the coming of God's Messiah. For Christians, his words resonate with the Passion story.

Zechariah, like his contemporary Haggai, was a prophet in a time of general revolt by the conquered states of the superpower Persia. Both prophets saw the events of their time as a sign that the oppressor was about to fall and the day of the Lord was about to come. The fact that the governor of Jerusalem, Zerubbabel, could trace his ancestry back to King David, the ideal king in the people's view, heightened the sense that the messianic kingdom was at hand. In the verse before this passage, which indicates destruction to come for the oppressors of Jerusalem, the prophet's message announces that a spirit of kindness and prayer will be poured out over the people. Such a spirit of kindness and prayer will enable the people to repent for a past wrong against some representative of God who has been abused and martyred. The day in which this great mourning enabled by the spirit will take place will be reminiscent of a past event of profound mourning.

The coming day will bring a great ceremonial cleansing of the abuse and martyrdom, as well as every other sin.

The Book of the Prophet Zechariah as a whole is a difficult book to get a handle on. It includes various kinds of material and seems to reference different time periods. It is definitely messianic, however, which further explains its significance to the Christian church and perhaps is the reason for its placement as the second-last book of the Old Testament, moving us into the New Testament. Christianity and Judaism share many biblical and theological realities; one of them is the understanding that whatever we believe about the messianic era, it is not yet completed. Our Jewish sisters and brothers await the coming of the Messiah; Christians believe that the Messiah, Jesus Christ, has come and we wait for him to return. For now, we live in the in-between time. The messianic kingdom is begun, but it is not fulfilled. What that fulfillment will look like is held in the wisdom of God; meanwhile, we endeavour to wait faithfully.

But what, exactly, will that faithful waiting look like in our time and place? Be specific in terms of the life, ministry and witness of your parish. It is not a passive kind of waiting, but an active one.[133]

---

133 See also Wright, *Surprised by Hope*.

Year C

Thirteenth Sunday in Ordinary Time – *1 Kings 19:16b, 19-21*

... then I will follow you

In this usage of "anointing," Elijah, the early prophet in the life of the people of Israel, is commanded by God to anoint several kings as well as Elisha, his successor. This anointing legitimates leadership. It establishes the lines of succession according to the will and purposes of God, and it situates Elijah as the one who acts on behalf of God in establishing such political and prophetic succession.

As this story moves on, it can lead us to reflect deeply on the nature of vocation. It is common in the prophetic canon for the prophets to strongly resist their calling by God, at least at first. Moses, Isaiah and Jeremiah all resist being called by God. Elisha verbally agrees to succeed Elijah, but first he must set his domestic affairs in order. (The fact that Elisha is plowing behind twelve yoke of oxen means that he comes from a wealthy family; he gives up much in following Elijah.) The "farewell" feast Elisha throws for his men before he heads off with Elijah indicates both his wealth and a mood of celebration and thanksgiving.

Vocation is a complicated subject – often murky for the person called and for the people around that person. When I became general secretary of The Canadian Council of Churches after serving as senior minister in a parish – preaching, celebrating communion, baptizing, doing funerals and engaging all the other realities that are part of parish ministry – I was startled at the number of people who said it was sad that I had "given up" ministry. For me, my new role was ministry! An Orthodox priest I know told me that many of the men of his tradition do not want to join the priesthood because they want to make money. How do we define a calling, a vocation to serve God? Through our work? By raising families? By caring for aging parents? By serving the poor? Once we have defined our vocation, how do we explain it or make its meaning visible so that it resonates with others, touching a deep longing they may barely understand within themselves? How do we proclaim a calling that doesn't pay well, can be difficult and lonely, can feel contrary to the general movement and mood of our society, and can even evoke opposition, yet is life-giving beyond all else? In response to God we say, "I will follow you."

Fourteenth Sunday in Ordinary Time – Isaiah 66:10-14c

Peace like a river

The beginnings of biblical books set the themes and tones for what is to follow. The endings of biblical books remind us of what has been said and move things forward in God's vision. This lectionary passage comes from the last chapter of the Book of the Prophet Isaiah. This poem in Isaiah 66 is a glorious statement of the intimate, passionate love of God for the people. It is found in what some scholars refer to as "Third Isaiah," the part of the book perhaps primarily addressed to the people in a time when they are returned from the exile in Babylon but still in the process of settling in. Chapters 56 to 66 deal with a community that is trying to reconstitute itself. As Walter Brueggemann says, the passage is trying to insist on a large and radical inclusiveness and a generous and concrete focus on neighbourly need.[134] It is clear in reading through the chapters, however, that disputes arise as those who are returned from exile and those who had remained in the land endeavour to settle in together. They are trying to balance the call for inclusiveness and focus on neighbourly need with the call to be a visible community with a defined and particular relationship to its God. This balance is something we continue to seek today.

This is the overall context for the lovely, oh so intimate, poem of Isaiah 66. It proclaims that in spite of any disputes the people are struggling with, in spite of the settling-in pangs they are facing, God's love is constant, total and very close. There is much focus on the city of Jerusalem in these words that clearly use female imagery for God. The nursing imagery is so explicit, some people may be uncomfortable hearing it out loud in liturgy. The tremendous joy that is Jerusalem's is interwoven with the joy of giving birth to and nursing a child. This kind of intense joy continues to resonate for us today: we have all experienced the great joy of new life, whether through having children

---

134 Brueggemann, *Isaiah 40–66*, 165.

of our own, or having family members or friends so blessed. Imagine, though, the impact of such new life in a time and a place in which a very large percentage of babies and mothers died in childbirth – as many in parts of our world still do. That is a hard statement to hear or say, but it is very much in the background of this text.

Read this passage that overflows with the deep and intimate love of God for the people, a love that is given to us as well and that reso-nates for us through the person of Jesus Christ. Feel the presence of God described by this passage as so close that it is physical. This is not an abstract, cerebral love but one that wants to give us all we need – a love that can be portrayed in very physical imagery, and means above all the peace of God (the Hebrew word for peace, "shalom," always encompassing wholeness, health and prosperity) flowing abundantly towards us like a river in a land in which water is a scarce resource. Rejoice indeed!

Fifteenth Sunday in Ordinary Time – *Deuteronomy 30:10-14*

It is doable

Moses the prophet, the lawgiver, wants to make sure that the people of the next generation have everything they need as they enter back into the land. They are going it alone; those freed from slavery in Egypt, who wandered amid the trials and tribulations of the wilderness and received the gift of the law in the ten commandments, will not return to the land. That includes Moses. The Book of Deuteronomy is his last shot at making sure that the new generation knows everything it needs to know. Most of the book is presented as Moses' farewell address. Scripture interprets Scripture in this text, as it does with so many other Old Testament and New Testament texts. Moses spells out what has gone before in the history and life of the people, but recognizes that the context has changed. It is not always possible for us to understand the exact ways in which those changes are reflected in the text, or why, but we can see that they are there.[135]

The point is that we have a living faith in which we understand God to be incarnational, deeply involved in the concrete realities of human life and life in our world – a truth to which biblical texts so powerfully witness. The core of our faith is unchanging: God loves us and the world, and we are to live in response to that love in ways of peace and just behaviour. The details of what that looks like in specific times and places can and do change, as the Bible itself declares.

A particular witness of the passage for this day is that the laws or guidelines God has given the people are doable. The heart and soul

---

135 One way to see that the faith is reinterpreting itself in a changed time is to compare the versions of the ten commandments in Exodus 20 and 34 with the version in Deuteronomy 5. For those who love this sort of thing, there is much scholarly material available that discusses the exact nature of the changes and what those changes might imply about the context.

of the people are to belong to God and the Law is within their reach. The "Word," which is used interchangeably with the "Law," is so close to the people that it is in their hearts and in their words. This kind of passage should banish forever the anti-Judaic way of speaking that Christians sometimes fall into, where the law is seen as a great burden under which our Jewish sisters and brothers struggle. Rather, the Law or Word is a gift of God's grace to guide and sustain the people. The specifics of the call to relationship between the people and God, and among the people, are doable. We have all had, and goodness knows the people of Israel had, times of failure. The biblical prophets could often think of little else except the times that the people had failed to walk in God's ways. The fact that God's laws are doable means we always have the opportunity to pick ourselves up, dust ourselves off and start again. Thanks be to God!

Year C

Sixteenth Sunday in Ordinary Time – *Genesis 18:1-10a*

See Year A, Proper 6, in the section on the Revised Common
Lectionary.

Seventeenth Sunday in Ordinary Time – *Genesis 18:20-32*

Sodom and Gomorrah

This is a difficult biblical passage. It has been used, misused, interpreted and misinterpreted for centuries; even today, it is possible to find wide differences of opinion about it. It is a passage to go carefully with, to be sure, especially given that the passage that follows it has an even more complicated interpretation. As with every biblical passage, setting the context is crucial. It follows immediately upon Abraham and Sarah's encounter with the three strangers at the Oak of Mamre, an encounter of hospitality in a harsh land, an encounter that reveals the will and promise of God.

The same three men set out with Abraham and arrive within sight of the city of Sodom. God, in a vibrant passage in which God speaks to God's self, declares that there is a great outcry over the sin of Sodom and Gomorrah. God is determined to know if the outcry is justified. What follows is an animated conversation between Abraham and God, much like conversations between Moses and God and Elijah and God, in which the speaker calls into question God's actions or plans. Abraham, somehow knowing that the outcry against Sodom will prove to be justified, challenges God's plan for consequences. After all, both those who act justly and those who sin will be destroyed as a result. God and Abraham embark on a bit of a numbers game, in which Abraham keeps pleading for the cities to be spared if 50 just men, then 45 just men, then 40, or 30, or 20, and finally ten can be found. Although continuing the "game," so to speak, God agrees to the lower number each time and does not have to be persuaded to be more merciful.

Abraham uses the argument that God is the judge of the whole earth. For that reason, God must administer justice. The implication is that destroying the sinners and the just alike is not justice. Abraham approaches God with a mixture of humility and the certainty that he is correct that God may be about to do something wrong. In the end, God promises not to destroy Sodom for the sake of ten just people.

There is much to comment on in terms of this passage. Much has been spoken and written about the sin of Sodom and Gomorrah. It has been said that the sin for which they are eventually destroyed is homosexuality. When we read the passage in the context of the previous one, however, the nature of the sin is revealed to be a grievous breach of hospitality. Verses 8 and 9 of chapter 18 show that it is the attitude of the men of the town towards strangers in their midst that is the problem, especially when compared with the first three verses of the chapter. Lot's behaviour towards his daughters is also despicable.

In the passage for this Sunday, two major issues emerge: the justice of God, and the vibrancy of the relationship between God and the people. How could God choose to destroy a whole town for bad behaviour, knowing that innocents will perish along with the guilty? One way to deal with this point is to see this passage in the light of Scripture as a whole. The message of other parts of the biblical canon, even the passage from Deuteronomy of two weeks ago, is clear: repentance and forgiveness are always possible.

Read this passage in the light of the Isaiah 66 passage from three weeks ago, too. Abraham challenges God and, in effect, changes the divine mind because he has a notion of what justice is in the first place from the judge of the whole earth.

The biblical text constantly challenges. It witnesses to the presence of the Divine in our lives and in the world; that overwhelming, awesome presence cannot be contained in easy, tidy answers. Ask the questions.

Year C

Eighteenth Sunday in Ordinary Time – *Ecclesiastes 1:2, 2:21-23*

The Bible is real

What makes the Bible so vital and relevant for us in our time and place is that it is so real about the human condition. God is revealed in it as our one God in three persons who loves us deeply and passionately, who has set up guidelines by which we are to be in relationship with Divinity and humanity. God is a God of justice and forgiveness. The Bible is also deeply honest about the realities of the human condition, showing our human weaknesses, our rebellions against God and the depths to which we can sink in despair.

The Book of Ecclesiastes is one of those parts of the Bible in which the possible depths of human despair are clearly set out for us. The implication in the first verse of the book is that it is attributed to King Solomon, the epitome of wisdom. But scholars who deeply examine such things say that the book was written after the time of the exile and therefore well after the time of King Solomon, and that it has resonances with Greek thinking. To attribute a book to someone already famous for the kind of subject matter in the book was a standard literary technique in the ancient near east. The book is made up of reflections, often in the first person, that deal with what the speaker sees as "the utter emptiness of human existence and the futility of a life in which good and bad must come to exactly the same end."[136]

The passage for this Sunday begins with the famous line "Vanity of vanities ... All is vanity." It then goes on to ask what a person gains for all the work and hardship, all the responsibilities and worry they have undergone. Like last week's passage, this one raises difficult questions and eludes easy answers. Like last week's passage, too, this one from Ecclesiastes must be seen in the context of the whole biblical

---

136 *The Jerusalem Bible*, Introduction to Ecclesiastes, 854.

witness of God's total love, justice, mercy and forgiveness – a love, justice, mercy and forgiveness that does not obliterate the realities of human thought and feeling, human weakness and despair.

When I was serving as the senior minister of a congregation, many people who found themselves in a dark, discouraged or despairing state would come to see me. Indeed, it was the most common reason that people came in to see me. Such feelings are real, whether caused by a tragedy in life or whether a kind of dark cloud in which people are surrounded. I have known people who have experienced the kind of despair that these verses from Ecclesiastes portray – the kind of feeling that all the efforts of life are useless. It is very hard indeed. After emerging from one of those very dark periods, one person said to me that two things I kept saying throughout the dark period had made a difference: that I loved them, and that someday they would feel better. I responded that those two things had not seemed to make any impact at the time, when the darkness was so real. Yet, deep down, those two truths were, in some way, believed. Have the courage to listen to the despair this passage portrays. Have the faith to speak love and light a candle in that darkness.

Nineteenth Sunday in Ordinary Time – _Wisdom 18:6-9_

Scripture on Scripture

The Exodus revisited. The third part of the Book of Wisdom is about the work of God in history. The broad context of this lectionary passage is a comparison between Egypt and Israel. Egypt is equated with darkness; Israel, with light. The broad context of this passage is a poetic one – not so much the format, though that is poetic, too, but the way the ideas are expressed and the language and images used. The passage sees the night of the Passover as something that had been promised to the ancestors of the people. The people expected that their enemies would be defeated and that "the virtuous," which in the Exodus story included all the people of Israel, would be saved. The text then moves into a recital of piety. The destruction of the Egyptians has the effect of calling the glorious people to God. Proper sacrifice, the Passover, is offered by the devout. The people are united in the joys and challenges of life, which they share.

All this is lovely, though the text, as it follows this passage, is pretty grim about what happens to the Egyptians. But what does it mean? It certainly points to the crucial importance of the Exodus in the recital of faith of the people. The event was a turning point that proclaimed God's sovereignty, God's relationship to the people and the people's response to their God, who had acted in such a great act of grace towards them. The event is still alive in the faith of Jewish people. It still holds the key meaning of their relationship with God. It still calls forth a response. But this is expressed in a new way for a different time and place in the life and faith of the people.

I have no desire to wade into what are sometimes called "the worship wars" – the debates around where exactly the line needs to be in the dialogue between traditional and more contemporary forms of worship. There is no easy determination of "right" or "wrong" in such conversations. At the time I was leaving my service as senior minister in a congregation, young adults were starting to drink coffee in the pews during the liturgy. Yet a magazine headline I saw recently proclaimed that young Christians of all denominations were wanting to go back to more "traditional" worship. The Book of Wisdom maintains a balance between the centrality of a key part of the faith and how it is expressed in the language of a very different time and place. It is attempting to speak the faith to the people of its day and age. Surely that is our calling as well.

Year C

Twentieth Sunday in Ordinary Time – *Jeremiah 38:4-6, 8-10*

It's not easy being a prophet

Sesame Street's Kermit the Frog used to sing, "It's not easy being green." Well, it's not easy being a prophet, either. In this passage from the Book of the Prophet Jeremiah, we have one of the few pieces of narrative chosen to be Old Testament lectionary passages. It is a pretty graphic and gripping story. Jeremiah is not popular – not at all. He prophesied the coming destruction of the southern part of the kingdom of Israel, Judah, by the Babylonians. He said to all the powers of his time that it was useless to resist and that the coming destruction was the will of God. Who wants to hear that? Not the powers of his time and place, that is for sure. One of the unique things about the Book of the Prophet Jeremiah is that it gives us a lot of biography of the prophet. It is mostly grim. Some of the powers of the time heard Jeremiah say, "Anyone who stays in this city will die by sword, famine or plague; but anyone who leaves it and surrenders to the Chaldeans will live; he will escape with his life. [God] says this: This city will certainly be delivered into the power of the army of the king of Babylon, who will capture it." The four powers go to the king wanting Jeremiah to be put to death for disheartening the remaining soldiers in the city, for not having the welfare of the people at heart. The king hands Jeremiah over; then comes the story of throwing him into the well, mud and all. Upon protest by another person of power, the king flip-flops and Jeremiah is removed from the well before he dies there.

The passage continues on in great detail about the rescue, including the "torn, worn-out rags" that are given to Jeremiah to pad the ropes so that his armpits will not be hurt during the rescue by ropes. The prophet does not exactly go free then, but lives under a kind of house arrest. And of course, ultimately, Jeremiah is proved right in all that he had prophesied.

This is a tough passage. A question that this passage raises for our time and place is the meaning of prophecy and the notion of prophets. Jeremiah's message was not well-received by the authorities. Before we rush too quickly to put ourselves or the church into the role of the prophet, we must remember that in our global society, many of us are the people with power and authority. In what ways do we resist the message that prophets are trying to get across to us? Here is a harder question: in what ways do we persecute the prophets whose message we do not want to hear? What is God saying through "prophets" in our time and place that we think is disheartening or does not have the welfare of God's people at heart? One answer to this question revolves around the environment and climate change. More difficult questions include homelessness and the call for the cancellation of the debts owed by developing countries. Let us face the hard question of how deep in the mud of distain, dismissal and unpopularity we are really willing to go for the sake of God's message of both continual forgiveness and consequences.

Twenty-First Sunday in Ordinary Time – *Isaiah 66:18-21*

Traffic jam

In a kind of twist on the story of the Tower of Babel, God is going to gather all the nations of every language to witness the divine glory. Messengers will be sent out to far and distant lands to proclaim God's glory.[137] By every form of transportation known at the time, given to us in complete and concrete detail, the messengers/missionaries will bring the people of the nations of every language to God's holy mountain in Jerusalem, the same holy mountain to which Isaiah has been referring since the second chapter of his book. They will be brought as a kind of offering. An offering, including the type of offering in this passage, is a response to the grace of God. The people of all nations will be a response to the love and grace of God, which is for them as well as for the people of Israel. They are so dear to the heart and purposes of God that God will even make some of them priests, those charged with special responsibility for the relationship between God and people.

As I have mentioned before, the beginnings and endings of biblical books are very important. These verses, which appear near the end of the Book of the Prophet Isaiah, describe part of the will and purpose of God. God is coming to establish total sovereignty on the earth; that total sovereignty will include all peoples. Like Isaiah 45, discussed in Year 1, Twenty-Ninth Sunday in Ordinary Time (Roman Catholic lectionary), this biblical passage is a key text in any interfaith conversation. The biblical text has been clear all along that the people of Israel are called to be a light to the nations, that they have a special role in witnessing to the reality of God. Passages like this one proclaim

---

137 Walter Brueggemann suggests "missionaries" (*Isaiah 40–66*, 258). It interests me that of the places listed in these verses, all but one, Rosh, can be identified by scholars in our time and place.

that people from all nations, of every language, are part of the culminating picture – some of them, in fact, in leadership roles.

What does witnessing to this passage look like in the everyday life we all lead?

One of the most powerful liturgies I ever experienced happened in the week after 9/11 – an attempt to light a candle in the face of the complicated darkness of that time and its aftermath. At the invitation of a Roman Catholic priest in my city, we gathered in the parish church where he served. We gathered as Jews and Christians and Muslims to read holy texts, to pray and to experience the music of each other's traditions. The Jewish rabbi began with a text from the Torah, reflected on it and led the very large, packed sanctuary in prayer. Then a piece of Jewish music was played. I, as the Christian representative, read Mary's Magnificat, reflected on it and led those gathered in prayer. Then a Christian hymn was played. The Muslim imam read a passage from the Qur'an, reflected on it and prayed. Then a piece of Muslim music was played. In a dark time, we witnessed together to God's vision, to God's glory which is for all people and includes all people as God, has always known.

Twenty-Second Sunday in Ordinary Time – *Sirach 3:17-18, 20, 28-29*

C.S. Lewis via Dante

Once upon a time, I preached a sermon in a major North American congregation on the Gospel as portrayed by Dante, one of the greatest Christian writers of all time. In three volumes – *The Inferno*, *Purgatory* and *Paradise* – he portrays a hierarchy of sins. The least serious of the sins he describes in graphic and creative detail are those of the flesh. One of the most serious sins, however, is Pride.

C.S. Lewis, who often writes in the tradition of Dante, says this about Pride:

> According to Christian teachers, the essential vice, the utmost evil, is Pride. Unchastity, anger, greed, drunkenness, and all that, are mere fleabites in comparison: it was through Pride that the devil became the devil: Pride leads to every other vice: it is the complete anti-God state of mind ... We say that people are proud of being rich, or clever, or good-looking, but they are not. They are proud of being richer, or cleverer, or better-looking, than others ... It is the comparison that makes you proud: the pleasure of being above the rest ... Pride is essentially competitive in a way the other vices are not ... It is Pride which has been the chief cause of misery in every nation and every family since the world began. Other vices may sometimes bring people together: you may find good fellowship and jokes and friendliness among drunken people or unchaste people. But Pride always means enmity – it is enmity. And not only enmity between man and man, but enmity to God ... In God you come up against something which is in every respect immeasurably superior to yourself. Unless you know God as that – and, therefore, know yourself as nothing in comparison – you do not know God. A proud man is always looking down on things and people: and, of course, as long as you are looking down, you cannot see something that is about you.[138]

---

138 C.S. Lewis, *The Business of Heaven* (San Diego: Harcourt Brace & Company, 1984), 90–91.

If C.S. Lewis writes in the tradition of Dante, surely they both write in the tradition of this passage from Sirach, or Ecclesiasticus. This late writing, which is part of the Roman Catholic Bible (though not official canon for Jews or Protestants), calls on us all to be gentle in carrying out the concrete realities of the way in which we earn a living. It speaks strongly to behaving humbly, something that has not always come easily to Christians when we have been part of the power structure of society. And it speaks very specifically about pride. It is easy to say that we reject proud behaviour in others, but much harder to correct it in ourselves. A colleague of mine, in a conversation about Dante and C.S. Lewis, revealed that she never tells her children that she is "proud" of them. She feels that if she were to do so, she would be encouraging and reinforcing competitiveness with others – including unknown others.

What do our behaviours and lives look like to us and to others when we remember that according to Dante and Lewis, pride is the most serious sin we commit against God?

Twenty-Third Sunday in Ordinary Time – *Wisdom 9:13-18b*

What is your intention?

I fire up the laptop again after something that resembled a Christmas holiday and find myself absorbed in wondering about the intentions of God. This was the Christmas season in which Benazir Bhutto was assassinated in Pakistan, with the resultant chaos and fears about the possibilities for democracy there; the same Christmas season in which the turmoil of the Kenyan elections has produced much uncertainty, death and destruction in that country. I was in Kenya only two months ago. I have colleagues and friends there. I also have many friends who hail from Pakistan; I have been in conversation with them and their concerns over the past weeks. What are God's intentions for those troubled and hurting places? What are God's intentions for our response to those troubled and hurting places? I wonder.

It is not God's will, ever, that people should die and suffer. God knows that it happens, sometimes through sin, sometimes through random events in nature, but the overall witness of Scripture is to a God of life – for all people. As I write these words, it is too early to say or know what the long-term future, or even the immediate future, is for Kenya and Pakistan. But what is God's intention for the people of those countries? The lectionary passage for this twenty-third Sunday in Ordinary Time tells us that it is not for us to know the intentions of God, for our reasonings are unsure and our own intentions unstable. Our bodies, our "tents of clay," press on our souls and weigh down our minds. It is hard enough for us to figure out what is going on in our own times, spaces and places. (At the same time, we need to be careful in preaching this passage not to let it sound as though we are somehow off the hook in terms of the biblical mandate to care for the "poor, the orphan and the sojourner.") But then the passage changes.

The great gifts of Wisdom and the Holy Spirit have enabled God's intention to be known. We have been taught what pleases God, and saved by Wisdom. What does this mean? The passage tells us that Wisdom and the Holy Spirit have taught us the truth that God is a God of love, *the* God of love, for all people, times and places. Wisdom, often attributed to King Solomon in the biblical text (even if written at a much later time, as this book was), is sometimes personified, but is always a kind of primer for how to live. Proverbs are Wisdom. The Books of Ecclesiastes and Sirach and Job are Wisdom. Stories such as the Joseph narrative in Genesis are Wisdom. These books contain guidelines for living a wise life of prudence, common sense, practicality and justice. Overarching everything, always, and something that cannot be stated in too many times and places, is the love and will for justice that is God.

I still struggle with what my response in wisdom might be for the pain of Pakistan and Kenya. I have written to colleagues in those countries and assured them of my constant prayer for their nations, their peoples. In the power of Wisdom and the Holy Spirit, may we embody the theme of the 100th anniversary of the Week of Prayer for Christian Unity: "Pray Without Ceasing."

Year C

Twenty-Fourth Sunday in Ordinary Time – *Exodus 32:7-11, 13-14*

See Year A, Proper 23, in the section on the Revised Common Lectionary.

Year C

Twenty-Fifth Sunday in Ordinary Time – *Amos 8:4-7*

See Year C, Proper 11, in the section on the Revised Common
Lectionary.

Twenty-Sixth Sunday in Ordinary Time – *Amos 6:1a, 4-7*

Ivory beds and wine by the bowlful

Woe to those who feel safe and snug, says Amos, a message that runs contrary to the kind of bombardment we receive from the media today. Amos's message also runs contrary to what we hear in our church congregations. Perhaps I am particularly aware of this because, as I write this entry, it is December 21st. The push to Christmas is real and noisy everywhere I turn. But it is not just the media that seem to be pushing us to a desire for safety and snugness in this season and throughout the year – though we certainly hear it in all those ads that emphasize the warmth, comfort and joys of home, a home filled with more food, drink, decorations and gadgets than seem possible. In our congregations, too, there is much talk about family and celebration, the warmth of community and the security of knowing who we are. Amos is not against all those things in principle, but his prophecies are clear throughout his book: it is not faithful to God if there is comfort at the expense of the poor, if there is comfort while others suffer.

As is usual with Amos, his critique and condemnation are concrete and graphic. Woe to those who feel safe and snug, who lie on ivory beds and drink wine by the bowlful and – the "and" is very important – do not care at all about the ruin of Joseph, about the impending ruin of the country. Clearly, the divine calling is to care about others and about the state of our nation. Not surprisingly, Amos was unpopular for saying these things.

I am frequently asked why Christian denominations would or should be involved in politics (the questioners are not always certain how they define "politics"). Recently I was interviewed, along with a Muslim colleague and a Buddhist colleague, on the question of whether faith communities should be involved in social justice. Both questions can be answered by reading this passage. How can we sit in a snug and safe church and hear these words, then go home to our snug and secure homes and ignore the needs of the world? I venture to say that Amos would be unpopular in our churches, just as he was in his own time.

No matter the time of year, our Christian calling is not about being snug and secure. It is about acting to prevent the ruin of our earth and to uphold our international governance systems.[139] It is about helping developing countries to become economically stable, lobbying for affordable, accessible health care at home and abroad, and advocating for those with low incomes or no incomes, with sub-standard housing or no housing. No matter what the time of year, we cannot eat, drink and be merry without acting on our caring for all our sisters and brothers.

---

139 The almost complete lack of any references to the UN in our churches deeply puzzled the former UN Secretary General, himself a faithful Presbyterian. Kofi Annan asked me during a visit that I and other international church leaders made to his office on the subject of Iraq why the churches never talk about the UN, which, imperfect as it is, is the only major international governance system that the world has. We in the west tend to be very critical of it, but I have heard many colleagues from developing countries talk about the UN being the only protection they have.

Twenty-Seventh Sunday in Ordinary Time – Habakkuk 1:2-3, 2:2-4

How long, O Lord?

The heading in the Jerusalem Bible for this Sunday's lectionary reading, from the Book of the Prophet Habakkuk, is "Dialogue between the prophet and his God." It is a vibrant dialogue, to be sure, in the tradition of Abraham, Moses, Isaiah and Job. They engage with God in a way that we would often hesitate to do. The prophet Habakkuk lives in a troubled time, a reality that often seems to call forth prophets. (Whether they are listened to in their time or, indeed, in our time, is another matter.) In Habakkuk's time, Babylon's power, influence and potential threat were increasing. In the prophet's opinion, the people of Israel were not being faithful to their calling as a people of justice. Habakkuk complains. He does not just complain about the people, he complains that he has been complaining to God and that God is not listening! There is violence, wrongdoing, trouble and a total lack of justice, and God seems not to be listening.

God *was* listening, but answers come in God's time, not Habakkuk's. God has a vision. God is well aware of all that is going on, both outside of and inside of the nation: that many people are living for themselves, but that others are living righteously, by their faith. There will be consequences for unjust and violent ways of living.

As we see so often in the Bible, God is a God, *the* God, of love and justice. God is also the God of consequences. Although we do not like it when the consequences happen to us, we would not really have it any other way. We, too, cry out for justice in situations of injustice. We, too, cry out when the consequences seem to be too long in coming, or when they do not seem to affect the nations and persons we think deserve them. This passage encourages us to be patient, to wait on the vision with its justice and consequences. But nothing in this passage says that either we or the prophet Habakkuk do wrong to complain. Our complaining to God, our protests that things in the world are not in line with God's vision, is a form of prayer. As Sir John Polkinghorne says,

> ... in prayer we offer ourselves to become fellow workers with God. We have been given some power to bring things about ... Prayer is seeking the alignment of our possibilities for action with God's possibilities for action ... when we pray [w]e are saying what it is we really want, what is our heart's desire. We are called upon to assign value, to commit ourselves to what comes first in our lives ... Honesty is an indispensable quality in prayer.[140]

Think of Habakkuk's complaints, think of ours, this way.

---

140 Polkinghorne, *Searching for Truth*, 101, 104, 106.

Year C

Twenty-Eighth Sunday in Ordinary Time – *2 Kings 5:14-17*

See Year B, Epiphany 6, in the Revised Common Lectionary section for commentary on the first part of the story, which begins at 2 Kings 5:1 and runs through to verse 27. Then read the entry below.

"No, thank you"

The first verse of this passage gives us, in detail, the healing of Naaman: the leper, the army commander of the king of Aram. After much going back and forth and much complexity and dispute, Naaman is healed by the prophet Elijah. As is not always the case in biblical stories of healing (definitely a sermon there, for another time and place), Naaman is immensely grateful to have been healed. His life has been transformed! He proclaims the God of Israel as the God of the whole earth, and he wants to give Elijah a present. Yet no matter how much Naaman presses Elijah to accept a gift in gratitude for the healing, Elijah's answer is "no." Clever Naaman then goes for plan B. There may be no God in all the earth except the God of Israel, but it is still easier, in the belief system of that time and place, to worship the God of Israel on the soil of Israel. So with "as much earth as two mules may carry," Naaman thinks he will be better able to worship the God of Israel when he gets back home to Aram.

What an intriguing image. Are we so different today? It is human to want to latch on to concrete objects that seem to facilitate our connection to God. When the congregation that I served as senior minister closed its doors some years after I left, it amalgamated with another congregation and moved into that congregation's building. The people took with them some things from their church, including a magnificent stained glass window, which was installed in the south wall of the other congregation's sanctuary. The items they took from one place to the other enabled their worship of God. Although God can of course be worshipped without these precious things, they facilitate our worship and form a tangible link with the divine.

Twenty-Ninth Sunday in Ordinary Time – *Exodus 17:8-13*

A rod in the hand ...

This is the kind of biblical passage that we are sometimes tempted to dismiss as obscure and not "worth" preaching the Gospel through. Resist the temptation![141] The biblical witness may be difficult. It may be beyond our understanding in some of its particular references and contexts, coming as it does from so many centuries ago. But every passage has been included in the canon for a theological reason. Why would we expect a holy text in which God reveals the divine self to be simple and straightforward? God as infinite wonder cannot be so contained, even by the text itself.

In the passage for this Sunday, there is conflict between the Israelites and the Amalekites, and bad behaviour on both sides. Moses appoints Joshua to a new leadership role and he is sent out to do battle with the Amalekites while the aging Moses surveys the scene with God's staff in his hand. As long as Moses held the staff high in the air, the Israelites were winning. But Moses was old and tired and could not hold his arms up for long. His companions in the faith and the journey, Aaron and Hur, sit him down and support his arms so the staff of God stays high. Ultimately, though we do not learn it in this passage, the Israelites win the battle.

This passage can be used as a springboard to talk about leadership: Moses delegating the battle to the new and young leadership of Joshua, and Aaron and Hur as leaders supporting the aging leadership of Moses. There is also the issue of what might seem like a kind of superstitious view of the staff of God. Like a royal sceptre, a rod for ritual offices in government, and a bishop's crosier, the object has rich

---

141 Biblical scholar Walter Brueggemann, whose ideas have permeated sections of this book, particularly the Isaiah sections, once dismissed chapter 38 of the Book of Genesis as having no theological value. He no longer does so. That chapter of Genesis has provided the church with much deep theological reflection in recent years.

symbolism. But to focus only on these aspects of the passage is to avoid its deep and difficult questions.

The greater question remains: Why does God take sides in a battle, especially when both the people of God and the "other" are guilty of wrong behaviour? Throughout history, people on both sides in a battle have often believed that God was on their side. We still hear that message in the rhetoric and conflicts of our current context. (The verses that follow the lectionary text are even more difficult: they record that the people believed that God has wanted the Amalekites to be wiped out.) The Very Rev., the Honourable Lois Wilson, a United Church minister and a former Canadian senator, who has served as ecumenist in residence of the Toronto School of Theology, says that sometimes biblical texts are a kind of a mirror. They show us human tendencies: by showing them, they encourage us in the overall light and witness of God to continue to strive to move through and beyond some of those human tendencies. This Sunday's challenging text can be seen as a mirror in our own difficult time.

Year C

Thirtieth Sunday in Ordinary Time – *Sirach 35:12-14, 16-18*

Faith and the public square

We all hear the comment from time to time – whether from the media, from people who are not church attenders, or from people involved in their faith tradition – that the church or the bishops or the priest or the parish social justice committee should not be involved in politics. Those comments puzzle me. Politics affect people's lives fundamentally – their opportunities, their choices, their needs. When politics have a negative impact on any of these areas, it becomes a question of justice and Christians are called to speak out, and always have been. A passage like this one in Sirach makes that imperative clear.

By whatever name it is known, this is a Wisdom book according to the categories set out in the Christian Old Testament. Although it was originally written in Hebrew, it was (as its own foreword tells us, with a vivid glimpse into the translation and transmission and study of Scripture) translated into Greek, perhaps in 132 BCE. It has never been a part of the Jewish TaNaKh (Scriptures) but is part of the Roman Catholic Scriptures. Like other books of Wisdom, it is about the art of living – living the concrete details of life through an overall understanding of the law and the traditions of our forebears. The passage for this Sunday clearly states that the wise life, the faithful life, is one that understands that God listens to the pleas and supplications and cries of the poor and vulnerable. Wisdom literature is always about human behaviour, human response. In reminding us that "[God] shows no respect of personages to the detriment of a poor man," the passage calls us to speak truth to power, and to remind us of our responsibility as members of a democratic society to act in ways that will bring justice.

A recent initiative sponsored by The Canadian Council of Churches is a direct response to Scripture passages like this one. It actively supports the new interfaith religious leaders' summit to be held in parallel with the G8 each year, a summit that aims to challenge the G8 nations to truly listen to the supplications of the orphan and to act on the stories of the widow. It actively supports and encourages the churches and faith communities of Canada to educate themselves about the United Nations' Millennium Development Goals and to push our politicians to lift Canada's voice for justice much higher in the G8 process. The initiative enters into dialogue with the G8 office of Canada about such transformation and works with the Munk Centre, which houses a leading global G8 research institute that studies the details of G8 commitments and the degree to which the G8 is fulfilling them. Through this work, the Canadian Council of Churches is, we believe, witnessing to this Sunday's passage from Sirach.

Thirty-First Sunday in Ordinary Time – *Wisdom 11:22-12:2*

The Lover of Life

This lectionary passage makes a good companion piece for the passage that comes two weeks later from Malachi. This part of the Wisdom tradition in the Old Testament, those books that focus on the concrete ways of living out our faith in everyday life, is part of the Roman Catholic Old Testament canon. (It is not fully accepted by the Protestant canon, because it is not part of the Jewish tradition.) This Sunday's passage lays out the people's belief that God is almighty. And yet, God is merciful to all and encourages repentance. God loves all things because God has created all things, and all things belong to the Holy One. God is the Lord and Lover of Life, whose spirit is in all. Correction and repentance are needed; there is no doubt of that. In this passage, God gradually admonishes and corrects the evil and establishes trust.

We all know that things are not as they should be in our lives and in the life of our world. We all know that things are not as God would have them be. So how do we hear God's admonishment and correction? How do we manifest our repentance to God and to the world? For the first question, living as a part of a Christian community is key. We must be engaged together in prayer, in the hearing of the Word, in the sacraments and in our response in justice and caring for the poor and vulnerable of our planet. We must be willing to challenge each other in love and respect, to engage each other in dialogue over the long-term, because much of the change that happens in our lives and in our world happens little by little. How we manifest our repentance to God and to the world is witnessed to by the very word "repentance." When translated from the Hebrew, this word means to "turn in another direction." In the biblical text when we repent, we repent to God. All things are from and in God; therefore, sins of omission or commission, whether against neighbour or planet, are sins against

God and against God's will for justice and right relationship. So when we repent, or turn in another direction, our action must be visible. We become on speaking terms with the neighbour with whom we were feuding. We become active advocates for a safe fuel source to supplement or replace fossil fuels.

I believe that we best hear God's admonition and correction, and we best manifest our repentance, not just in our own faith traditions but with our sisters and brothers in Christ of different traditions. The 21 denominations that compose The Canadian Council of Churches (representing approximately 85 per cent of Christians in Canada) gather regularly to hear the voice of God in each other's traditions, faces and voices, to manifest unity in diversity, and to encourage and inspire each other to always, in all that we say and we do, turn towards God.

Thirty-Second Sunday in Ordinary Time – *2 Maccabees 7:1-2, 9-14*

I am the resurrection and the life

The story from 2 Maccabees told in this lectionary passage requires both some context-setting on the part of the preacher and some courage on the part of the congregation. Much of the Bible is graphic; it does not spare the details of what happened to people in times and situations of violence. People suffer terrible violence, like the brothers in this story in Maccabees, because of their faith. This passage is particularly graphic.

Because this is the only reading from one of the books of Maccabees in the lectionary, it is crucial to preach on it.[142] The period covered includes decades in the last two centuries before the Common Era, a time of resistance by the Jewish people to the Hellenization of their nation by oppressor kings wanting to impose such Greek-based culture upon them. Both books of Maccabees may be said to be a combination of historical context and religious history. They are addressed to the expatriate Jews of Alexandria for the purpose of arousing their concern for the danger threatening the Temple in Jerusalem with historical incidents placed to serve that purpose, not the kind of chronological ordering that we favour today.

This particular passage relates part of the tale of seven brothers and their mother who are arrested for refusing to eat pork, which is prohibited by Jewish faith. This story follows another story of martyrdom, and precedes the stirring story of the triumph of the Maccabees and their followers against the Greek-culture oppressors. (This triumph ultimately includes the purification of the Temple, the event

---

142 The books of Maccabees are included in the Roman Catholic Old Testament but are found in what Protestants call the Apocrypha, as they have never been in the Jewish TaNaKh. However, the history of the books of Maccabees is commemorated in the Jewish celebration of Hanukkah.

upon which the Hanukkah story is based.) In this Sunday's passage, the brothers resist the king no matter what torture they are subjected to. They resist by dying nobly, uttering words that express both their resistance and their faith in God. I think that this one passage, of all the passages available in Maccabees, has been chosen for its two references to life after death, to resurrection. As he dies, the second son proclaims, "The King of the world will raise us up, since it is for his laws that we die, to live again for ever." And as the fourth son nears death he cries, "Ours is the better choice, to meet death at men's hands, yet relying on God's promise that we shall be raised up by him; whereas for you there can be no resurrection, no new life."

A word about martyrdom. The church has long commemorated those who chose death rather than compromising their faith. We are all called to be faithful, to work against oppression for the sake of all people. Martyrdom might occur because of such efforts, but it is not to be sought for its own sake. Though some may be called to give up their lives for the sake of life and freedom for others, we are to seek life first and foremost.

Thirty-third Sunday in Ordinary Time – *Malachi 4:1-2*

The end of the beginning

We end Year C with what are close to the final verses of the final book of the Old Testament, the Book of the Prophet Malachi.[143] The final verses of Malachi proclaim that the people are to remember the law of God's servant Moses. (How did it come to pass that some Christians want to discard the importance of the law, when the order of our canon holds it up for us?) The people are also to know that God is going to send the prophet Elijah before the coming day of the Lord: in Christian thinking, this is often understood as John the Baptist.

In the verses just before those chosen to close Ordinary Time, we hear that God is preparing a day to come. On that day, those who have stood in awe of God and taken refuge in the holy name will be God's special possession. (In the wide witness of the biblical canon, to be the people who are God's special possession means not privilege but the responsibility of being a light unto the world.) On that day to come, there will be a winnowing of the people who serve God and those who do not serve God. (The description calls to mind the Christian text of Matthew 25.) As we move into the lectionary verses for this Sunday, we hear that the consequences for those who do not serve God will be dire. For those who stand in awe of God, who fear God's name, there will be healing in the rays of the sun of righteousness.

How can we set this passage in the context of our time and place? Most people do not take it literally, as if evildoers will literally be burned up, though Christians might hear a few echoes between this

---

143 The order of Scriptural books in the Christian Old Testament is deliberately different from that of the Jewish TaNaKh. The latter ends with the books of Chronicles to dream forward to an ideal kingdom, modelled on that of King David, but more ideal than is portrayed in the books of First and Second Samuel. The Christian Old Testament ends with the Book of the Prophet Malachi, whose name means "my messenger," to set up the birth of the ultimate messenger in the next book in the canon, the Gospel according to St. Matthew.

passage and the Book of Revelation, two books of endings and forward vision. What the prophets always declare, however, is that there are consequences for bad behaviour. God is a God, *the* God, of justice. Ultimately, evildoing cannot be part of what God envisions for us and for the world. This passage sounds harsh, as the prophets often do. In Malachi (3:1), the messenger must be sent to restore people and the world to the way God has intended them to be. In spite of many harsh prophetic passages, the overall witness of the prophets is that repentance and forgiveness are always possible. The messenger must come, and will come, as a refiner's fire to bring about a restoration. The restoration will leave neither root nor stalk of evil, but righteousness and justice will be healed. The question for us is how will we, individually and as a community, participate in that restoration as we are called to do? Our participation will be bound up with the healing rays of the sun of righteousness, so all will ultimately be restored to God's intention. In the fulfillment of God's time, evil will be banished forever. Yes.

Year C

Third Sunday in Lent – *Exodus 3:1-8a, 13-15*

See Year A, Proper 17, in the section on the Revised Common Lectionary.

The Three-year Cycle –

Canon Within the Canon:
The Revised Common Lectionary[144]

Genesis

Exodus

Leviticus (once)

Numbers

Deuteronomy

Joshua

Judges (once)

Ruth

1 Samuel

2 Samuel

1 Kings

2 Kings

1 Chronicles

2 Chronicles

Ezra

Nehemiah

Esther (once)

Job

Psalms (separate part
of the lectionary)

Proverbs

Ecclesiastes

Song of Solomon (once)

Isaiah (45 times)

Jeremiah

Lamentations (once)

Ezekiel

Daniel

Hosea

Joel (once)

Amos

Obediah

Jonah (once)

Micah (once)

Nahum

Habakkuk (once)

Zephaniah (once)

Haggai

Zechariah

Malachi (once)

---

144 Old Testament books in the Revised Common Lectionary appear in bold type. Old Testament books *not* in the Revised Common Lectionary appear in regular type. It is also noted in brackets when a book appears very infrequently or very frequently.

The Three-year Cycle –
Canon Within the Canon:
The Roman Catholic Lectionary[145]

Genesis
Exodus
Leviticus
Numbers
Deuteronomy
Joshua
Judges
Ruth
1 Samuel
2 Samuel
1 Kings
2 Kings
1 Chronicles
2 Chronicles
Ezra
Nehemiah
Esther
2 Maccabees
Job
Psalms (separate part
of the lectionary)
Proverbs

Ecclesiastes
Song of Solomon
Wisdom of Solomon
Sirach
Isaiah
Jeremiah
Lamentations
Ezekiel
Daniel
Hosea
Joel
Amos
Obediah
Jonah
Micah
Nahum
Habakkuk
Zephaniah
Haggai
Zechariah
Malachi

---

145 Old Testament books in the Roman Catholic Lectionary appear in bold type. Old Testament books *not* in the Roman Catholic Lectionary appear in regular type.

Bibliography

The Abingdon Bible Commentary. New York: Abingdon-Cokesbury Press, 1929.

Akenson, Donald. *Surpassing Wonder.* Chicago: University of Chicago Press, 2001.

Armstrong, Karen. *The Great Transformation: The Beginning of our Religious Traditions.* Toronto: Alfred A. Knopf, 2006.

Brueggemann, Walter. *First and Second Samuel.* Louisville, KY: John Knox Press, 1990.

———. *Ichabod Toward Home: The Journey of God's Glory.* Grand Rapids, MI: William B. Eerdmans, 2002.

———. *Isaiah 1–39.* Louisville, KY: Westminster John Knox Press, 1998.

———. *Isaiah 40–66.* Louisville, KY: Westminster John Knox Press, 1998.

———. *Theology of the Old Testament: Testimony, Dispute, Advocacy.* Minneapolis, MN: Augsburg Fortress Publishers, 1997.

Buechner, Frederick. *The Magnificent Defeat.* New York: HarperOne, 1985.

———. *Secrets in the Dark: A Life in Sermons.* New York: HarperOne, 2007.

———. *Wishful Thinking: A Seeker's ABC*. San Francisco: Harper Collins, 1993.

Cahill, Thomas. *The Gifts of the Jews*. New York: Doubleday, 1998.

Childs, Brevard. *Introduction to the Old Testament as Scripture*. Philadelphia: Fortress Press, 1979.

Feiler, Bruce. *Abraham: A Journey to the Heart of Three Faiths*. San Francisco: Harper Perennial, 2004.

Jenkins, Philip. *The Next Christendom: The Coming of Global Christianity*. New York: Oxford University Press, 2007.

The Jerusalem Bible, reader's edition. Garden City, NY: Doubleday, 1966.

The Jewish Publication Society Torah Commentary: Exodus. New York: The Jewish Publication Society, 1991.

The Jewish Publication Society Torah Commentary: Genesis. New York: The Jewish Publication Society, 1989.

Lewis, C.S. *The Great Divorce*. New York: HarperOne, 2001.

———. *The Last Battle*. New York: Harper Collins, 2007.

———. "On Forgiveness," in *Fern-Seed and Elephants and Other Essays on Christianity*, Walter Hooper, ed. London: Fount Paperbacks, 1975.

———. *The Voyage of the Dawn Treader*. New York: Harper Collins, 2005.

———. as quoted in *The Business of Heaven*, Walter Hooper, ed. New York: Harcourt Brace and Company, London, 1984.

Neil, William. *One Volume Bible Commentary*. London: Hodder and Stoughton, 1962.

Plaut, Gunther. *The Torah: A Modern Commentary*. New York: Union of Hebrew Congregations, 1981.

Polkinghorne, John. *Searching for Truth: Meditations on Faith and Science*. New York: Crossroad Publishing Company, 1996.

Ratzinger, Joseph. *The God of Jesus Christ: Meditations on the Triune God*. Fort Collins, CO: Ignatius Press, 2008.

Sawyer, John. *The Fifth Gospel: Isaiah in the History of Christianity* (Cambridge: Cambridge University Press, 1996).

Williamson, Clark M. *A Guest in the House of Israel: Post-Holocaust Church Theology* (Louisville, KY: Westminster John Knox Press, 1993).

Wilson, Lois Miriam. *Miriam, Mary and Me* (Northstone Publications, 2000).

———. *Stories Seldom Told* (Northstone Publications, 2002).

Wright, N.T. *Surprised by Hope: Rethinking Heaven, the Resurrection, and the Mission of the Church* (New York: HarperOne, 2008).